# No 230 Squadron Royal Air Force

## Kita chari jauh – We search far

**Guy Warner**

Colourpoint

6 5 4 3 2 1

© Guy Warner 2004

Designed by Colourpoint Books, Newtownards
Printed by W&G Baird Ltd

ISBN 1 904242 33 2

Colourpoint Books
Colourpoint House
Jubilee Business Park
21 Jubilee Road
NEWTOWNARDS
County Down
Northern Ireland
BT23 4YH
Tel: 028 9182 0505
Fax: 028 9182 1900
E-mail: info@colourpoint.co.uk
Web-site: www.colourpoint.co.uk

**Guy Warner** has been a regular contributor to *Ulster
Airmail*, the journal of the Ulster Aviation Society, for
eight years and has also written for *Aircraft Illustrated,
Air Enthusiast, Air Pictorial, Aviation Ireland* and *Northern
Ireland Travel News*. He is also co-author of *In the Heart
of the City: The History of Belfast's City Airport, 1938–1998,
Flying from Malone: Belfast's First Civil Aerodrome, Belfast
International Airport: Aviation at Aldergrove since 1938*
and *Army Aviation in Ulster*. Guy is a teacher at Ben
Madigan Preparatory School, Belfast, is married with two
daughters and lives in Co Antrim.

*Cover pictures:*

*Front:* Sunderland Mk III EJ143/S, the aircraft flown by
Alan Deller during 1944 and featured on pages 61 and 62, is
depicted preparing to alight on a calm sea 'somewhere in the
Indian Ocean', while EJ141/R taxies to its mooring, in this
painting by Norman Whitla.

*Rear:* In 1991 Puma XW224 was adorned with this
magnificent Tiger colour scheme, credit for which must go
to Mrs Lesley Palmer (the wife of Flying Officer 'Harry'
Palmer), Flight Lieutenant Simon Roberts and Flying Officer
Andy Turner. Indeed the effect was so striking and unusual
that the then AOC-in-C, Air Marshal Sir Andrew Wilson
KCB, AFC was rendered speechless.

Flt Lt 'Harry' Palmer

*Frontispiece:* In March 1937 the Squadron Badge was
approved by HM The King. The crest was designed by the
Squadron and was inspired by the label on a bottle of Tiger
Beer. This featured a tiger under a palm tree and was adapted
and improved upon by the addition of the motto, in Javanese,
'Kita Chari Jauh'.

The royalties from this publication are being donated
to The Royal Air Force Benevolent Fund and the
British Limbless ex-Service Men's Association.

# Contents

It is with particular pleasure that I provide my contribution to this comprehensive history of No 230 Squadron of the Royal Air Force. The Squadron was formed some 86 years ago but it can draw on a heritage which goes back to the origins of military aviation. The War Flight of the Royal Naval Air Service based at Felixstowe had been mounting operational patrols since 1914 and it was from this small pioneering unit that the Squadron was formed soon after the formation of the Royal Air Force.

Few RAF Squadrons have had such a long and almost continuous history of operational service, nor have many served in just two principal roles and in so many parts of the world. Until the late 1950s, the seaplanes and flying boats of 230 Squadron performed a vital role in the maritime defence of the United Kingdom and our overseas interests. Its illustrious exploits during the Second World War built on an already fine reputation and many operations are recorded in the history which recount outstanding and brave performances by the unit's air and ground crews.

Since 1958 the Squadron's role has been exclusively one of army support. Initially light aircraft capable of operations from tiny airstrips were used and then from 1961 until the present day, the Squadron has been equipped with helicopters. With lengthy periods of overseas service in Borneo during the Indonesian Confrontation, in Germany during the Cold War, in the Gulf War and for the last 12 years in Northern Ireland, the Squadron has been highly successful in its work for army formations and at the forefront in the development of operational techniques and procedures in both battlefield support and internal security operations.

In 1964, my father presented No 230 Squadron with its first Standard recognising twenty five years of active service. In 1994 I was very pleased to further the connection between my family and the Squadron by presenting the unit with its second Standard when it qualified for the award having completed another twenty five years of operations in the Royal Air Force.

It is very important that the details of such a long and distinguished history are recorded for future generations and to acknowledge the deeds of former members of the Squadron. This book fulfils that purpose admirably and I believe its publication will be of great interest to the general public as well as military and aviation historians.

## 10 DOWNING STREET
### LONDON SW1A 2AA

Since 1997 I have visited Northern Ireland on many occasions. After arriving at RAF Aldergrove the next stage of the journey has often been a flight in a 230 Squadron Puma to Hillsborough. So it can be said that the Squadron has been a vital cog in the Peace Process. I have always been impressed by the professionalism and expertise of all the Squadron aircrew and groundcrew.

For the last decade and more the Squadron has been based at RAF Aldergrove, serving the people of Northern Ireland with quiet efficiency and dedication. We should all be grateful for the service given by the Squadron not only in support of the Army, Police Service of Northern Ireland and Royal Ulster Constabulary in maintaining security through often difficult times but also in a range of humanitarian duties which have saved many lives. The job of securing the peace that we all desire is not yet complete but all members of the Squadron, past and present, can take a great pride in its contribution to the restoration of more stable conditions for the benefit of the entire community.

I wish No 230 Squadron continued success and good fortune and would like to express my sincere thanks for all its valuable work.

Rt Hon Tony Blair MP

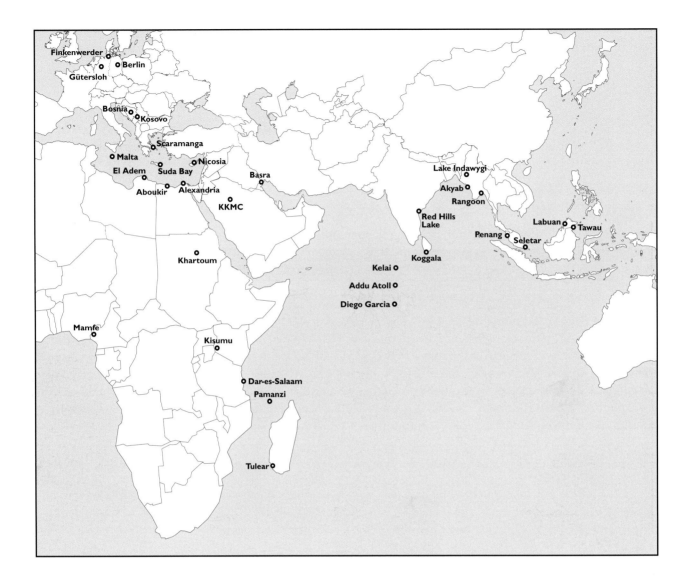

No 230 Squadron RAF has operated in many theatres worldwide, in war and peacetime. These maps give an indication of the global nature of 230's service and also of the many locations in the United Kingdom at which the Squadron has served. The Americas also received visits from 230 with detachments being sent for service in Belize.

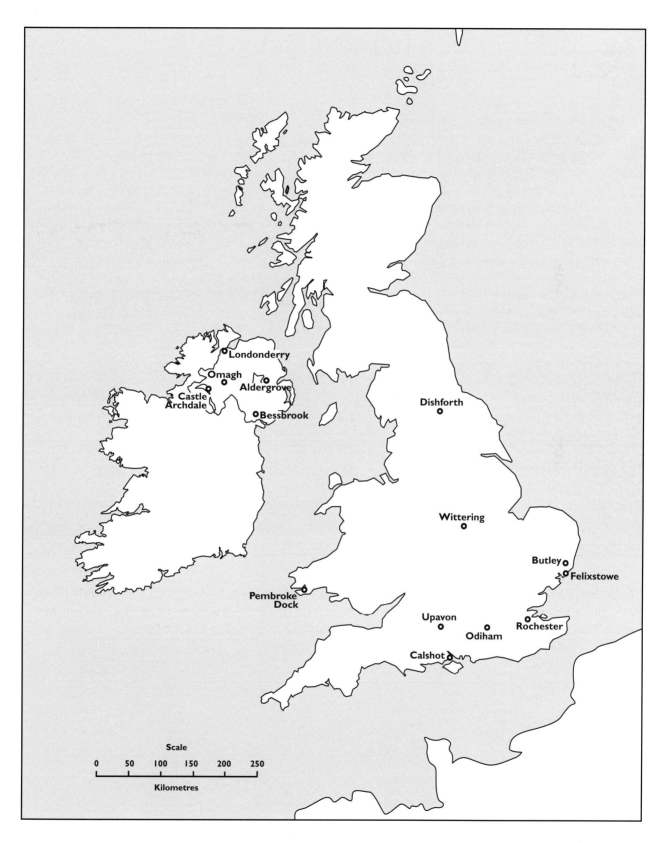

Londonderry

Omagh

Aldergrove

Castle
Archdale

Bessbrook

Dishforth

Wittering

Butley

Felixstowe

Pembroke
Dock

Upavon

Rochester

Odiham

Calshot

Scale

0    50    100    150    200    250

Kilometres

# Introduction

It was with great pleasure that I accepted the invitation of Wing Commander Bob Turner, the Chairman of the Squadron Association, to write the history of 230 Squadron. Seldom can any unit have been blessed with so prophetic a motto – 'Kita Chari Jauh', a Javanese phrase which may be translated as 'We search far' or 'We seek afar'.

In 1937 when the Squadron badge and motto were created, 230 Squadron was in Singapore, having already served in Egypt and in the United Kingdom. The succeeding years would find the Squadron travelling even further in peace and war, back to the Mediterranean, far across the Indian Ocean, to tiny tropical islands, to Africa, India, Burma, Australia and Japan, to the heart of Europe, boldly going where no flying boat had ventured before, to Greenland's icy mountains, back to the steamy heat of Africa, to Borneo, South America, the Middle East, Northern Ireland – the list is long.

In 2004 it celebrated its 86th Anniversary. For twelve of those years – 1923 to 1934, briefly in 1957/8 and again in 1971/2 – it was in suspended animation. Remarkably two aircraft types dominate more than 70 years of active life – the Short Sunderland between 1938 and 1957 (no squadron flew this aeroplane for longer) and the Westland/Aerospatiale Puma from 1972 to date – over 50 years altogether.

Originating out of the Royal Naval Air Service, and for many years a Coastal Command squadron, 230's history has a strong nautical flavour. For the last 40 years operational activities have involved close support to the Army – a graphic illustration of the versatility of air power.

My thanks are extended to Westlands, Bombardier Aerospace Belfast, 230 Squadron Association and also the Squadron itself for their generous support for this project. I must also record thanks to the team at Colourpoint Books for turning the text and photographs into such a splendidly produced book. Finally, as ever, special thanks must go to my wife, Lynda, without whose support, coffee and biscuits this work would not have been possible.

This tale has been a pleasure to write and to research; I hope that it does justice to the heroism, commitment and service of this fine squadron.

Guy Warner
Carrickfergus

August 2004

# CHAPTER 1
# 1913–1928

The menace to allied shipping presented by the U-Boat Service of the Imperial German Navy was still a major threat in 1918. A large and well-protected submarine base had been created at Bruges in the occupied territory of Belgium and U-boats were able to proceed to exit points on the coast of Flanders at Ostend and Zeebrugge by means of the Belgian canal system. From there they could pass through the English Channel to prey on merchant shipping all around the British Isles.

In order to combat the submarines, various methods were used – the convoy system, naval vessels, minefields and aerial patrols. As well as attacking U-boats on the surface, aircraft would also force them to hide below the waves and so use up valuable air and electricity. In the last year of the war antisubmarine patrols by aircraft increased four fold. Such a growth required greater resources in men and machines to be made available and, accordingly, a number of new squadrons were formed, including Numbers 230, 231 and 232, on 20 August 1918, at Felixstowe, in Suffolk, on the east coast of England.

Felixstowe was one of the original Royal Naval Air Service (RNAS) stations and also became a centre for trials and development of flying boat designs under the leadership of Squadron Commander John C Porte RN. Felixstowe Air Station had been established in August 1913. The first officer appointed to command there was Flight Commander Charles Risk of the Royal Marine Light Infantry (RMLI). Nautical terms were much in evidence:

> The ship's company numbered 23 hands and the facilities were rudimentary. Sheds A and B were standing at this time but little else. There were no slipways or fences, no concrete, no quarters for officers or men, all of whom were billeted ashore. C Shed was erected shortly before the outbreak of war. The first machine on the station, so far as can be learned, was a Borel monoplane, of which great things were expected, but unfortunately, on its maiden trip to greet the Hon.. Winston Churchill (the

First Lord of the Admiralty) on HMS *Enchantress*, which was entering the harbour, the monoplane collapsed after taxying halfway to the guardships.

The following year, on 18 July, Risk was the leader of one of the five flights of naval aircraft which flew over the Fleet at Spithead during a review by King George V.

By the outbreak of the Great War in August, the RNAS had more aircraft under its control than the Royal Flying Corps (RFC). The main role of the RNAS was fleet reconnaissance, patrolling coasts for enemy ships and submarines, attacking enemy coastal territory and defending Britain from enemy air raids. The duties allocated to Felixstowe were patrolling and scouting under the direction of the Senior Naval Officer, Harwich and the defence of the port against attack by hostile aircraft.

By this time Risk had been promoted and was succeeded by Flight Commander Charles Rathbone RMLI. Rathbone's aircraft, the Maurice Farman Seaplane 115, had taken part in the Royal Fleet Review but had suffered engine failure on the way home. It alighted on the water off West Worthing and was completely wrecked. Rathbone and Telegraphist Stirling were rescued by boat.

The Felixstowe aircraft were a mixed batch of Maurice Farman pusher propeller driven seaplanes and land planes. One of these aircraft, the Maurice Farman S7 Longhorn serial No 70 is recorded as having been fitted with bombs and a rifle and to have made patrols in the early stages of the war. Four pilots were available plus an intelligence officer. The store of offensive weapons consisted of 12 Hales grenades. A contemporary source asserts:

> Aviation was a public spectacle in those days and on occasions the aid of the local constabulary had to be invoked to save the populace from the consequences of its over-rash curiosity.

Two Sopwith Pusher Seaplanes with 100 hp Anzani engines, serials 123 and 124, were delivered to Felixstowe in August 1914. Both were fitted with bomb-dropping gear

*Maurice Farman Seaplane 115 (on right) with a Henry Farman Seaplane at Felixstowe in 1914.*

JM Bruce / GS Leslie Collection

*A Maurice Farman Seaplane made armed patrols from Felixstowe in the early stages of the war.*

JM Bruce / GS Leslie Collection

and No 123 was also converted to land plane configuration. This aircraft is known to have flown an armed patrol in January 1915. Rathbone handed over to Porte when he was posted to take over command of the seaplane element of 1 Wing at Dunkirk. He was later awarded the DSO and bar, became a prisoner of war and eventually attained the rank of Air Commodore. He died in 1943.

Felixstowe grew into a substantial base with three large aircraft sheds measuring 200 feet by 300 feet. In front of these was an expanse of concrete reaching to the water's edge and then there were the slipways – three wide wooden gangways running out into the harbour and sloping down into the water – which were used for launching the flying boats. It was but 110 miles or an hour's flying time from there across the North Sea to the Hook of Holland, from where U-boats from the North German ports left the security of the coast to set out into the English Channel looking for prey. A little further south

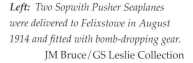

*Left: Two Sopwith Pusher Seaplanes were delivered to Felixstowe in August 1914 and fitted with bomb-dropping gear.*
JM Bruce/GS Leslie Collection

*Below: A good idea of the development of Felixstowe as a base can be gained from this aerial photograph.*
JM Bruce/GS Leslie Collection

were the occupied Belgian ports of Zeebrugge and Ostend.

As well as the U-boats, Zeppelins and seaplanes added to the menace. As previously mentioned, coastal patrols had been undertaken from the station since the beginning of the war. A variety of seaplanes, manufactured by Short Brothers and Sopwith, operated from Felixstowe in 1915 and 1916. Aircraft are recorded as carrying out combat

patrols along the shipping channels ten or twenty miles out to sea, on the look out for enemy activity. Two of the pilots are known to have been Flight Sub-Lieutenants JL Gordon and GR Hodgson, both from Montreal.

At this stage it may be worth pointing out the essential difference between a flying boat and a seaplane. A seaplane is an aeroplane equipped with floats enabling it to land

*Seaplanes manufactured by Short Brothers operated out of Felixstowe from 1915 onwards and included Type 184s, pictured above, and Type 827s, below.*
Rolls-Royce plc (above) / JM Bruce / GS Leslie Collection (below)

upon the water; a flying boat is a boat shaped hull with wings. The earliest flying boats to serve with the RNAS included the single-engined Donnet-Leveque, which was of French origin and from which was developed the Franco-British Aviation FBA Type 'B'. Over 150 of these were used by the RNAS, including those flown by Rathbone at Dunkirk. Many future flying boat pilots would have their initial training on this type at Calshot.

Larger flying boats, the Curtiss H1s, were delivered from the USA and were flown from Felixstowe in 1915 on coastal patrols but the engines gave constant trouble and the boats rarely reached home under their own power. Flight Sub-Lieutenant John Galpin (another Canadian, who hailed from Ottowa) and his crew suffered engine failure on patrol which resulted in 18 hours riding out a gale on the North Sea. On a subsequent patrol he sighted a U-boat but his observer was too excited to pull the bomb release!

Curtiss H4 'Small Americas' were erected at Felixstowe and the first 'Large Americas' – the Curtiss H8s – were imported from the USA. To begin with the H8 had a tendency to shed its propellers in flight, which did little to gain the confidence of those pilots who had to test fly the aircraft; these included Commander Porte, Flight Commander Ralph Hope-Vere, Flight Lieutenant Arthur Cooper and Flight Sub-Lieutenant CL Scott.

During 1915 and 1916 night patrols were also carried out by Felixstowe pilots from the Landguard range just outside the gates, a rather rough strip which featured such hazards as rifle pits and gravel holes. The aircraft used were BE2c biplanes and Deperdussin monoplanes. The regular pilots were Flight Commander Hope-Vere, Flight Sub-Lieutenant Scott and Flight Sub-Lieutenant WR Mackenzie.

In the summer of 1916 Flight Sub-Lieutenant Day carried out a remarkable experiment, flying a Bristol Bullet biplane from the top centre section of a Porte 'Baby' flying boat. Not long afterwards the first attempt at a rendezvous with a destroyer flotilla was made but the weather conditions were so bad that the only result was the loss of the flying boat as it was being towed and the narrow escape of the crew – Flight Lieutenant Cooper, Flight Sub-Lieutenant Hobbs and Lieutenant Erskine Childers RNVR. Childers was the author of the popular prewar novel *The Riddle of the Sands* which predicted a German invasion. He was also a skilled yachtsman who

brought his knowledge of North Sea coastal waters to good use as an intelligence and aerial reconnaissance officer. He was shot by the Irish Government in 1922 for being on the wrong side in the Civil War. Many years later his son, also Erskine Childers, became President of the Irish Republic.

The Curtiss H8s were improved when their twin 160 hp Curtiss engines were replaced with Rolls-Royce 260 hp Eagle VIIIs, with the result that they were redesignated H12. The pilots began to lose much of their distrust of long sea patrols and became reasonably certain that after six, seven and more hours of work over the sea, the aircraft would return to base under its own power.

It was not until April 1917, however, that the War Flight was established on a proper footing under the command of Flight Lieutenant TD Hallam DSC, RNAS. Two aircraft were allocated to the flight, Curtiss H12s 8661 and 8663. Hallam later wrote:

> I had No 2 Shed. There was no intelligence hut, no flying office, no telephone in the shed, no pigeons and Flight Sub-Lieutenant 'Billiken' Hobbs, who was the only pilot at this time turned over to the flight, had never seen an enemy submarine. And I was in like case myself; besides which, I had never flown one of the big twin-engined boats.

Douglas Hallam and Basil Hobbs flew the War Flight's first operational patrol in 8661 on the morning of 13 April 1917. Both men were Canadians – Hallam was from Toronto and Hobbs from Montreal, adding yet more names to the list of distinguished flying boat and seaplane pilots from the Dominion. Hallam had already seen action with a machine-gun unit at Gallipoli, where he had been wounded three times and had earned his first DSC. On 16 April Hobbs and Flight Sub-Lieutenant FW Bryans spotted a U-boat and repeated John Galpin's experience:

> It must be admitted that the surprise was mutual, for Bryans was so struck by buck fever that he did not reach for the bomb release until his Hun had dived.

On 23 April, 8661, flown by Hallam, bombed a U-boat, which he claimed to have "bent very badly". Hallam later described a typical daily scene at Felixstowe:

> At 10 o'clock on an overcast day and a twenty-knot westerly wind blowing, I sounded off five sharp taps on the bell, the signal for patrol. The chiefs of the engineer, carpenter and working parties reported for instructions. The working party of twenty men gathered around

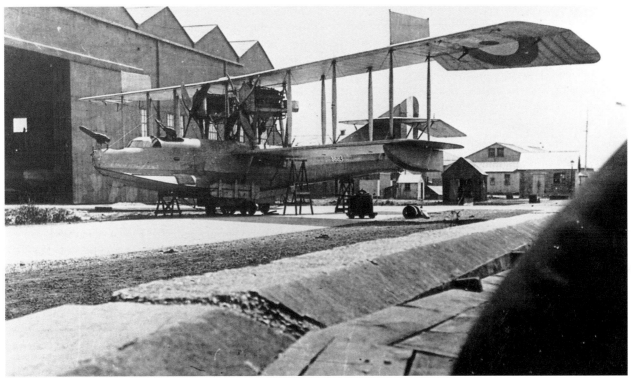

*The Curtiss H8 was much improved when fitted with Rolls-Royce Eagles and redesignated H12. This is 8683 which was delivered to Felixstowe in March 1917.*
JM Bruce / GS Leslie Collection

*Douglas Hallam pictured in the cockpit of a Curtiss Jenny, the type in which he learned to fly.* Defence Forces of Canada Archive

*Old '61* and rolled her out of the shed to the concrete area. Here they chocked her up under the bow and tail to prevent her standing on her nose when the engines were tested. In the meantime the armourer's party had fitted on the four Lewis machine-guns and had racked up into place under the wing roots, two on each side of the hull, the four one hundred pound bombs. The crew then boarded. The first pilot sat in a cockpit covered by a transparent wheelhouse, so that he did not have to wear goggles, since these were thought to interfere with efficient observation. If a submarine was sighted the second pilot was supposed to move to the open forward cockpit with its machine-gun, bomb-sight and bomb-release levers. The wireless operator sat facing forward on the right-hand side of the boat behind the first pilot, with his wireless cabinet, code books, Aldis signalling lamp and carrier pigeons. The engineer sat in the cockpit amidships. The working party then rolled the boat out onto the slipway. Here six waders, in waterproof breeches coming up to their armpits and weighted boots to give then a secure foothold when the tide was running, steered the boat down into the water, the working party easing her down by tailing her on the

line. As the flying boat entered the water the thrust of the engines urged her forward and she taxied clear. Under good conditions a boat becomes airborne at about 35 knots but landing and taking off in bad weather makes exceptional demands on the pilot. This was also true of long patrols. Coming back against a headwind, it took so long that I thought somebody had moved England.

The Felixstowe-based flying boats were most closely associated with the 'Spider Web' patrol. This was an area of sea on which an imaginary octagonal shape was drawn. It was some 60 nautical miles (nm) in diameter, with radial arms 30 nm long and chords crossing the arms 10, 20 and 30 nm from the centre. It covered 4000 square miles of sea. Its centre was the red, rusty *North Hinder* light-vessel, which the U-boats used as a navigational mark when proceeding on the surface to their hunting grounds.

When a U-boat was spotted or detected by radio fix, the flying boats attacked with bomb and machine gun. One flying boat could search a quarter of the 'Spider Web' in five hours, well within the endurance of these machines but what of the crews? The wooden-hulled 'boats' had open cockpits and were cold, spartan and wet.

In-flight catering was limited to bully beef sandwiches and water, supplemented with a personally provided Thermos flask of hot tea, coffee or Bovril. One of these pilots later wrote:

> The flying boats were terribly overloaded and it was amazing how the engines stood up to the extra demands that were made on them. One of the curses of these long patrols was that one couldn't smoke. The bulk of the petrol was stored in large tanks inside the hull just behind the pilot's seat and the risk of a disastrous explosion was too great.

Another regular duty was escorting fifteen or sixteen cargo boats making the 'Beef Trip' two or three times a month between England and the Hook of Holland.

On 14 June 1917 the Zeppelin L43, commanded by Captain Kraushaar, was destroyed off the Dutch coast by machine-gun fire from the War Flight H12 8677. The pilots of the 'Large America' were Flight Sub-Lieutenants BD Hobbs and RFL Dickey and the crew, Air Mechanics HM Davis and AW Goody. On 15 September Hobbs and his crew in 8677 attacked an enemy submarine on the surface, the flying boat's two 230 lb bombs hitting ten feet ahead of

*The rusty* North Hinder *lightship – the centre of the 'Spider Web' described above.*

Imperial War Museum, London (HU 67691)

the conning tower. Large oil patches were seen. However, post-war German records indicated that, although damaged, the submarine survived. Another submarine was encountered on 28 September and a bomb was seen by Hobbs to strike the submarine's deck. It is probable that this was UC-6 which sank in the North Sea that day.

In its first year of operations the War Flight made 605 patrols in the course of which it flew 105,397 nautical miles and sighted 47 submarines, attacking 25 of them with bombs. By then it consisted of nine flying boats. Hallam paid tribute not only to the aircrews but also to:

> . . . the carpenters who true-up, inspect and repair the machines; the engineers who clean, test and keep the engines in order; the armourers who adjust the bombs and machine-guns and the working party who push about the boats and fill the tanks with petrol. The work of these men often gets overlooked – work which is hard and exacting, and with little honour and reward.

In the New Year of 1918 the first American pilots joined the flight – Ensigns Vorys, Fallen, Potter, Sturtevant, Hawkins and Scheffelin USN. They were fresh and full of enthusiasm – "charming messmates, splendid pilots and

very gallant gentlemen" – and indeed one of their number performed the feat of looping a six-ton flying boat.

In February 1918 King George V made his third visit of the war to Felixstowe to hold an investiture ceremony, where gallantry awards were made to Squadron Commander Hallam and 22 other officers and men.

The German Naval Air Service's well-armed, fast and manoeuvrable Hansa-Brandenburg W29 seaplane, designed by Ernst Heinkel, was a particularly effective opponent. One of the most formidable German airmen operating from Zeebrugge was Oberleutnant Friedrich Christiansen. On 23 April 1918, leading a flight of seven W29s, he encountered and attacked two Felixstowe-based flying boats. A German account related:

> The Oberleutnant shot down a Curtiss flying boat after a long combat. After fire had been opened and the machine-gunner in the stern of the flying boat killed, Christiansen flew parallel with the boat and his observer opened fire with his machine-gun at the oil tank at the rear of the port engine, setting the tank alight. The pilot of the flying boat then tried to land on the water but as he was at a height of only ten feet,

*A Hansa-Brandenburg W29 crosses low over the sea bathers near Zeebrugge, watched closely by German military personnel.*

Imperial War Museum, London (Q 54387)

*Captain Norman Magor was killed flying Curtiss H12 8677 on 23
April 1918.* National Archives of Canada

he could not turn into wind, so that she crashed on
alighting and burst into flames.

So perished 8677 flown by Captain Norman Magor
and Ensign S Potter. Magor's loss was a poignant one as
he was, "a very gallant and efficient pilot and a charming
messmate". Magor, who hailed from Montreal, had been
the pilot of 8695 on 22 September 1917. When operating
on detached duty at Dunkirk, a submarine was sighted;
two bombs sent the UC32 to the bottom, the first U-boat
sunk by bombing from a RNAS aircraft.

Revenge for the loss of Magor and his crew came
six weeks later, when on 4 June five flying boats – four
Felixstowe F2As (two from Great Yarmouth, N4295 and
N4298, and Felixstowe's N4302 and N4533) and the Curtiss
H12 Convert 8689 – went looking for the enemy. A dogfight
ensued in which at least three of the Germans were shot
down. The action was summarised by CF Snowden Gamble:

> So ended the greatest action that was fought between
> seaplanes during the War. The flying boats after having
> flown for nearly three hours fought right on the enemy's
> doorstep and defeated him. The enemy were defeated
> by the leadership and tactics of Captain Robert Leckie
> and by the flying skills and gunnery of the officers and
> crews under him.

On 1 April 1918, the RNAS had been merged with the
RFC to form a new service, the Royal Air Force. Therefore
there was a distinctly nautical flavour to 230 Squadron's
origins, as well as a fine war-fighting heritage, when it
was formed from Numbers 327, 328 and 487 Flights in
August. It was part of No 4 Group and along with No 231
Squadron it formed the 70th Wing.

The Squadron's first CO was Flight Lieutenant
Cecil Clayton, from Victoria in British Columbia, who
had been commissioned into the RNAS after gaining
his Royal Aero Club Aviator's Certificate as a civilian
on 6 September 1916. He had joined the War Flight
in the summer of 1917 and was the pilot of 8661
on 5 February 1918, when a German seaplane was
shot down in aerial combat over the North Sea, Air
Mechanic GH Robinson being the successful gunner.
Clayton recorded in his diary:

> My machine had over 25 holes in her. A good group of
> 15 in the tail, one of the sliding doors at the rear shot
> away, six holes in the starboard prop, two or three holes
> in the planes, two landing wires nearly severed, one
> bracing wire shot away and one hole through the hull,
> two feet back of my head. Some glorious little scrap
> alright. The fellows made more fuss of me than if I had
> got a submarine.

Some authorities give Clayton's rank as Captain
which is symptomatic of this transitional period when the
two services were being combined and the new ranks and
uniforms still had to be established. In any case, he was
soon promoted to Major.

On 21 August the Squadron had to test fly the H12
N4344 which had been fitted with balanced ailerons and two

gun positions on the top wing. The idea was not a success as it reduced the flying boat's top speed by 10 knots and also resulted in one of the control wires being shot away.

The first aircraft types to equip the new squadron were Curtiss H16s and Felixstowe F2As. Both were flying boats and had many similarities, as John Porte had worked closely with Glenn Curtiss, adapting and improving the original American design. Flying boats offered long range and endurance, as well as the ability to carry a good payload. The sea provided a virtually limitless takeoff run for these larger, heavier craft. The trade off was that they had a relatively slow speed, even for 1918.

The Curtiss H16 'Large America' was a substantial machine with an upper wingspan of 95 feet and a hull length of 46 feet. Powered by two 400 hp Liberty 12 engines and carrying a crew of five (a pilot, two observers, a mechanic and a wireless operator) it was armed with four Lewis guns and could carry four 230 lb bombs, with an endurance of nine hours and a maximum speed of 95 mph.

The F2A had a longer two-stepped planing bottom with a much deeper v-shaped hull, designed by Porte. His design changes resulted in much better hydrodynamic behaviour - ie when moving on the water. The effect of

a step running across the hull assists in reducing the natural downwards suction induced by a convex shape as its speed increases in the course of a flying boat's takeoff run. A vacuum is created behind the step, air is sucked in and gradually a cushion of air is built up from the step to the stern, separating the hull from the water. At the same time lift and speed are overcoming weight and drag and so the flying boat will pull clear of the surface.

The F2A was a very impressive machine of similar dimensions to the 'Large Americas', powered by two 360 hp Rolls-Royce Eagle VII engines, having a good armament of six Lewis guns, an endurance of eight hours at 65 knots cruising speed and was highly manoeuvrable – though in those days of manual controls, it required strength and stamina from the pilots too. It had twin guns mounted on a Scarff Ring in the nose compartment, one for the second pilot above the cockpit, one in the dorsal position aft of the wings and, covering previous blind spots, one to either side firing through ports covered by sliding doors. Over 100 F2As were built.

Towards the end of the war many of the large flying boats based at Great Yarmouth and Felixstowe were painted in bizarre and gaudy colour schemes, emulating the 'dazzle painting' of warships – blues, yellows and

*The Felixstowe F2A was a large and heavy aircraft for its day but looked very graceful in flight.*                    JM Bruce/GS Leslie Collection

**Above:** *During 1918 the flying boats were dazzle painted in a variety of imaginative ways. This is F2A N4545, which served with 230 Squadron from August 1918.*                    JM Bruce/GS Leslie Collection

reds, stripes, bars and chevrons. There was a practical purpose behind this riot of colour and pattern; it aided identification of friend or foe in the air and assisted in the easier location of an aircraft forced to land on the water. It was also hoped that "it would put the wind up the Hun".

At the end of August the activities at Felixstowe since April were summarised: 19 fights, eight flying boats lost, 14 personnel killed, six personnel wounded, three personnel prisoners of war, nine enemy machines destroyed, 15 enemy personnel killed, 949 patrols, 3007 hours in the air, 178,333 miles flown. The lack of mention of submarines provides graphic evidence of the success of the RNAS in neutralising their menace. The higher casualty figures are a result of a tactical change to hostile patrolling, trying to bring enemy aircraft up to fight.

Further types of aircraft were added to the new squadron's strength in September and October – though it must be stated that the records for this period are a little

insubstantial and that no corroboration is available in the form of serial numbers. The aircraft were the Sopwith Camel, a flight of which was detached north of Ipswich at Butley, the Felixstowe F3, Short 184 and Fairey IIIB/C.

The Camel was, of course, one of the classic fighters of the Great War. The 2F1 version was designed for use on ships, it had a shorter wingspan and a detachable rear fuselage. The type operated successfully from ships adapted to carry aircraft and from platforms (lighters) towed by destroyers.

One of the more remarkable exploits carried out by a 'Ship's Camel' was on 11 August 1918, when Lieutenant Stuart Culley RNAS (another Canadian) took off in N6812 from a lighter towed by the destroyer HMS *Redoubt*. (The lighter was a flat-bottomed steel barge fitted with thirty feet of deck, which could be towed at 30 knots.) Part of the Harwich naval force was carrying out an offensive sweep in the Heligoland Bight when a

*Sopwith Camel N6812 is pictured being towed, at speed, on lighter H3.*                    JM Bruce / GS Leslie Collection

Zeppelin was spotted high overhead. Culley was able to lift the Camel off the lighter's deck after the shortest of runs. He strived for an hour to climb close to the airship, which was at 19,000 feet. At extreme altitude, with the Camel hanging on its propeller, Culley pulled back on the stick and fired his specially mounted twin Lewis guns into the belly of the Zeppelin. The Camel stalled and fell away but the incendiary bullets had struck home. The L53 was ablaze and plunged, flaming, into the waters of the North Sea, near Terschelling, along with Kapitanleutnant Prölss and his crew of 31. As planned, Culley ditched his aircraft near the ships and both were recovered. Culley did not even get his clothes wet. He was subsequently awarded the DSO. The Camel survives to this day in the Imperial War Museum.

Lighters were also used to position flying boats nearer the Heligoland Bight and so increase their effective patrol range. Cecil Clayton was one of the pilots taking part in the trials in January 1918 and in the first operational use in March, when three F2As on lighters were towed out of Harwich harbour by destroyers. Two enemy seaplanes were encountered off the Dutch coast, one of which was

shot down. On return to base Clayton's dairy records:

> We were all marched up to Rear Admiral Cayley (the Senior Naval Officer, Harwich), who complimented us on our work. Both he and Commander Porte are rather bucked up about it and we are to have a holiday tomorrow.

The Felixstowe F3 was heavier and longer-ranged than the F2A but was less manoeuvrable and slower. It was not popular with aircrew as it was unable to defend itself against German seaplanes as well as the F2A. The Short 184 was a large, single-engine, rather ungainly looking seaplane. Its looks belied its utility and it gave valuable service throughout the war. In home waters its main tasks were antisubmarine patrols and bombing attacks on enemy North Sea coastal bases. A pilot of the time, Flight Commander AH Sandwell, commented, "It was a physical impossibility to fly a Short at much more than 75 miles an hour." It was, however, "the pilot's dream for putting in hours – docile, stable, obedient, and thoroughly deserving its affectionate nickname – Home from Home'." The Fairey IIIB and C were developed from a basic two-seat bomber design. In the closing stages of the war they were

used for mine-spotting patrols. Later marks of this very practical design served with the RAF and the Fleet Air Arm for many years post-war.

During the last year of the war out of 7000 convoys that had an escort of aircraft, only six were attacked by submarines. In 1917 and 1918, ten U-boats were known to have been sunk and 21 seriously damaged. Antisubmarine air patrols were greatly feared and much detested by U-boat commanders and their crews, as captured documents subsequently showed. A convoy with an air escort was much less likely to be attacked. The concept of marine aviation had been rigorously tested in combat and been proven efficacious. These lessons were, of course, to be re-learned the hard way in the early stages of the Battle of the Atlantic twenty years later.

The fighting men of Felixstowe also paid tribute to those who worked just as hard but received much less of the credit:

> In the Dope Shops, the Armoury, the Offices, the Garage and a hundred other places, wherever one wanders on the Station, one is sure to find a Wren. She will perhaps be hard at work on her job, or may be earnestly discussing it with a colleague; or she will be proceeding to, or coming from it. They have fully entered into the varied labours of the Station and there is hardly a place where they may not be seen.

There were more than 80 Wrens employed at Felixstowe by the war's end.

Following the Armistice on 11 November 1918, 230 Squadron's CO had to contend with boredom. He recorded in his diary on 13 November, "Dull weather. Good enough for patrol in wartime, but not good enough now, so patrols were washed out." Some relief from this was given by the task of photographing surrendering U-boats from the air. Clayton also visited one of the 122 U-boats moored in ranks on the River Stour. Other tasks included surveys and fishery patrols but there was a general desire to be demobilised swiftly.

The extra spare time was put to very good use in the production of a special issue of *The Wing*, the station magazine, which gave a fascinating, illustrated history of Felixstowe during the war, along with character sketches and descriptions of lighter moments.

Two of the Squadron's leading lights were soon to retire into civilian life. Douglas Hallam became the Secretary-Treasurer of the Canadian Woollen and Knit

*Lighters were also used to position flying boats nearer the Heligoland Bight. The first such operational use was in March 1918, when three F2As were towed out of Harwich harbour by destroyers.*

Imperial War Museum, London (Q 69380)

*A surrendered U-boat is caught by the camera near Harwich – perhaps one of those seen later by Cecil Clayton.*

Imperial War Museum, London (HU 70331)

Goods Manufacturers Association in Toronto, while Cecil Clayton embarked upon the study of dentistry in the same city. Also back in Canada, Basil Hobbs and Robert Leckie set a post-war record in October 1920 when they flew 3265 miles in 10 days, spending 45 hours in the air in making the first trans-Canada flight. They used no less than six float and land planes on the way, including a Fairey IIIC float plane, G-CYCF, and a Felixstowe F3, G-CYEN. Hobbs also flew the Curtiss HS-2L flying boat for the Forestry Service during the dawn of bush flying. He served as a Group Captain in the Royal Canadian Air Force in the Second World War, while Leckie rose to the rank of Air Marshal and was RCAF Chief of the Air Staff from 1944 to 1947.

Having been reduced to a cadre in March 1919, the Squadron was re-established at peacetime strength by the end of the year. Post-war the Squadron's aircraft were the familiar Felixstowe F2As, F3s plus an improved version, the Felixstowe F5 and possibly Fairey IIICs.

The F5 was to become the standard RAF flying boat in the immediate post-war years. A peacetime colour scheme was applied. The wooden hulls were varnished and polished, the superstructure and the planing bottoms of the hulls were doped white. The F5 been involved in an ambitious plan made in 1919 to start

transport services to the Azores, the USA and Egypt. One F5 had made a successful 14-hour endurance trial but the project was abandoned. 230 Squadron was the first RAF unit to be equipped with this aircraft.

At that time the RAF in the United Kingdom was reorganised into three commands – Northern, Southern and Coastal Area. Coastal's duties were defined as the protection of UK waters to ensure free passage of shipping, protection of the Fleet, assistance to the RN in minesweeping and spotting, possible offensive capability against hostile naval forces and, at the bottom of the list, antisubmarine duties. The role of service flying boats was further elaborated as being to defend the country's trade and to maintain communications with all parts of the Empire. In March 1920 the force in being to carry out these tasks comprised just three squadrons!

Following Major Clayton, the Squadron's next Commanding Officer was Wing Commander CE Risk, who had commanded Felixstowe Air Station in 1913–14. He was an officer of some versatility, as may be shown by his work during the war as an expert designer and commander of armoured cars.

A tragic event happened on 29 April 1920 when the Felixstowe F5 N4044, piloted by Squadron Leader ER Moon, spun into the water from 1800 feet, a quarter of a

mile from the shore. (Rowland Moon had been a noted prewar aviator in the Southampton area, flying his Moonbeam 1 and 2 monoplanes from North Stoneham Farm between 1909 and 1912.)

Risk was replaced by Squadron Leader FGD Hards DSC, DFC in May 1920. Squadron Leader Hards had extensive combat experience with the RNAS, including attacking the Zeppelin L9 "with bombs and darts", while flying the BE2c 8326 on 25 April 1916 and bombing a U-boat with four 100 lb bombs from the Curtiss H8 8668 on 27 June 1917. He eventually attained the rank of Air Vice Marshal and was the AOC British Forces, Aden from 1941–1943.

In December 1920 Wing Commander IT Courtney took over the Squadron. In 1915, as a member of No 1 (Naval) Squadron, Courtney took part in one of the world's first long-range bombing missions. Long-range being a relative term, it was nevertheless a courageous and impressive feat. The Squadron was based at Saint-Pol, near Dunkirk, and the target was the German submarine depot at Hoboken, near Antwerp, in occupied Belgium. On 24 March Squadron Commander Courtney was the leader of a force of five Avro 504Bs which despite bad weather carried out a hazardous low level attack, destroying two submarines and setting the shipyard afire. The mission took four hours and covered 250 miles nonstop.

Risk and Courtney were two of the three Royal

Marine officers who, in August 1912, had commenced flying instruction on the first course at the new Central Flying School at Upavon. They were both awarded their Royal Aero Club Aviators' Certificates, numbers 303 and 304 respectively, on 1 October 1912. Courtney retired in the rank of Group Captain in 1932 and died in 1978 at the age of 93. Risk retired as a Wing Commander in 1922. Colonel Porte deserved a better fate. Following malicious accusations of taking bribes from the Curtiss company, he was, after a long trial, exonerated and awarded the CMG. Sadly he died in 1919 of tuberculosis.

In May 1922 the Squadron moved to Calshot which was the foremost training establishment for marine aircrew. It was built on Calshot Spit, which is the most southerly point on the west of the Solent. Until the construction of the aircraft sheds, slipways, jetties and the 'Calshot Express' narrow gauge railway, it was dominated by the ancient bulk of Henry VIII's Calshot Castle. The Squadron's main task was to exercise with the Portsmouth Submarine Flotilla and was concerned with the operational evaluation of new tactical techniques in air-sea warfare.

In less than a year, on 1 April 1923, the Squadron was disbanded and re-numbered as No 480 Coastal Reconnaissance Flight, under the command of Squadron Leader WB Callaway AFC. The flying log book of Flight Lieutenant WJ Daddo-Langlois records that on 26 July

*BD Hobbs flew as a pioneer bush pilot in Canada after the war. He is pictured here beside the Curtiss HS-2L flying boat G-CYDS.*
Defence Forces of Canada
Archive

*N4838 is a Felixstowe F5 which served with 230 Squadron firstly at Felixstowe and then at Calshot from 1921 onwards.*

JM Bruce / GS Leslie Collection

1924 he was the pilot of the Felixstowe F5 N4634 which flew as part of a formation fly-past at Calshot as part of a Royal Review. Later that summer he paid a visit to HMS *Warspite* with the CO in the same aircraft. The F5 was retained until July 1926, when Daddo-Langlois notes flying N4048 for 35 minutes on a local test and reconnaissance flight.

In the summer of 1925 the Flight had been partially re-equipped with Supermarine Southampton Mk Is, the first major military design of RJ Mitchell, later to gain fame as the creator of the Spitfire. The manufacturer's works at Woolston were but a short distance from Calshot and the Flight was the first RAF unit to receive the type. This twin-engine, open cockpit, biplane flying boat gave faithful service to the RAF for more than a decade. It was described in the contemporary magazine *The Aeroplane*:

> In the bow is the cockpit for gunner and bomb aimer, provided with a machine-gun on a Scarff mounting; behind are two cockpits for the pilots, in tandem, with dual controls. The after pilot also has a complete set of navigating equipment. Below the wings is the wireless compartment, which opens out into two staggered cockpits aft of the wings, each equipped with Scarff gun-mountings. A crew of five is normally carried. The inside of the hull may be equipped with hammocks and cooking apparatus, so that the aircraft can remain in the air for long periods. Ventilation is arranged by means

of adjustable portholes hinged to the hull plating and, with a view to reducing the hull temperatures when moored in hot climates, a specially designed awning can be supplied.

The Mk Is had wooden hulls but the main production Mk IIs introduced a hull made from duralumin which improved performance as, not only was it lighter, it did not soak up and retain water in the way that a wooden hull did. An experienced flying boat pilot, Group Captain GE Livock commented:

> The Southampton was a pleasant aircraft to fly but it was not designed for comfort and at the end of a long flight the crew would arrive very deaf and rather dishevelled. In their open cockpits, the pilots had little protection from sun or rain and none from the noise of the engines, two reliable 450 hp Napier Lions. There were no flying aids of any kind, no automatic pilot or blind-flying instruments.

In order to show off the attributes of this new machine as widely as possible, four Southamptons set out on a 20 day cruise of 10,000 miles around the British Isles which included exercises with the Royal Navy in the Irish Sea and visits to coastal towns in Northern Ireland and southwest Scotland.

The first Southampton Mk I to be delivered was N9899 – the fuselage of which is preserved to this day in the RAF Museum at Hendon. Flight Lieutenant JH

Bentham made the first flight in N9899 on 20 July 1925, going solo the next day. Later in the month he flew a series of fruitless searches for oil patches from the submarine *M1* which had been lost with all hands.

Early in September, after giving flights to officers from HMS *Royal Oak*, he commenced his part of the cruise as copilot to Flight Lieutenant Shoppe. They flew by way of Portland, Cattewater and Pembroke Dock towards Belfast. However engine failure 15 miles southeast of Wicklow Head forced them to alight on the water. They were rescued and towed to Belfast by the light cruiser HMS *Calliope*. Repairs were effected on one of the slipways at Harland and Wolff's shipyard and a trial flight was made from Belfast Lough on 21 September. *The Belfast Evening Telegraph* reported that a 'flotilla' of

similar flying boats alighted on the lough that same day, doubtless as part of the cruise mentioned above. The officers were brought ashore at Carrickfergus in the motor launch *Zaida* and the next day they flew on, by way of a landing on Lough Neagh, not far from the RAF station at Aldergrove. N9899 flew to Pembroke Dock in "thick mist, rain and fog" on 25 July, returning to Calshot, after a further delay due to more engine trouble, two days later.

In October 1925 the Air Ministry issued a special communiqué:

> Under conditions of weather which must throughout be considered distinctly bad, the Southampton flying boats have been proven to be capable of keeping in the air and carrying out such observations as visibility will permit. What is more important, the cruise has demonstrated

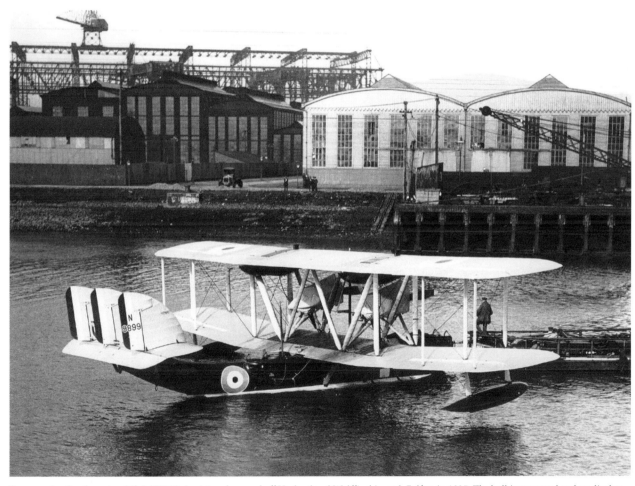

*Supermarine Southampton Mk I, N9899, is pictured moored off Harland and Wolff's shipyard, Belfast in 1925. The hull is preserved and on display at the RAF Museum.*

E Cromie Collection

that a programme once having been drawn up, it can be adhered to practically independent of the weather. Refuelling at sea was carried out on all occasions without a hitch and, provided a certain amount of shelter is available when the flying boats are not flying, it has been shown that they can function successfully quite separately and independently of their land bases.

In the following year navigational exercises to the Channel Islands and Normandy were a regular feature, as were training flights with HM ships using camera guns. Both Flight Lieutenants Bentham and Daddo-Langlois recorded in their log books flights in Fairey IIIDs (N9485, N9640 and N9733) and Supermarine Seagulls (N9607, N9646 and N9647). These may not have been on the official strength of the Flight but may instead have been attached to the Calshot Aeroplane Park.

A return visit was made to Northern Ireland in July 1926, when the five aircraft made a fine sight moored on Lough Neagh, off the town of Antrim.

Squadron Leader Callaway was succeeded by Squadron Leader A Durston AFC in January 1926, then in late 1928 Squadron Leader IT Lloyd handed over command of the Flight (which was by this time equipped with the metal-hulled Southampton Mk II) to Squadron Leader DG Donald DFC, AFC. Less than a month later, on 1 January 1929, No 201 Squadron was reformed from a coterie of nine officers, six NCO pilots and two Chilean naval officers on attachment. Callaway, Lloyd, Durston and Donald all achieved air rank in WW2. Air Vice Marshal Callaway was Senior Air Staff Officer (SASO) at Fighter Command in 1942, Air Marshal Durston was Deputy Chief of the Air Staff in 1945, Air Commodore Lloyd served at Coastal Command Headquarters for much of the time and Air Marshal Donald was AOC-in-C Maintenance Command at the end of the war.

*Officers and men of 480 Flight in front of Supermarine Southampton Mk II S1232 in 1928.*    RAF Museum

# CHAPTER 2
# 1934–1939

More than a decade was to pass before darkening skies in Europe due to the rise of the Dictators caused a hitherto complacent British government to change tack. On 30 June 1934, in the 'night of the long knives', Hitler eliminated a possible rival by using Heinrich Himmler's SS (Schutz Staffeln or Storm troopers) to liquidate the SA (Sturm-Abteilung or Brown Shirts) of Captain Ernst Roehm. On the death of President Hindenburg on 2 August, Hitler was proclaimed 'Fuhrer of the German Reich' to whom all officers had to take an oath of loyalty as head of state and supreme commander. In Italy, Mussolini was pursuing an aggressive foreign policy.

A rearmament programme was initiated and the Royal Air Force was increased in size. In 1934 only 42 of the 52 squadrons authorised in 1923 had been established; the front-line strength was less than 500 aircraft. An immediate dispensation to grow the RAF in size to 75 squadrons was made and it was intended that this would rise to 128 squadrons within five years. 230 Squadron was reformed at Pembroke Dock, in west Wales, on 1 December 1934 and it was equipped with perhaps the most successful biplane flying boat to serve with the RAF – the Short Singapore III. At this early stage Flight Lieutenant RW Hill assumed temporary command until he was replaced by Wing Commander WH Dunn DSC and bar, on 6 March 1935.

Wilfred Dunn was no stranger to marine aviation as he had been a gallant member of the RNAS during the Great War. The citation for the award of his DSC was announced in the Special Supplement of *The London Gazette* dated 22 February 1918:

> Distinguished Service Cross – Flight Commander Wilfred Henry Dunn RNAS. In recognition of his services while employed in East Africa. He did splendid work during the operations in the Lindi area and carried out valuable gun spotting, reconnaissance and bombing flights.

Lindi is on the coast of what is now Tanzania and was then German East Africa. It was the scene of confrontation between British forces and those of General von Lettow-Vorbeck. No 8 (Naval) Squadron was equipped with Voisin 5 pusher biplanes and Short 827 seaplanes, which carried out a variety of tasks, as mentioned in the citation. It is also of interest to note that the senior RNAS officer in that theatre was Squadron Commander Frederick Bowhill, who from 1937 to 1941 was AOC-in-C of Coastal Command and of whom it was said, "salt water ran in his veins".

Dunn was awarded a bar to his DFC "For conspicuous courage and skill in carrying out an extraordinary amount of flying, both in sea and land planes." He flew Bristol Fighters in India, on the North-West Frontier, in the 1920s and later served on the aircraft carrier HMS *Glorious*.

There was a certain mystique about being a flying boat pilot in the 1920s and 1930s. The "Flying Boat Union" encouraged the belief that it was the preserve of but a few with special talents not given to ordinary mortals. They sported uniform buttons and cap badges stained green from verdigris and slipped easily into nautical jargon.

It has to be admitted that there were indeed particular skills to be mastered, especially when manoeuvring the craft on the water. A flying boat, as the name implies, had the characteristics of both an aeroplane and a surface vessel. It was moored to a buoy, it carried an anchor and conditions of wind, wave, current and tide had to be assessed correctly. A good eye for the weather was essential, as was the ability to read a chart and to recognise ships of every kind and sort from the air in every degree of visibility. The skills honed and passed on by these dedicated airmen paid dividends in the conflict to come.

Flying boats were big and impressive machines, they had large crews, they went on long journeys across the oceans of the world to the far-flung corners of the Empire. The Skipper was the master of all he surveyed. It was

*Wing Commander WH Dunn won a DSC while flying Voisin biplanes in East Africa during the Great War.*

JM Bruce / GS Leslie Collection

*Short Singapore III K4579, the first to be received by 230 Squadron.*

Dennis Bracey

small wonder therefore that some had a tendency to delusions of grandeur (though not, of course, any of 230's pilots!). The undoubted cachet attached to flying boats was further fostered by the almost film star prominence given to Imperial Airways captains. The biggest aeroplane in the world was a flying boat – the German Dornier DoX, a twelve-engined monster. The flying boat was an icon of the art-deco age.

The Squadron received the first of its new aircraft, Short Singapore III K4579, on 26 April 1935 when it was flown to Pembroke Dock from the manufacturers at Rochester. Between 10 and 14 June, two aircraft, K4580 (Flight Lieutenant Grierson) and K4579 (Flight Lieutenant Mitchell) took the GOC-in-C Western Command to Ireland for his annual inspection visit. By August the Squadron had its full complement of five aircraft.

The contemporary manufacturer's sales brochure gives an excellent description of the Short Singapore III:

> The Singapore III is a high performance flying boat suitable for long-range, open-sea reconnaissance duties. It is a development of the Singapore II from which it differs in some details, the chief of which being the complete re-design of the internal equipment to bring it into line with modern requirements.
>
> Type:                Four-engined reconnaissance and coastal patrol flying boat.
>
> Wings:                Unequal span biplane. Ailerons on top and bottom wings.
>
> Hull:                Two step type. Underwater planing surface specially designed to eliminate any tendency to porpoise. Wing tips floats of similar construction to hull.
>
> Tail Unit:        Monoplane adjustable tail plane mounted on the rear end of the hull. Triple fins and rudders. Tracking central fin operable from cockpit.
>
> Power Plant:        Four Rolls-Royce Kestrel twelve cylinder water-cooled engines mounted in tandem pairs. The petrol for normal range is accommodated in the upper centre section with gravity feed to the engines. The overload petrol is carried in stainless steel tanks in the lower centre section whence it is pumped by means of the engine pumps to the main tanks. The oil tanks, each of nine gallons capacity, are situated in the nacelles. An auxiliary power unit is fitted in one nacelle for refuelling, bilging etc.
>
> Accommodation:                Bomber's position in nose cockpit with Scarff ring and stowage for mooring gear. Enclosed pilot's compartment with side-by-side seating and complete dual control. Second pilot's seat and control unit made detachable. A central gangway between the seats gives access to the front compartment. Aft of the pilots is a compartment used as the officers' quarters and is fitted with two bunks. The navigator's chart table is situated in this compartment. The space between the spar frames is occupied by the engineer and the W/T operator. Behind the rear spar frame is located the crew's quarters, which is fitted up with three bunks. Provision is arranged for cooking apparatus, work bench with vice, stowage for drogues, dinghy, engineers' ladders etc.
>
> The midship gun is arranged on a sliding mounting so that vertical fire can be obtained on both sides of the aircraft. At the extreme aft end of the hull, behind the tail, is a further gunner's cockpit.

| | |
|---|---|
| Maximum Speed: | 145 mph |
| Minimum Speed: | 65 mph |
| Initial rate of climb: | 700 ft./min. |
| Ceiling: | 15,000 ft. |
| Time to take off in flat calm: | 22 sec. |
| Range in still air at a cruising speed of 105 mph : | 1000 miles |

The excellence of this aircraft is not confined to her amazing performance, for her design embodies all the desirable qualities of seaworthiness and stability, both in the air and on the water. The workmanship and material that have been utilised in her construction are the finest available in Britain, and research experiments on models both in the wind tunnel and on the firm's own Experimental Tank were zealously pursued to their finality. The resulting full-scale product has more than amply recompensed the labour so spent.

A noteworthy incident occurred on 2 September when K4580, flown by Flight Lieutenant Hill, suffered a failure of its tailplane incidence gear over Edenbridge in Kent. It was forced to alight on the waters of the ornamental lake at Hever Castle, where it remained for eleven days as a somewhat unusual water feature. Having been repaired in situ by a team from Short Brothers, takeoff presented something of a problem, as the lake was only 700 yards long. The flying boat was roped to a tree while the engines were run up to full power by Flight Lieutenant Hill. He was accompanied only by a fitter, Corporal Lewis. (It is not recorded if the corporal volunteered for the position!) A spectacular departure was then made, thankfully not in company with the tree.

On the very same day, 13 September 1935, the

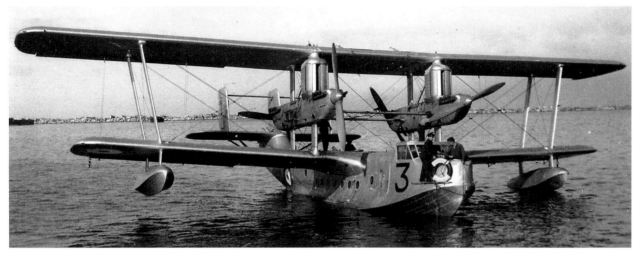

*A Short Singapore III of 230 Squadron at its mooring, with work in progress.*                    Dennis Bracey

Squadron received orders that it was to proceed to the Middle East "with all dispatch". The reason for the haste was what has become known to history as the 'Abyssinian Crisis'. The Italian dictator, Mussolini, wished to establish an East African empire and was sabre-rattling with hostile intent. The crews of the four aircraft were as follows:

K4580 – Wing Commander Dunn, Flight Lieutenant Barrett and Sergeant Pilot Powell;

K4579 – Squadron Leader Moulton-Barrett, and Pilot Officer Pettit;

K4578 – Flight Lieutenant Bainbridge, Pilot Officer Maguire and Sergeant Pilot Squire;

K4585 – Flight Lieutenant Grierson and Pilot Officer Oliver.

On the same day that three 230 Squadron aircraft arrived at Aboukir in Egypt (2 October) Italian forces invaded Ethiopia and began a brutal campaign. By the end of the month the four Singapores had shifted moorings to a permanent base in Alexandria harbour.

The routine tasks of patrols checking on Italian shipping movements and the carrying of dispatches were punctuated by taking senior officers on tours of inspection. There was also time for some sightseeing and trips were made into Cairo and to visit the Pyramids.

On 1 January 1936 K4580 undertook a search to locate the Imperial Airways Short Calcutta G-AASJ *City of Khartoum*, which had suffered engine failure on approach to Alexandria harbour. The sole survivor was the pilot, Captain Wilson.

A potentially catastrophic event was averted on 28 June 1935 when a fire occurred on the port wing of K4579 owing to an engine backfire. Only prompt action by Flying Officer Pettit and Corporal Berryman saved the fire from spreading to the complete aircraft and from there to the rest of the squadron.

Later that year, as the result of an Anglo-Egyptian Treaty, a survey was carried out of the Bitter Lakes region selecting possible sites for RAF bases. By then the Ethiopian army had been defeated by the Italians and the matter rested in the well-meaning, but ineffectual, hands of the League of Nations. In Germany, Hitler had achieved the military reoccupation of the Rhineland and the creation of the Rome-Berlin 'Axis' would soon follow. Accordingly 230 Squadron prepared to return to the UK.

The flight home was not trouble free as on passage between Lisbon and Mount Batten in August 1936, K6912, flown by Flying Officers Oliver and Wills had to force land off Vigo in Spain. The Spanish Civil War had begun and there was the real possibility of a diplomatic incident. Luckily the problem was not severe and the crew were able to keep the engines running on the water for the 17 minutes it took to rectify matters. An 'official looking' rowing boat approached but could not come alongside as K6912 was being guarded by K4580 which had landed beside; this aircraft was being flown by Wing Commander Dunn.

The Squadron did not remain in home waters for long, as on 14 October 1936, K6918 (Wing Commander Dunn,

*The Singapore III was a most graceful looking aeroplane in flight,*                    Dennis Bracey

Flying Officer Jenkins and Sergeant Pilot Powell), K6912 (Flight Lieutenant Cecil-Wright, Flying Officer Pettit and Flying Officer McBratney), K6916 (Flight Lieutenant Bainbridge and Flying Officer Maguire), K4585 (Flight Lieutenant Grierson and Sergeant Pilot Squire) and K6917 (Flying Officer Oliver and Flying Officer Wills) departed Pembroke Dock on the long haul to Singapore.

The island of Singapore, located at the southern extremity of the Malay Peninsula, was a base of immense strategic importance in respect of British interests in southeast Asia. Its position gave command of the Straits of Malacca, the main sea lane connecting the Indian and Pacific Oceans. The journey took three weeks and the route was as follows:

Pembroke Dock – Mount Batten – Berre – Malta – Aboukir – Lake Habbaniya – Basrah – Ras El Kaimah – Karachi – Allahabad – Calcutta – Mergui – Singapore.

K4585 had to make a forced landing at Kotah, between Karachi and Allahabad but was able to proceed to rendezvous with the Squadron at Allahabad the next day. All arrived safely in Singapore on 6 November. The international situation grew ever more threatening, later that month after Japan signed the Anti-Comintern Pact with Nazi Germany.

Meanwhile the Ground Party (the rest of the Squadron) was making a more leisurely way east by sea. A flavour of this long gone experience, shared by so many sent to defend the outposts of the Empire, can be gained from the memoirs of Corporal SL Manfield. He made the same journey on being posted to join the Squadron in 1938. He boarded the SS *Amra* at the King George V Dock (now part of the location of London City Airport) and sailed down the English Channel and across the Bay of Biscay, passing Gibraltar before stopping, briefly, at Malta. After nine days at sea they reached Port Said and commenced coaling. His impression of the passage through the Suez Canal is worth quoting in full:

> A large searchlight had been hung over the bow of the vessel as part of our passage was to be made during the hours of darkness and we had also picked up a pilot, a very skilled man, as it was easy to imagine the chaos that would ensue should the canal at any time be blocked. I was once given a quick rule of thumb regarding the statistics of the canal, 100 miles long, 100 yards wide and 100 feet deep; about half way along its length are the Bitter Lakes near Ismalia and it ends at Port Suez which is at the entrance to the Red Sea. The Bitter Lakes are used as lay-bys, as the ships wishing to make passage of the canal are formed into convoys at either end. Going

*The SS* Manela *in Alexandria harbour with one of 230 Squadron's Singapore IIIs at moorings.*     Dennis Bracey

*A pair of 230 Squadron Singapore IIIs, K4583 and K4578, fly over Alexandria harbour.*     Rolls-Royce plc

*On 4 February 1936, Dennis Bracey (in back row fourth on left) visited the Pyramids with other squadron members.*

Dennis Bracey

south there is quite a lot of habitation and vegetation on the starboard side but on the port side it is just desert.

Once into the Red Sea the order was given to change into the tropical issue drill uniforms, which fitted where they touched. The heat rose rapidly and at Port Sudan, "a God-forsaken place", some relief was gained by a trip in a glass-bottomed boat to view the coral and by the sight of what Manfield quaintly termed in the language of the times, 'fuzzy-wuzzies' on the shore. The highlights of the passage across the Indian Ocean were a tropical storm, a water spout, shoals of flying fish and Palethorpe's Tinned Pork Sausages for lunch. The arrival in Colombo was described graphically:

> Our first sight of the eternal dark green of the Tropics. It was a dark olive green everywhere, only changing where there were buildings, cultivation or where mountains or hills rose above the trees. My impressions

of Ceylon were that it was a lovely place, its people serene, courteous and graceful.

After a further two days at sea landfall was made again in Madras and the party transferred to the SS *Rhona*. It was a somewhat less salubrious vessel, particularly after picking up a cargo of small purple onions, so the RAF party opted to sleep on deck:

> We had to be up early in the morning before the crew started to scrub the deck but it was worth it. We had no need to worry if there was an occasional tropical shower and could luxuriate in the cool breezes, with just the sound of the waves on the side of the ship, the slight vibration of the ship's engines and the easy motion of the vessel as it slid through the phosphorescent waters. The wake of the ship was a path of light, if you dipped your hand in the sea, the water dropped off your fingertips like a cascade of crystal drops.

Having crossed the Bay of Bengal, the next stop was Penang, one of the Straits Settlements of the Federated Malay States:

> As one approached from the sea, on the port side was the mainland with mountains in the hinterland and palm trees, jungle and mangrove swamps down to the water's edge; ahead and to starboard the sandy, palm-fringed beaches of Penang island, with a large hill in the centre.

The quayside scene was exotic and unforgettable:

> . . . literally piles of tropical fruit in all colours of the rainbow - durian, lichees, mangoes, mangosteens, rambultans, papaya, breadfruit and limes. The population mix was predominantly Chinese, with Malays, Indians (Sikhs, Tamils and Bengalis) and Europeans, each race was wearing distinctive styles and colours.

Journey's end was almost at hand. After a further stop at Port Swettenham, the port for Kuala Lumpur, another 24 hours served to bring the SS *Rhona* close to Singapore:

> We were cruising very slowly through a mass of very small islands, all with palm trees and some with a Chinese temple, the sea was calm and green and gradually Singapore Island came into view. All we could see were more palm trees and buildings with bright red tiles, the occasional tree-topped hill and literally hundreds of ships of every description lying in the Roads outside the harbour. There were passenger liners, American, Japanese, Scandinavian, Dutch and French. There were junks by the hundred, bugalows from Indonesia, small coasters from the Straits Steamship Company and a host of small lighters being used to transport goods to and fro.

Having disembarked and been allocated a space for kitbags and suitcases on a waiting fleet of Morris lorries, it was time to proceed to RAF Seletar. The drive out of the docks and through the city left an indelible impression:

> . . . noise, bustle and smells. The Chinese en masse are great chatterers, always talking and arguing, motor horns were constantly being used, everyone seemed to be in a terrible hurry. Mind you they were working loading or unloading a ship at a rate that would fill European workers with horror, as would the loads that individuals carried. And then the smells, a combination of curries, spices, joss sticks, fruit, dried fish, drains and swamps. I loved it, there can have been no other place quite like it.

Leaving the city behind, the convoy drove through a rubber plantation and past the guardroom at the entrance to RAF Seletar, stopping on the parade ground. The barracks allocated to the new arrivals, 'F' Block, was a pleasant surprise:

> This was about 400 yards from the parade ground and looking down towards the Straits of Johore about 150 yards from the water's edge. Each barrack block was three stories high, no windows but louvred doors between each pair of beds. There was also a verandah about eight feet wide which ran around each floor. The views from the first floor were marvellous, with the spacious sports grounds to one side and the Straits to the other in which were moored the flying boats of Numbers 205 and 230 Squadrons.

Photographs taken of the Squadron personnel assembled formally in front of an accommodation block show the officers with pith helmets on their knees and the other ranks in old style tunics, which buttoned to the neck. All ranks wore shorts and long stockings and give the appearance of having visited local tailors rather more skilled than the makers of the standard issue kit.

Early in 1937, soon after the arrival of the Ground Party in the SS *Agamemnon*, a long-range flight was made by one aircraft, flown by Flying Officers Oliver and McBratney, taking Air Marshal Sir Edgar Ludlow Hewitt on a visit to Calcutta via Mandalay, a journey of over 2000 miles. Later in the month exercises in preparation for Combined Operations were carried out, including live bombing practice. Thus was set the pattern for the next eighteen months.

One very important occurrence out of the ordinary took place in March, when the Squadron Badge was approved by HM The King. The crest was designed by the Squadron and was inspired by the local brew, in the preparation of which the little purple onions were a vital ingredient. The label on a bottle of Tiger Beer featured a tiger under a palm tree, this was adapted and improved upon by the addition of the motto in Javanese 'Kita Chari Jauh' - translated as 'We search far' or 'We seek afar'. This was no idle boast, as was proven within a matter of days.

On 8 March, the CO led a flight of four aircraft to Hong Kong, which was 1600 miles away as the crow flies. A distinguished passenger was Air Commodore AW Tedder (later Marshal of the Royal Air Force Lord Tedder). A press report described the return journey around the South China Sea:

> At 11am on Tuesday 6 April, four flying boats of No 230 (FB) Squadron alighted at Pending, bringing with

*The mangrove swamps were a feature of the coastline in the Federated Malay States.*

Dennis Bracey

*The imposing entrance to RAF Seletar in 1936.*

Dennis Bracey

**Below:**  *A Squadron group photograph outside 'F' Block at Seletar in 1936. Wing Commander Dunn is seated in the front row, fifth left.*

Dennis Bracey

them Air Commodore AW Tedder CB, RAF. The flying boats were on their way back to Singapore after a flight to Hong Kong, their return journey having included stops at Manila, Sandakan, Kudat, Jesselton, Brunei and Miri. Since this was the first visit to Sarawak of the Air Commodore, he was accorded an official landing and was received by a guard of honour and a salute of eleven guns from Fort Margherita battery.

The flying boats were met by HHMY *Maimuna* which brought the Air Commodore and his officers to Astana, where the official landing took place. After inspecting the guard of honour, the Air Commodore was received by His Highness the Rajah; a small reception was held on Astana verandah, in the course of which His Highness welcomed the flying boats to Kuching and proposed the health of the Royal Air Force. During their stay Air Commodore Tedder and Wing Commander WH Dunn RAF, who was in command of the squadron, were the guests of His Highness the Rajah at Astana.

On the following evening a dinner and dance was held at Astana. The flying boats left for Singapore on the morning of 9 March.

It requires only a little imagination to picture the scene, the flying boats at anchor on a balmy tropical evening, soft light glittering on the water, the dance band playing, the guests in tropical mess kit, the 'White Rajah', Sir Charles Brooke, urbane, elegant and hospitable.

Dennis Bracey, who served with the Squadron between 1935 and 1938, recalled an encounter with Air

Commodore Tedder at Seletar. Bracey had been adopted by the CO as an unofficial clerk (in addition to his regular boat handling duties) as the avuncular Wing Commander Dunn had discovered that the young Aircraftman knew shorthand. When Air Commodore Tedder visited the Squadron offices, Dennis was specially introduced and praised for his skill – much to the discomfiture of the Corporal in charge.

King George VI was crowned on 12 May 1937, an event which was celebrated across the Empire, and by No 230 Squadron. One aircraft, K6917, flew to Kuala Selangor and gave flights to local native headmen. The other three aircraft performed a special formation fly-past over the Pedang in Singapore during the Coronation parade. Another similar fly-past took place the next month on the occasion of the King's official birthday. A further guest appearance was made a couple of days later at the opening of the new civil airport at Kallang, with an aerial escort being provided for His Excellency The Governor.

In October 1937, K6918, crewed by Flying Officer McBratney, Pilot Officer Alington and Sergeant Pilot Powell, acted as safety escort for the Vickers Vildebeests of No 100 (Torpedo Bomber) Squadron which were carrying out mock attacks on the 'County class' heavy cruiser HMS *Dorsetshire*. Sadly, six months later, the same aircraft conveyed a party from No 100 Squadron to perform a funeral ceremony at sea, where one of the Vildebeests had crashed. Five wreaths were deposited over the scene of the crash and 'The Last Post' was sounded by a bugler.

*The label on a Tiger Beer bottle was adapted and improved to become the Squadron badge.*

Dennis Bracey

Colonial Officers were regular passengers on inspection trips to North Borneo, Sarawak, Port Swettenham, Penang, Mergui, Kuantan, Sibu Island and the Endau River Japanese iron mine. Training cruises, navigation and parallel sweep exercises were interspersed with the annual 'Combined Operations' which usually took place in February, when good weather was likely.

In 1938, K6912 (Squadron Leader Carr and Flying Officer McBratney), K6916 (Flight Lieutenant Cecil-Wright and Pilot Officer Alington), K6918 (Flight Lieutenant Oliver and Flight Sergeant Squire) and K4585 (Flight Lieutenant Maguire and Flight Sergeant Powell) took part in three days of activities, which involved eleven separate patrols, eight night takeoffs, 48 hours and 50 minutes day flying and 16 hours 40 minutes night flying. Soon afterwards, Flight Lieutenant Cecil-Wright and Flight Sergeant Powell won the coveted Sassoon Bombing Trophy. Aerial photography was also undertaken; K6912, flown by Flying Officer McBratney, was used to take a vertical mosaic of the area whilst on a training cruise to Muar.

Although operating the Singapore III in exotic locations was undoubtedly an attractive proposition, there was a down side. The four Rolls-Royce Kestrel engines had no fewer than 96 sparking plugs, which had to be serviced, cleaned and checked. As well as 96 spare plugs an engineer was also carried. His tasks were often laborious, and without the benefit of workshop facilities. One engineer recalled another aspect of flying boat operations:

> Although these aeroplanes were marvellous weight-lifters, it was often very difficult to get off in a placid sea, which often occurred abroad. I had my first experience of a circular takeoff under these conditions. There was nearly always plenty of water and a takeoff in a large circle created a wash which helped to break down the suction under the step.

However, the Singapore's time with the Squadron was drawing to a close. In June 1938 Wing Commander Dunn was advised to expect the imminent arrival of new aircraft, the Short Sunderland. The RAF's modernisation programme was gathering speed and not before time, as the latest fruit of the policy of appeasement was the Nazi occupation of Austria by the German Army and the proclamation of union on 13 March 1938 – the Anschluss.

The prototype Short S25 Sunderland K4774 first took to the air in the hands of Short's famous Chief Test Pilot, John Lankester Parker, from the River Medway, at Rochester on 16 October 1937. The contemporary account in *Flight Magazine* described the new type:

> Essentially the Sunderland is a development of the Empire or 'C Class' of flying boat designed for Imperial Airways. The fitting of more powerful engines has permitted an increase of normal all-up weight and, despite the larger hull with its gun turrets and other military equipment, an even higher performance.

The article went on to describe the interior accommodation of the new boat:

> The pilots' compartment is generally similar in design to that of the Empire flying boat, but is placed much further aft in relation to the bow. The hull is divided into two decks, the upper accommodating two pilots side by side, a navigator, a wireless operator and engineer. Towards the rear of the upper deck, which extends to a point just aft of the main plane, is stowage for flares and maintenance cradles. The lower deck embodies the mooring compartment, lavatory, officers' wardroom, galley and quarters for the crew. The wardroom and crew's quarters have bunks and folding tables. The upper deck is reached either by a stairway adjoining the lavatory or by a ladder from the galley.
>
> Apart from the usual marine equipment (anchor, drogues, bollards etc), there is a fitter's work bench with vice; flares, with an appropriate launching chute; and provision for a camera. Other items of service equipment include marine distress signals, smoke puffs, microphone and telephone system, four rifles, two collapsible dinghies and awnings for use while at moorings in hot climates. The galley has a cooker, fresh water tanks, paraffin tank, draining rack and an ice chest.
>
> Apart from a heavy bomb load of 2000 lb, which can consist of bombs, depth charges or mines, accommodated in the hull and run out large side hatches under the wings for dropping, there are two Nash and Thompson power-driven gun turrets (bow and stern) and two midships gun mountings. There is a single Vickers gas-operated machine gun in the nose and four Browning 0.303 machine guns in the tail, two further 0.303 machine-guns can be mounted in the midships positions. The turret in the nose is arranged to be retracted rearward to permit mooring operations. This is effected manually.
>
> The floor of the front gun position is hinged; when this is folded down the position may be used for mooring and, when up, the floor acts as a footrest for

the gunner. There is a small flap which forms the bomb aimer's seat.

The production machines have four Bristol Pegasus XXII engines, which are rated at 840 hp at 4000 feet, the maximum power for all-out level flight being 890 hp at 6500 feet. For takeoff 1010 hp is available. De Havilland three-bladed, two-position, variable-pitch airscrews are standard. The Sunderland has six fuel tanks in the wing, three on each side of the hull. The inboard pair of tanks hold between them 1058 gallons; the intermediate pair 711 gallons; and the outer pair (employed for overload condition) 265 gallons. Oil is carried in four tanks, one in each engine nacelle, the normal capacity of each being 23 gallons. The maximum speed is 210 mph at 6250 feet, the maximum cruising speed (normal rpm) is 178 mph at 5750 feet, the minimum flying speed is 80 mph, the rate of climb from sea level is 1200 feet per minute, the service ceiling is 20,500 feet, the time to take off in a 10 mph wind is 23 seconds, the normal range in still air is 1670 sea miles and the overload range in still air is 2500 sea miles.

Despite its great bulk, the hull was so well designed aerodynamically by the Shorts team under Arthur Gouge that its drag was actually less than that of the Singapore III. Hydrodynamic performance was also improved by introducing a vertical knife-edge at the rear of the second step on the planing bottom.

The first Sunderlands were issued to No 210 Squadron at Pembroke Dock and it was crews from that squadron and No 209 Squadron which delivered the initial aircraft allocated to No 230 Squadron. The first departed the UK on 9 June 1938 and was the second production model L2159. Captained by Flight Lieutenant WA Hughes, it flew by way of Gibraltar, Malta, Alexandria, Lake Habbaniyah, Bahrain, Karachi, Gwalior, Calcutta, Rangoon and Mergui, arriving at Seletar on 22 June, in record time. There was much paperwork to be completed; manuals, forms and records to be updated and copied. Dennis Bracey's clerical skills were called into use; he was allocated an attap thatched hut, a typewriter, a duplicator, mounds of paper, piles of stencils and gallons of ink. He emerged blinking into the sunlight – very tired and extremely inky, what seemed like a very long time later.

Further Sunderlands arrived at intervals over the next few months until the Squadron reached its full strength of eight aircraft on 22 December. By this stage the international situation had worsened with the annexation, by Germany, of the Sudetenland, ratified by the Munich

Agreement of 29 September 1938. Nor was the position in the Far East any more encouraging, Japan had invaded China in 1937 and in the following year Japanese forces were engaged in combat with Soviet troops.

One of the first tasks for the new aircraft was to operate Close Convoy Patrols to the submarine depot ship HMS *Medway*, the old 'V & W Class' destroyer HMS *Westcott* and the more modern destroyer HMS *Diana*. Another duty to arise in September was the visit by L2164, flown by Flight Lieutenant Maguire and Pilot Officer Smith, to Sarawak and British North Borneo. The objects of the mission were threefold – to convey the Senior Air Staff Officer, to carry out photographic exercises and to train crews in operating away from base.

The purchase of several of the Sunderlands had been funded by a gift of £300,000 from the Sultans of the Federated Malay States. Accordingly these aircraft were flown to christening ceremonies by the Sultans of Perak, Selangor, Pehang and Negri-Sembilan. On each occasion the Air Officer Commanding, Air Vice Marshal JT Babington CBE, DSO was present, as well as the newly promoted Group Captain Dunn DSC. Considerable favourable newspaper coverage was given in *The Straits Times*, Singapore. Excited crowds witnessed the events, as members of the ruling families and colonial officials were taken for inaugural flights.

During the latter part of 1938, two Vickers Wellesleys of the Long Range Development Flight, led by Squadron Leader R Kellet, made a successful world distance record-breaking, 48-hour, 7158 miles, nonstop flight from Ismalia in Egypt to Darwin, Australia. 230 Squadron's L2160, with Flight Lieutenant Oliver and Pilot Officer McCall took part in this by flying to Kuching in Sarawak on 5 November to act as security aircraft.

The Squadron's new Commanding Officer, Wing Commander GM Bryer OBE, AFC arrived on board Sunderland L5801 on 15 November. Born in 1897, he had first been enthused by flight after meeting Cody and Bleriot in 1912. Subsequent service with the RNAS had included early deck landing trials with Sopwith Pups, for which he was awarded the AFC. In the 1920s he flew Westland Wapitis on the North-West Frontier.

One of the new CO's first duties was to lead a 'Colonial Development Cruise' of three aircraft – L2161, L2160 and L5801 – taking the AOC to Ceylon. As well as the useful purpose of 'showing the flag', the aim

*The first Short Sunderland to arrive with the Squadron made quite an impression on Dennis Bracey, as regards paperwork.*

Dennis Bracey

of the expedition was also to examine the harbours at Trincomalee, Galle and Colombo as potential flying boat bases, to enable the AOC to inspect the Air Ministry works at Trincomalee and to carry out some long distance operational training. In Colombo the opportunity was taken to give a few VIPs, including the Governor, a pleasure flight.

In the middle of these pleasant diversions the chance for a task of a more operational nature arose, and which resulted in a potentially very dangerous incident. On 12 December the formation was asked to locate and report on the whereabouts of an Italian cruiser reported to be on its way to Singapore. Adverse weather conditions arose which caused the aircraft to split up. Then the port outer engine of L2161 seized, causing the airscrew to shear off and remove the propeller from the port inner as well. The crew set course for the Nicobar Islands and landed at Nancowry, accompanied by L5801. Meanwhile L2160 had successfully located and shadowed the cruiser, making the first nonstop flight from Ceylon to Singapore in the process. It is a testament to the flying qualities of the Sunderland and to the airmanship of the crew that L2161 survived the loss of two engines and was flying on the starboard pair

alone. Nancowry was approximately equidistant between Trincomalee and Seletar, being about 900 miles away from each. *The Straits Times* reported that only one man on the island, a Bengali hospital dresser, could speak English.

It took a month of activity before L2161 was able to return to Seletar. Firstly, the Senior Engineering Officer had to be flown in to inspect the damage, then stores and supplies had to brought to the marooned aircrew. Next, the good ship RAFA *Aquarius* made passage to Nancowry with four spare engines and two airscrews. It also brought Pilot Officer Smith, in the capacity of second mate, who then relieved Pilot Officer Alington as the captain of L2161. More supplies, doubtless of a festive nature, were flown in on Christmas Eve. Five days later another supply flight brought fuel and uplifted the Native Quartermaster of the *Aquarius*, who was suffering from appendicitis.

This relief aircraft, L2160, nearly came to grief the next day when it suffered a massive drop in oil pressure, forcing it to make an emergency landing at Great Nicobar Island. Having lashed the propeller to avoid further damage, L2160 returned to Nancowry. One of the engines intended for L2161 was fitted to L2160, with considerable

urgency and it was able to leave for Seletar with the sick seaman on New Year's Day 1939. A further reinforcement machine set off from base, bringing another replacement engine, more fuel and fitters to replace the overworked personnel on Nancowry. Meanwhile the *Aquarius* had

departed to Sabang for refuelling and re-provisioning, from whence it returned on 8 January. Having had enough shenanigans, Wing Commander Bryer decided to remain on the island to direct operations. Yet another Sunderland, L2164, brought the final load of fuel. After an

unsatisfactory flight test on 10 January, L2161, escorted by L2164 finally took off for home the following day. Only a short stop had to be made en route to rectify a slight defect in the lubrication system.

At this point it may be instructive to record a description of Nancowry as it was in 1939, made by Corporal SL Manfield, whom we met earlier:

> The Nicobar Islands are a group of three, one of which is called Nancowry – Isle of the Naked. The natives lived in huts, shaped like beehives, thatched with palm leaves and standing on poles to keep out the rats and alike. Their religion was Animist, ie they worshipped spirits. They lived on fish, coconuts and rice grown in the forest clearings. Most of the land was jungle, right down to the water's edge.

He went on to record his impressions of a tropical night:

> It is full of the sound of crickets and frogs which abound in the jungle, the wind soughs through the trees and the leaves make crackling noises. All sorts of night birds call, mainly nightjars and owls. Mammals also occasionally call to each other, monkeys and deer. The sea is phosphorescent and glows in the starlight, one can hear it breaking on the beaches and also there is the hollow sound of waves entering caves on the cliffs beneath us. The final glory is the sky which is absolutely magnificent – a very deep purple colour covered with thousands and thousands of stars. The Milky Way really is a creamy river across the sky and there are always shooting stars everywhere. There is always an electrical storm somewhere in sight, constant vivid flashes of light and sometimes a rumble of thunder. The dawn indeed does "come up like thunder", one moment it is night and the next it is day.

Further details were added by TD Crompton:

> The coral beds surrounding the shores make the sea appear to be an exquisite assortment of colours from pale green to deep blue. Queen Ishlon, the ruler of nearby Champion Island, was very interested in our welfare and even presented us with a cooked pig on Christmas Day. She received our people in her palace. Her courtiers did a series of war dances to the tune of Clementine, which Doctor Sapre, the Indian District Officer thought must have been introduced into the islands by a visiting Methodist missionary years previously. The natives are short in stature the males usually being sturdily built. The women, when young, are quite attractive but get large and flabby at an early age.

*One of the ground crew surveys a steamer coming up the creek, from an excellent vantage point.*
Dennis Bracey

It is worth noting that 230 Squadron was the first to become operational on the Sunderland and that much useful work was being done during the intensive work-up period, proving the type in the challenging conditions of the Far Eastern climate.

Another non-routine occurrence happened in the middle of February, when following a navigation exercise over the South China Sea, four aircraft were ordered to carry out a parallel track search south of Singapore Island, "to locate a submarine of a foreign power believed to be in the vicinity without Admiralty sanction". Despite three days of intense activity nothing was sighted.

Further evidence of heightened tensions was given by another operation in March, taking the AOC and the Command Signals Officer to Borneo, with a view to surveying locations for Direction Finding (D/F) stations for use in war and as emergency landing grounds. A few days later, three aircraft were dispatched to exercise with the China Seas Fleet and, in particular, the aircraft carrier HMS *Eagle* and two escorting cruisers. Two mock dive bombing attacks were carried out by Flying Officer Smith in L2164.

Tragedy was to strike in June when L5801 crashed on takeoff in the Johore Straits. Pilot Officer Barnes and Aircraftman Mills were drowned, while Aircraftman Cook died in hospital the same morning. The aircraft was written off as a total loss. The replacement N9029 arrived at Seletar from the UK on 25 July – camouflaged and modified with a new bomb-aimer's hatch.

The storm clouds were growing. In March Germany annexed the Czech provinces of Bohemia and Moravia and on 23 August the Nazi-Soviet treaty of non-aggression was signed in Moscow by Foreign Ministers Molotov and Ribbentrop. Two days later the British Government signed a Treaty of Mutual Assistance with Poland. Steadily, the preparations for hostilities marched on. Two squadrons Nos 11 and 39, both flying Blenheim light bombers, were moved from India to reinforce Singapore. 230 Squadron was deployed to cover the move. From 28 August one Singapore III (from No 205 Squadron) and one Sunderland were continuously maintained at 60 minutes notice and one Singapore III and one Sunderland at two hours notice between 0630 and 1830 daily.

On 1 September 1939 the Luftwaffe initiated the German invasion of Poland and war with Germany was declared on 3 September. The Operations Room at Seletar was placed on continuous duty and the Squadron commenced flying antisubmarine patrols.

A week after Mr Chamberlain's announcement, the CO lectured his men on the subject of Efficiency of Personnel in Wartime. A more informal lecture delivered to Imperial Airways staff a little later may have been more entertaining – the Squadron Record notes laconically, "Squadron told to vacate a buoy by Imperial Airways, CO refused." In October there was a scare that the German heavy cruiser *Admiral Scheer* was in the area but searches proved fruitless. Routine duties, convoy and anti-sabotage patrols took up most of the time.

On 27 October a major detachment of six aircraft was sent to China Bay on the northeastern side of Ceylon and developed facilities for the opening up of flying boat stations there and also at Koggala in the southwest.

*Sunderland Mk I L5801 overflies a Far Eastern landscape, possibly Seletar. Note the No 230 Squadron badge on the forward end of the 'boat's fuselage.*

John Elms / John Evans Collection

# CHAPTER 3
# 1940–1942

In February 1940 Ceylon officially became the
Squadron's base and the remnant remaining at Seletar
was absorbed by No 205 Squadron as 'S' Flight. Some
convoy patrols were flown but there was very little action
in this theatre at this stage of the war. Flying Officer Alan
Lywood later described this early experience of Ceylon:

> There were no marine craft in Ceylon, we brought our
> own dinghies, we took over a lake, put the level of water
> up and had our own elephant to move things around.

Thought was given to establishing a detachment in the
Seychelles and, indeed, Squadron Leader Geoffrey Francis
was sent to the islands to reconnoitre a base. However
this was not to be, which, in the light of Squadron Leader
Alan Deller's later description of the charms of the
islands, may have been something of a blessing:

> The local women were almost uniformly lovely, mostly
> exceedingly friendly and, regrettably, in very many cases
> carrying a particularly virulent form of VD.

On 1 May the order was received, by signal from
the Air Ministry, to prepare for an immediate move to
Alexandria. Naturally this was operationally sensitive
and was classified secret. Wing Commander Bryer, many
years later, told of how the cover was blown by the
freighter carrying much of the Squadron's heavy material;
it moored at Colombo proudly displaying its purpose and
destination to any interested parties, one of whom was
Lord HawHaw, William Joyce, who was able to announce
the fact within 24 hours in a propaganda broadcast.

During the war, the Air Ministry produced an
account of the work of Coastal Command in which
it described the character and duties of the General
Reconnaissance (GR) crews:

> In temperament they resemble their comrades in
> Bomber rather then those in Fighter Command. This
> is natural, for their duties have this much in common
> – they involve flights of many hours' duration in almost
> all weathers, and during much of that time the main

preoccupation must be whether the aircraft is on its
right course or not. Then, however, the resemblance
grows thin. The crew of a bomber are concerned to find
a target, which is usually stationary and to hit it with
their bombs. Those of an aircraft of Coastal Command
have first to find what is very often a moving target and
then to hit it or to keep it under observation so that a
striking force may do so. Moreover, if they are on convoy
protection – and this form of patrol is one of their main
duties and entails the spending of many thousands of
hours in the air and the covering of many millions of
miles over the sea – they may never see a target at all,
though they must constantly be on the look out for one.
They are therefore, generally speaking of a phlegmatic
turn of mind. The chief enemy is boredom, which may
provoke first inattention, then indifference. The crews
must spend hundreds of hours with nothing to look
upon but the expanse of sea and sky. The largest aircraft
operated by Coastal Command is the Sunderland, which
is impressive and commodious but has less room inside
it for the crew than a small fishing smack.

Operating flying boats was a much more demanding
life for aircrew than was the case with land-based
aircraft. Takeoff procedure had to be completed without
the assistance of ground crew – there was no team with
a generator at hand to start the engines. Instead the
Sunderland's petrol driven auxiliary power unit (APU)
was contained in a housing in the wing, by No 3 engine,
onto which crew members had to clamber to start it up
with a pull cord – in much the same fashion as a lawn
mower. When the outboard engines had fired the APU
could be shut down. When these engines were running at
the correct temperature the captain would then give the
order to slip the buoy – to release the rope attaching the
aircraft to it. As the aircraft taxied towards takeoff point
the inner engines were then started. One engineer kept
watch on his instrument panel while the other stood at
the Plexiglas astrodome keeping a good lookout astern.

The captain then called out "Clear take off!", to which the engineer would reply, "Clear above and astern, standing by the booster pumps." The two pilots began to open the four throttle control levers to full power. As the speed through the water increased, so the noise level increased until the aircraft rose onto the 'step' and the transition from waterborne to airborne craft was made. (The 'step' was a lateral division of the hull halfway along its bottom designed to raise the after part clear of the water, thus reducing water-drag and making it easier for the aircraft to obtain the increased speed necessary to enable it to 'plane' over the surface of the water instead of ploughing through it.)

Landing was another seminal experience for the novice, as the noise level on touchdown could be quite alarming. The pilot then had to approach the buoy with great care. In difficult conditions it was not unknown for a crew member to be left clinging to the buoy while the captain taxied around for another go.

The long day of a flying boat crew was not yet over. Even after an eight or ten hour patrol, the aircraft still had to be refuelled, the engine covers put on, watertight doors fastened and everything made secure. The crew would then repair ashore in a dinghy for debriefing and the completion of the necessary paperwork. At night the taxying required in the ill-lit flare path area could add another hour on the water. Teamwork and a close comradeship was vital, as they would be spending many hours in each others company – almost literally in a world of their own.

At this time the Mediterranean theatre was considered to be second only in importance to the defence of the United Kingdom. Britain maintained bases and forces in Egypt, Palestine and Trans-Jordan and the Royal Navy had vital anchorages at Malta, Gibraltar and Alexandria. Moreover trade routes to India, the Far East and the oil supplies from Iraq and Persia came through the Suez Canal and the Red Sea.

230 Squadron arrived in Alexandria on 6 May, in the words of Alan Lywood, "a little Imperial Airways staging post with one slipway and a small dirt standing area next to the yacht club". It was soon to be under the command of Wing Commander Geoffrey Francis. He was described by Alan Lywood as follows:

> He was the best pilot we had, I should think the best navigator, a very good wireless operator, a canny

engineer and a courageous man. He exemplified the RAF training before the war – which was that you couldn't or shouldn't be allowed to command or tell anyone what to do, unless you could do it yourself.

On promotion to Group Captain, Wing Commander Bryer became OC of 201 Group at Alexandria, consisting of 228 and 230 Squadrons. These were the only long-range maritime reconnaissance assets available to RAF Middle East Command at that time. The AOC-in-C was Air Chief Marshal Sir Arthur Longmore, who had been an early airman of considerable distinction with the RNAS, having flown Naval Biplane No 2 as early as December 1911. His deputy was Arthur Tedder, who was later appointed to replace Longmore in May 1941.

The overall war situation was far from comfortable. Seizing the opportunity for easy pickings with minimum effort at what was perceived as a time of maximum weakness, Italy declared war on Britain and France on 10 June 1940. Mussolini was much more keen on the prospect than the Italian Naval Staff who had not planned to go to war before 1942 at the earliest. They were to find that they had bitten off rather more than they could chew. The Italian fleet was well-equipped – better armed, faster and more modern than the RN's Mediterranean Fleet under Admiral Sir Andrew Cunningham. It also possessed more than 100 submarines. The balance of power was fairly even if the French fleet was added to the equation. But the calculations were soon to change, as on 22 June the Franco-German armistice was signed. Britain was now fighting against the odds.

One asset which Britain had to maintain was the island of Malta. It was vital as a base and a fortress in the midst of waters which would otherwise have been dominated by the enemy. Both 228 and 230 Squadrons supplied detachments to the island. Their base on the island was at Kalafrana. The naval historian Donald MacIntyre wrote of the island during this period:

> The contest largely revolved around the ability of the British to build up and preserve the little island of Malta. This involved the supply and replenishment of the fortress and the efforts by the enemy to eliminate it.

The strategic position of the island dictated its use as a base to provide cover for the replenishment of British forces in North Africa and for the denial of the same to enemy supply convoys.

The Squadron wasted little time getting into the

thick of the action. On 20 June the CO was on an early morning patrol in L2160/X when he was attacked by four Italian fighters – Fiat CR32s or Fiat CR42 Falcos. These highly manoeuvrable biplanes and the well-armed flying boat had quite a fight, which ended with one of the enemy aircraft being shot down by the rear gunner. Leading Aircraftman Jack Beauchamp, the gunner in the front turret wrote many years later of the Sunderland's fuel tanks being holed and of a great shower of petrol cascading down the ladder leading from the top deck to the galley. He added:

> I scrambled up the ladder and found the top deck about an inch deep in petrol. After much plugging of holes which we could reach through the wing root we settled down to make our way back to 'Alex'. In my mind it was a miracle that we did not burn as there must have been quite a flash when the bullets exploded.

So 230's first taste of action in World War Two had a successful conclusion.

Even better was to follow a week later, when Flight Lieutenant WW Campbell in L5804/S attacked and sank the Italian submarine *Argonauta* on 28 June. He repeated the dose the next day, when he sank another, the *Rubino*. The first action was described graphically by one of the crew, Roy Diss:

> The majority of alarms were due to birds or fish but on this day, way off on the beam, was a sub travelling at periscope depth. We turned away to wind out the bomb racks and prepare for the attack. In the early marks of boat the loading and winding out of the racks was manual and our earlier practise paid off. As armourer I had the responsibility for the bombs and all weapons on board and acted also as tail gunner. We turned to come out on to the sub from astern, which was oblivious of our presence. The attack was made with four 250 lb A/S bombs which fell close enough to damage and disable; the second attack finished it off. The debris and oil were positive proof to us but the claim of the sinking was not confirmed "as there is no knowledge of a submarine in that area".

This was later changed. Diss then went on to describe the second attack:

> It was spotted on the surface, our preparation time was now much shorter and again from astern. The bow turret was instructed to pour concentrated fire into the conning tower. No-one could be seen on watch on the submarine. The first four bombs dropped two on either side of the sub which promptly broke in half forward of the conning

tower; the second four almost lifted the stern section out of the water. We stood off and wound in the bomb racks and as we circled, survivors were seen in the water. Bill Campbell calmly advised us over the intercom, that he was landing to pick up our proof from the sea. Against normal practice I was to remain in the tail turret in case we were attacked. How we managed to land and take off in that swell I shall never know. Our message to Malta to lay on a POW escort caused confusion; we arrived with only three survivors, to be met so it seemed, by most of the 'Brass' of Malta.

A few days later *The Times* carried a report of Sunderland L5804's exploits:

> While patrolling, the aircraft sighted the periscope of an enemy submarine, whereupon it immediately conducted a dive-bombing attack and released some special bombs. The force of the explosion almost blew the submarine out of the water. Her nose rose sharply to the surface and then the boat appeared to slide vertically downwards. Huge air bubbles were seen at once while smaller ones continued to rise for some time and oil also appeared on the surface of the sea. Returning two hours later, the pilot saw a huge patch of oil, 300 by 500 yards in extent. The next day the same flying boat, with the same crew, again sighted an Italian submarine on the surface. Again a dive-bombing attack with special bombs sank the submarine. Some of the crew of the submarine were blown into the sea by the force of the explosion. The pilot brought his aeroplane down and picked up three lieutenants, all suffering from shock. A search for more survivors had to be abandoned as a local storm was blowing up. While returning to its base the aircraft spotted yet another Italian submarine. All its bombs having been used, the aeroplane swooped down and raked the conning tower and bridge of the submarine with all its available machine-guns. The operation was repeated a second time before the submarine crash-dived.

Arnold Hutchison was part of the crew on both of these attacks, he recalled the Skipper as "a big, happy go lucky character, a real gentleman". The survivors from the *Rubino* were:

> . . . put into the wardroom between the front door and the kitchen, one in each corner. An armed guard was put in the kitchen to keep an eye on them. As we were working away from base, all of us had spare clothing on board so we dug around and gave them some dry clothes to wear then made them a pot of hot tea to warm them up. Before going ashore in Malta, the Captain of the submarine

thanked us for saving their lives. Two days later our spare uniforms were delivered to us all nicely laundered.

His next encounter with Italians was less friendly, as the aircraft in which he was flying as nose gunner was attacked by two Breda fighters:

> It wasn't nice sitting a few feet off the water, being shot at by some evil-minded Italian and thinking if the pilot gets hit, I'm going to be first in the drink.

Luckily they shook off the attackers and made it safely back to Malta.

A few days later a new pilot joined the Squadron as Navigation Officer. His name was Flying Officer Dundas Bednall and he subsequently wrote about his experiences during two wartime tours of duty with 230. His initial impressions were very favourable:

> The Squadron scene was one of hustle and bustle and great activity. Nevertheless I was warmly greeted and made to feel at home immediately. I never really found out what the old sea dogs really thought of a landlubber bomber pilot being posted to them as Navigation Officer. They would have been quite within their rights to have raised an eyebrow or two but to their credit, they never showed it.

The Squadron was based in Alexandria harbour on board the SS *Dumana*, which was moored between the battleship HMS *Warspite* and HMS *Medway*, a submarine depot ship. The engineering facilities were ashore but as bringing a Sunderland up the slipway by attaching a beaching chassis was a time-consuming operation, much servicing and maintenance was carried out afloat. For this purpose sections of the wing leading edge were designed to fold down as platforms about a foot square on which a fitter could perch. If the front of the engine or the airscrew needed attention frames were attached on to the little platforms and a light alloy plank, eight inches wide, was passed under the engine and located on the frames at the side. If a tool or part was dropped, it fell into the water and was lost forever. For major servicing the aircraft was taxied close to the slipway, a hawser was then attached to the aft end of the keel and was hooked up to a mobile crane which hauled the aircraft around ready to be pulled backwards up the slipway and onto the hard standing. In the meantime a wading party had fitted the beaching legs on either side of the hull and the steerable tail trolley close to the hawser attaching point.

Each aircraft had its own dedicated team consisting of engine fitters, riggers, electricians, instrument fitters and an armourer. When flying the fitters and riggers became air-gunners and on the water they acted as seamen carrying out mooring operations.

A good example of the skill and dedication of these men is the courage shown by the crew of L5804/S on 28 July. It was on patrol between Alexandria and Malta, flown by Squadron Leader C Ryley, when it was attacked by four Italian Macchi MC200 fighters. The engagement lasted nearly an hour. One fighter was destroyed and another damaged. Three of the air-gunners were wounded but stuck to their posts. The Sunderland was also badly damaged and was only kept flying by LAC Campbell, who climbed into the wings and plugged the

*Sunderland Mk I N9029/V is seen is this air-to-air shot. The pilot is recorded as Flight Lieutenant Alan Lywood.*
JL Watson/John Evans Collection

holes until overcome by petrol fumes. The front turret gunner was LAC Jack Beauchamp, who by this time must have been getting quite used to aerial combat.

Flying Officer Bednall had been allocated to N9029/ V as second pilot and navigator, the captain being Flying Officer Alan Lywood. This partnership was to last for nine months throughout a very active period of the Squadron's history although it began somewhat inauspiciously with a 'rocket'.

Lywood and Bednall had been tasked to a routine patrol of the Ionian Sea, south of Italy and east of Sicily when a convoy of five ships, escorted by an Italian destroyer was sighted. Lywood decided to attack and could certainly claim to have – at the very least – 'put the wind up' the enemy and shown the right aggressive spirit. On return to base the next day, instead of the expected hearty congratulations, they were told off in no uncertain terms. The Navy in Malta was concerned lest the Italians became 'irritated' and retaliated. Fortunately this attitude did not prevail for long and 230 was allowed to act in a warlike manner.

While hunting submarines, bombing ships and shooting down fighters attracted the headlines, much of the Squadron's work was equally valuable but unsung. Fourteen transport trips carrying much-needed supplies were flown into Malta. Admiral Cunningham himself recognised the value of long hours of sometimes monotonous reconnaissance patrols over the sea. He told Wing Commander Francis that each Sunderland was as valuable to him as a cruiser and praised the gallantry and dedication to duty of the hard-worked crews. Patrols could last from 10 to 12 hours – out of sight of land except for glimpses of the enemy coast and, due to the need to keep radio silence, out of touch with the rest of the world. There were no artificial aids to assist with the search other than binoculars; eye-strain was a particular hazard, bearing in mind the glare of the sun's rays on the sea. To help the time pass as comfortably as possible in the circumstances, the Sunderland was well-equipped as regards catering facilities. Hot tea, coffee or cocoa was in plentiful supply. The main meal would usually consist of the infamous Machonachie's tinned stew but often a crew member would reveal talent as a chef by the preparation of such delights as corned beef fried in thick batter.

Good navigation was a vital skill. The main methods used were the taking of astronomical sights with a marine sextant, when the visibility was suitable or a bubble sextant when the horizon was obscured, followed by calculations from the book of tables and Dead Reckoning. Dead Reckoning involved two factors: the extent to which the wind was causing the aircraft to drift from the track plotted on the navigator's chart, in other words the angle between the course actually flown and the course plotted (track) and the true speed at which the aircraft was flying, that is the speed at which it was passing over the sea. The drift sight was aligned on an object in the sea such as a wave cap until the object appeared to travel along the wires of the sight; the drift of the object could then be read off on a scale. Ground speed could be worked out by the calculation of wind velocity. The resulting figure would then be added to the air speed if it was a tailwind or subtracted if it was a headwind. The navigator was constantly at work taking sights, calculating and plotting. It was vitally important for the navigational plot to be highly accurate not only to enable a safe return to base but also to ensure that the position of any enemy shipping spotted could be reported exactly.

The Squadron achieved another notable success on 30 September 1940 when Flight Lieutenant PH Alington in L2166/U was signalled by the Australian destroyer HMAS *Stuart*. Attacks had been made by warships on the Italian submarine *Gondar* which had been seriously damaged. A bombing run made by the Sunderland was the last straw, with the crew scuttling the submarine and abandoning ship.

In October 1940 Italy declared war on Greece in the expectation of a quick and easy victory over a weaker opponent. This was not to be, as the Italian forces, though numerically superior, proved incompetent. The effect of this action on 230 Squadron was to further broaden its area of operations. A new base for detached duty was established at Suda Bay on the north coast of Crete. Dundas Bednall describes the scene:

> After the barren rocks of Malta and the deserts of Egypt, Crete seemed like an oasis to us. We were encamped in an olive grove a short distance up the slope of a hill from Suda Bay. Ours were the normal RAF pattern tents and the ripened olives falling from the trees went plop, plop throughout the night. On the rare occasions when we had an hour or two to spare, several of us would walk up the steep escarpment to the ridge, where there was a typical Greek village set amid breathtaking views of the Cretan mountains.

The Sunderlands were by now armed with depth charges rather than bombs, which proved to be much more efficient when attacking submarines. As well as antisubmarine and general reconnaissance patrols, providing air cover for Aegean Sea convoys and supporting the Mediterranean Fleet in its Ionian Sea actions, the Squadron also flew a number of VIP transport missions. Passengers carried included such notable figures as General Sir Archibald Wavell (Commander in Chief Middle East), General Sir John Dill (Chief of the Imperial General Staff) and Anthony Eden (the Foreign Secretary), taking them to confer with the authorities in Athens and Cairo, as Britain prepared a military force to assist Greece. By a strange coincidence, the pilot carrying Eden and Dill reported seeing "a small grey ship with a number of ragged seamen gesticulating wildly". This was HMS *Dolphin* – a small sailing vessel employed on clandestine operations. One of the "ragged seamen" was Alan Deller, whose name will appear again in this narrative.

A further base was set up in January 1941 at Scaramanga, on the shores of Lake Eleusis, near Athens, again described by Dundas Bednall:

> A most impressive feature of Scaramanga was the marvellous feeling of well-being on breathing the cool, scented airs descending from those pine clad mountains. The majority of patrols took us along the Gulf of Corinth past the mystical Delphi.

The detachment commander was Squadron Leader Pat Alington.

In the meantime, on the night of 11 November the Italian fleet had been dealt a severe blow by an attack at Taranto, using torpedo-armed Fairey Swordfish aircraft of the Fleet Air Arm. On the other hand the Germans were also making plans to take a hand in Greece and the Balkans. Arrangements were also made to alter the balance of power in the air by the deployment of Fliegerkorps X of the Luftwaffe to Sicily. By January 1941 it was in position and ready to strike at Malta. A British success was gained on 7 February when the forces commanded by Major General O'Connor defeated the Italians and captured all of eastern Libya. However in the same month Lieutenant General Erwin Rommel arrived in North Africa in command of the Afrika Korps. Once more the Germans were having to bail out their incompetent ally. Rommel attacked in March pushing the Allied army back. Britain and the Empire were beset on all sides.

The vital role played by one of 230 Squadron's crews in opening an opportunity for a tactical and strategic victory on 28 and 29 March 1941 has, perhaps, not been fully appreciated. Sunderland N9029/V, flown by Flight Lieutenants Alan Lywood and Dundas Bednall was ordered to take off from Scaramanga to search the seas to the south of Crete. The previous day Flight Lieutenant Ian McCall in L2161/P had spotted elements of the Italian Fleet at sea but in the misty conditions had lost contact. The Royal Navy at Alexandria immediately prepared to leave port but Admiral Cunningham needed to know where the Italians were heading. The crew of N9029/V made sightings of two squadrons of Italian cruisers and for the next thirteen hours shadowed the enemy and reported their position to HQ in Alexandria. Guided by these reports the Royal Navy closed in. The Battle of Matapan was a heavy defeat for the Italians and was of considerable assistance in improving British morale at one of the war's darkest periods.

One of the young naval officers serving with the Fleet at Matapan, in the battleship HMS *Valiant*, was Midshipman Philip Mountbatten. 230 Squadron was asked to give him a little air experience flying; Dundas Bednall remembered him as "a most likeable man" and wondered if he recalled his time on patrol in NM/V.

An army of 60,000 British, Australian and New Zealand troops was sent to Greece on 5 April 1941. The next day, as the Greek Government had feared, the Germans invaded Greece and Yugoslavia. The German force proved irresistible as it swept down through the two countries. Within three weeks Yugoslavia was overrun and the Allied forces in Greece had withdrawn to Crete. On 18 April N9029/V flew from Scaramanga to Alexandria via Suda Bay carrying King Peter of Yugoslavia, General Simonovitch, other members of the Royal Family, as well as political and military staff, into exile. Worse was to follow, as Crete was subjected to the first really large, sophisticated, well co-ordinated airborne assault in history, commanded by the German General Karl Student.

During the months of April and May RAF Sunderlands of 230 and 228 Squadrons, Bristol Bombays of 216 Squadron, Lockheed Lodestars of 267 Squadron and two BOAC Empire flying boats G-AEUI *Coorong* and G-ADUV *Cumbria*, flew many sorties between Greece, Crete, Yugoslavia and Egypt, evacuating more than 2000 personnel and saving tons of valuable stores.

*Flight Lieutenant Dundas Bednall alights Sunderland Mk I T9050/Y at Suda Bay, Crete in April 1941. This aircraft was lost in September 1941 in a crash at Aboukir Bay.*

Wg Cdr Dundas Bednall/John Evans Collection

*Two Mk I Sunderlands of No 230 Squadron moored off the south coast of Crete during the evacuation of British and Commonwealth troops in May 1941.*

Imperial War Museum, London (CM 759)

There are many individual tales that can be told including Flight Lieutenant Bednall being ordered to give priority to the AOC's wife and her pet parrot, the evacuation of the Greek Royal Family by Alan Lywood and the embarkation of 74 passengers by Wing Commander Francis in T9050/Y, including six standing in the lavatory. One of the passengers was Captain James Roosevelt, the son of the US President, who had been in Greece and Crete as a 'military observer and adviser'. A three mile takeoff run was needed to break free of the water with this overload. Other members of the Squadron contended that Squadron Leader PH 'Scruffy' Woodward must have had a throne in L2160/X's wardroom, so many royal passengers had he uplifted. It should be noted that as well as this heavy commitment, the Squadron also had to carry out its normal vital reconnaissance duties.

On 23 April L2161/P was riding at anchor at Scaramanga when it was attacked by seven Junkers JU87 Stuka dive bombers. Despite the falling bombs and resultant fire, the two waist gunners, Sergeants VC Cordery and GC Starkey remained at their posts and fired

back to such an effect that one Stuka was shot down and others damaged. Both were awarded the Military Medal. NM/P, however, burned out and sank.

An unusual evacuation vessel was 230's re-fuelling barge at Scaramanga. It was fitted with four salvaged Vickers machine-guns and was manned by Squadron Leader Alington, three other RAF personnel, a Colonel and a private soldier of the Greek Army and three nursing sisters. It reached Suda Bay safely.

By the end of May 1941 the battle for Crete was over; the Germans had won but both sides had paid a heavy price. 230 Squadron was now back at Aboukir. Wing Commander Francis was awarded the DSO for his leadership during this period and also for a daring attempt to make contact with British forces thought to be holding out on Crete after its fall. Flying at night off an unfamiliar coast, he landed in rough sea five miles offshore and taxied in closer. A dinghy was launched and was greeted with enemy machine-gun fire on nearing the shore. The Sunderland was hit but Geoffrey Francis was able to take off and drop messages to the British troops.

In May, Flight Lieutenant Brand and L2166/U were sent to Basra during the revolt in Iraq. A pro-German faction had taken over and vital oil supplies were threatened. This was swiftly disposed of by General Wavell with the British occupation of the country and the reinstatement of a more co-operative government. Later, in June, Britain seized Syria and Lebanon from the Vichy French to prevent a flanking attack by the Germans from that quarter.

The conflict in the Mediterranean had crystallised into the following key objectives:

the Africa Korps drive towards Egypt;

the Axis need to reinforce and resupply the Afrika Korps;

the British attempts to cut this lifeline from its base in Malta and

the British efforts to reinforce and resupply Malta from Gibraltar and Alexandria.

This was the crucible of war in which 230 Squadron was now operating.

The Squadron received some new aircraft but of a most unusual type and from a very unexpected quarter. A number of Yugoslav airmen and their aircraft had escaped from the German occupation of their country following the April War of 1941 and were keen to carry on the fight. The aircraft flew from their bases at Krtole and Orahovac via Athens, Corinth, Kefalonia, Patras and Crete to Egypt. They were re-designated as No 2 Yugoslav Squadron of the Royal Yugoslav Navy Air

*Royal Yugoslav Navy personnel being inspected at Aboukir in the summer of 1941.*

Crown copyright

Arm, the CO of which was Commander LV Petrovitch. It was relocated with No 230 Squadron at Aboukir and was administered by the Squadron. It was a virtually self-supporting Flight with some RAF maintenance assistance. Some 15 Royal Yugoslav Navy officers and 11 NCOs escaped with their aircraft. Eight Free French fitters were also found by the RAF and posted to service the Dorniers' Hispano-Suiza engines. Its activities were recorded in the normal manner with details of missions, aircraft serial and crew in 230 Squadron's Operational Record Book – the Form 540.

The aircraft were eight Dornier Do22s and a single Rogozarski SIM XIV. The Do22s were three-seat, single-engine float planes, with a single wing set above the fuselage. Four machine guns were fitted, one fixed and firing forward, one in a ventral position and two in the rear cockpit. A torpedo or four 100lb bombs could also be carried. The maximum speed was 217 mph and the type had a range of 1429 miles. Other examples were sold to the Greek and Latvian air forces.

The Rogozarski was a product of Yugoslavia's most significant aircraft manufacturer. The company had been established in Belgrade in 1924 and had also designed and constructed fighters and light bombers, as well as float planes. The SIM XIV-H was a twin-engine, monoplane, coastal reconnaissance seaplane. Its designation derived from the initials of the designer, Simo Milutinovic, followed by the 14 project number and 'H' for hydro. The fuselage could accommodate three passengers and three crew. It was armed with two machine guns, one in the fully glazed nose and the other on a dorsal mounting behind the pilot and could also carry up to 2200lbs of bombs. It had a maximum speed of 151 mph and a range of 522 miles.

After a number of training flights, the first operational patrol was flown by a Dornier on 3 June 1941. To begin with the aircraft flew in pairs on flights of between two and three hours duration. Over the course of the next two or three months the entries in the Operations Record (OR) Book show that the Yugoslav crews took part in the normal antisubmarine patrols with regularity and their activities became part of the Squadron's routine. Other duties included search and rescue as well as the calibration of the harbour's defences.

The Sunderlands had not been idle; on 15 June the Vichy French destroyer *Cavalier Paul* was spotted and shadowed by Flying Officer Bohm in L5806/Q. An attack by Fairey Swordfish of 815 Squadron, Fleet Air Arm resulted in the sinking of the vessel. Some 80 sorties were flown in July.

Two aircraft were lost in August. First, Sunderland L2166/U was involved in an encounter with the Italian submarine *Delfino* in which the aircraft came off second best, being shot down in flames; six bombs released from the Sunderland caused a certain amount of damage to the submarine when they exploded in the water in close proximity to it. Four of the crew – Flight Lieutenant Brand, Flying Officer Packington, Sergeant Yates and Sergeant White – were rescued from the sea by the Italians, then on 22 August Dornier 311 had to force land at sea. The crew sent a radio message asking for help but the aircraft could not be found.

The submarine threat in the Mediterranean was increasing as in September the Germans began to deploy U-boats diverted from their normal Atlantic hunting grounds. In the same month Wing Commander Geoffrey Francis came to the end of his demanding and successful tour as CO. He was replaced by Wing Commander TWG Eady, who was swiftly followed in October by Wing Commander MC Collins. Alan Lywood's tour of duty came to an end in October. During the first year and a half of the Mediterranean war he had flown over 1000 operational hours with his crew in N9029/V. They never failed to take off or complete a task, landing at sea but once to carry out repairs. He described it as a complete life revolving around the aircraft and crew:

> From the hour our war started, there were no Saturdays or Sundays or leaves. We made great fun of our leisure time when it arose but our energies and thoughts were concerned with our aircraft and Squadron tasks in a unique single-mindedness.

Two of his 2nd Pilots, Lionel Powell and Dundas Bednall, commanded the Squadron later in the war. His navigator, Pilot Officer Tony Jillings had a unique claim to fame. In August 1914, his father, Sergeant-Major DS Jillings, flying as an observer in No 2 Squadron, had been the first British soldier to be wounded in an aeroplane, when hit in the buttocks by a bullet from a German cavalryman's carbine!

The struggle for mastery of the Mediterranean continued in deadly fashion. The British convoys to Malta had to run a gauntlet of attack by submarines, Luftwaffe

**Right:** *Dornier Do22 No 309 is recovered to the beach for maintenance. No mechanical assistance here though, just brute force!*
Captain Vladimir Isaic

**Below:** *Rogozarski SIM XIV-H No 161 is pictured here on home territory in Yugoslavia before the war.*
Captain Vladimir Isaic

units based in Sardinia and Sicily, torpedo boats in the Sicilian Channel and minefields, not forgetting the still dangerous, though somewhat demoralised, Italian fleet. Punishment was inflicted in return on Italian convoys to North Africa by aircraft based in Malta, and Royal Navy submarines. Major blows against the Allied cause were struck in November with the sinking of the aircraft carrier HMS *Ark Royal* and the battleship HMS *Barham* by torpedo. In December a daring attack by Italian frogmen caused substantial damage to the battleships HMS *Valiant* and HMS *Queen Elizabeth* in Alexandria harbour. During that month the course of the war turned mightily with the attack on Pearl Harbour bringing in both the United States of America and Japan.

On 22 December 1941, Flight Lieutenant Hughes and the crew of T9071/M began a remarkable escapade. The aircraft was flying from Aboukir to Malta with ten passengers on board when it was attacked by twin-engine Messerschmitt Bf110 fighters. One was shot down and the other damaged but the Sunderland was forced to alight on the sea. One of the passengers had been killed and Pilot Officer Odhams mortally wounded. The 20 men sat on the wing of the aircraft as it drifted shorewards on a friendly tide and landfall was made on a rocky beach on the Libyan coast halfway between Benghazi and Tobruk. They were greeted by 20 armed Italian soldiers, the closest of whom threw his rifle away and advanced with outstretched arms. The two parties exchanged greetings and cigarettes. Meanwhile the aircraft, having done its duty as a life raft, was being battered by the waves and with its back broken, was breaking up on the shore. Another larger force of rather more aggressive Italians arrived soon afterwards and took the British as their prisoners.

The following day 20 more Italian officers appeared on the scene, complaining bitterly that the Germans had seized their vehicles and left them to fend for themselves as best they could. They were in such a state of high dudgeon that they proposed to the leader of the British party that in exchange for their help, he would put in a good word for them if captured by the Allies. In due course the motley band arrived in the Arab village of El Hamla. The RAF persuaded one of the Arabs to seek help from the British lines, whereupon he disappeared into the desert night never to be seen again. Horses were then procured along with some reliable guides and soon the airmen, passengers, their Italian prisoners and a little dog

which two of the officers had adopted were safely behind the British lines. This is not a tall story, it was recorded in writing and photographs by one of the aircrew, Sergeant Robinson, and a few months later it featured as an article in the *Illustrated London News*.

1942 brought immediate success for 230 Squadron. On 9 January Squadron Leader Garside was flying W3987/X on patrol west of Aboukir when his ASV operator reported a contact. The Sunderland Mk II had been equipped with Air to Surface Vessel radar, the visible external evidence of which was the fitting of four vertical dipole mast antennas along the top of the fuselage, aft of the new mid-upper turret, and long horizontal aerials under the outer wings to give azimuth guidance. Following the initial radar trace, Garside altered course and was soon rewarded by the sight of a conning tower rapidly submerging. Three depth charges and four bombs were released in two separate attack runs. A large bubble was seen to appear on the surface along with a widespread oil patch. The submarine, Type VIIC U577, was commanded by Kapitan Leutnant Herbert Schauenburg and neither he nor any of his 41 crew survived. Many years after the war some doubts were raised and it was suggested that U577 may have been sunk some days later by a Swordfish strike. The official record still stands, however, crediting the kill to the crew of NM/X. Garside was inspired by this success and over the next couple of months the OR Book records a succession of his sightings and attacks.

The Rogozarski (serial number 157) made its first operational patrol with 230 Squadron on 26 January 1942, a sortie of four hours and ten minutes duration to investigate an oil patch on the sea. One of the crew, Lieutenant Ivkovic, had a busy morning as he had already been on a dawn antisubmarine patrol between Alexandria and Tobruk in Dornier 308 for two hours. Sadly No 157 was lost on 2 February while on antisubmarine patrol. A radio message reported 'sandstorm'. In the resultant crash into the sea the pilot and the wireless operator/air gunner were killed. The observer was able to swim ashore. The final Yugoslav patrol under the auspices of 230 Squadron was made in Dornier 309 on 28 February by Lieutenants Beran and Filipovic. Operational sorties were henceforth carried out as No 2 Royal Yugoslav Air Force Squadron until the end of April when all personnel were transferred to RAF units.

These pictures show Sunderland T9071/M after its encounter with a Messerschmitt Bf110 on 22 December 1941, as detailed on page 53. In the upper picture it lies beached on the Libyan coast whilst below we see it, with its back now broken, washing up on the rocks.

Crown copyright

Meanwhile the Sunderlands continued making several attacks a month on submarines in the course of the usual lengthy patrols over the sea, searching for hostile warships and protecting convoys. On land, Rommel had reached the apogee of his fortunes as the Afrika Korps swept all before it in its drive to conquer Egypt and reach its goal of the Suez Canal. Malta had not fallen, however, and was being reinforced by sea and by air, including transport missions flown by 230 Squadron, ferrying cargo and passengers to the beleaguered island. One of these passengers was the AOC-in-C, Air Marshal Sir Arthur Tedder KCB. In June Malta received vital replenishment and Rommel was correspondingly starved of supplies. On 1 July he was halted in his progress at El Alamein by General Auchinleck and a German breakthrough to Cairo, the Nile Delta and beyond was prevented.

The most costly attempt to break the siege of Malta took place in August. 'Operation Pedestal' was a convoy of 14 fast merchant ships escorted by a formidable naval force. Only five of the convoy made it to the island but their cargo was sufficient to ensure the island's continuing survival. The Royal Navy lost the aircraft carrier HMS *Eagle*, the cruisers HMS *Manchester* and HMS *Cairo* and the destroyer HMS *Foresight*.

230 Squadron continued to fly antisubmarine and surface vessel escort sorties as the summer wore on and autumn approached but without any incidents of great note apart from a temporary move to Fanara, on the shore of the Great Bitter Lake, for most of July. In September, however, there were two tragic losses. Flight Lieutenant Howell and eight of his crew of thirteen were killed when W3987/X crashed on takeoff from Aboukir on 7th,

*Squadron Leader Garside's attack on U577 on 9 January 1942 is depicted in this painting by* Fred Mock.

while on the last day of the month T9050/Y, captained by Flying Officer Murphy crashed on landing, resulting in the deaths of three of the crew. Some months later Pilot Officer AG Richmond was awarded the George Medal for his "courage, determination and devotion to duty" in connection with the crash of NM/X.

The tide of the war was turning and between 23 October and 4 November 1942, the Eighth Army, under General Montgomery, at the second Battle of Alamein, began the process which resulted in an advance of over 1400 miles and which in six months ejected the Axis forces from North Africa. At the same time US and British Forces had landed in French North Africa on 8

November in 'Operation Torch', eventually linking with the victorious Desert Rats.

230 Squadron had played a full part in this momentous struggle, flying thousands of hours, combating the German and Italian air and naval forces, not forgetting the brief land campaign of Flight Lieutenant Hughes and his men. In the time-honoured words of Winston Churchill, who said in his Mansion House speech on 10 November 1942, "This is not the end. It is not even the beginning of the end. But it is, perhaps, the end of the beginning." Certainly it was very far from the end for 230 Squadron. There was a new theatre in which to fight and many more thousands of square miles of sea to cover.

*The 230 Squadron badge endorsed with the signatures of some who served in the Squadron's Mediterranean campaign.*

Mari Davis/John Evans Collection

# CHAPTER 4
# 1943

In January 1943 the Squadron moved to Dar-es-Salaam, Tanganiyka, which was a large and well-equipped base, as well as being a beautiful palm-fringed location. Maintenance work was carried out at Tabora Creek just off the main harbour. All the aircraft were by this time the Sunderland Mark III which had an improved planing bottom and streamlined step. The armament was also progressively enhanced. The engines were also uprated by the addition of two-speed superchargers which allowed an increased all-up weight of almost 5000 lbs. However the workload of the engineers also increased due to the inability of the Bristol Pegasus XVIII engines to cope with the climate – though there is another school of thought which believes that the engines were not to blame, it was the poor quality of engine oil available.

First to depart for Dar-es-Salaam was Flight Lieutenant PD Squires in EJ136/Y on 9 January on a route which took in Wadi Halfa, Khartoum, Kisumu and Mombassa. He was followed by the middle of the month by the CO, Wing Commander CR Taylor in EJ132/X. On 12 February Taylor flew 150 miles down the coast to Lindi in W4021/W with the AOC and Group Captain Bryer to inspect the alighting and mooring area there. It is of interest to remember that the former CO of the Squadron prewar, Wing Commander Dunn had served at Lindi in 1917. Between 17 and 27 February Flight Lieutenant Squires flew a tour of the Indian Ocean islands seeking out suitable anchorages and also conveying the GOC-in-C Lieutenant General Sir William Platt, Major General Smallwood and the AOC East Africa, Air Vice Marshal Wrigglesworth on an inspection visit. The itinerary followed was an attractive one – Mombassa, Pamanzi, Diego Suarez, Mauritius, Rodriquez and the Seychelles, a succession of tropical islands on leaving Kenya.

The protection of convoys along the east coast of Africa was the Squadron's most vital task. All supplies from the UK to Egypt had to come the long route around the Cape of Good Hope and U-boats were lurking in the eastern Indian Ocean. The range and effectiveness of the attack boats were enhanced by the presence of the mother ships *Charlotte Schliemann* and *Brake*, as well as submarine tankers, which provided them with fuel, spare parts, food, clothing, ammunition, torpedoes, water, medical care and crew replacements, much increasing the length of time they could remain on patrol.

Flying operations began in February with convoy escorts and antisubmarine patrols. A routine was established in which the flying boats flew tours of the islands, patrolling as they went. A detachment was also established at Tulear in Madagascar. The Squadron Headquarters at Dar-es-Salaam was affected by a malaria epidemic which peaked in May; the humid conditions and the encircling palm trees provided an ideal breeding ground for the mosquitoes which spread the disease.

A further commitment was placed on the Squadron in June when it was ordered to provide six aircraft for transport, reconnaissance and air-sea rescue duties in support of the forthcoming 'Operation Husky' – the invasion of Sicily. They were based at Bizerta in Tunisia, which had just been captured by US forces. The 3000 mile journey from Dar-es-Salaam was broken at Aboukir, where the aircraft took part in fighter affiliation exercises with Hurricanes. In command was Wing Commander Taylor, who was accompanied by his successor designate, Squadron Leader Dundas Bednall, who had just returned to the Squadron. Bednall was not impressed by the conditions which he found at Bizerta:

> It was still a mess as the town had only just been taken and the harbour was littered with sunken ships and debris, including the odd dead body.

The living conditions were little better, as the tented accommodation allocated to the airmen was subjected to nightly air raids.

*Sunderland Mk III EJ141/R, which features on the cover painting, is pictured on patrol.*

Wg Cdr Dundas Bednall/John Evans Collection

The main task for the Sunderlands was to run a shuttle service between Bizerta and Malta. This went smoothly enough but one particular air-sea rescue mission did not. On 17 July one aircraft, JM659/Q, flown by Flying Officer DW McNichol, was tasked to search the Bay of Naples for a the crew of a ditched American aircraft. As he approached the north coast of Sicily, enemy aircraft were detected by radar and then visually. A dinghy was located but as McNichol was preparing to land, a Junkers 88 attacked the Sunderland. He tried to shake off the German but was handicapped by the fact that his mid-upper turret was unserviceable, being capable of firing only single shots. He returned several times but always found the Ju 88 circling the dinghy. Aware that landing under attack would result in the loss of his aircraft McNichol turned for home. A second Sunderland, EJ141/R flown by Flying Officer GOP Watson, was detailed to set off at dawn, this time escorted by USAAF P38 Lightning fighters. In the meantime Bednall was given a tremendous rocket by the AOC, Air Vice Marshal HP Lloyd, which he considered most unjustified. All ended well as Watson effected the rescue of the six crew from the downed Martin Marauder.

On the same day the fighter escort of another air-sea rescue flight made by Flight Lieutenant Middleton in JM659/Q also enjoyed some success when it intercepted a formation of Junkers Ju52 transports and shot down 15 of them. Watson and McNichol were later awarded DFCs.

Another good effort was made on 19 July when Flying Officer FJ Statham in EJ143/S landed in a heavy swell off

the coast of Sardinia. Contact was made with the dinghy by flare pistol and Aldis lamp. However the sea conditions proved just too rough, contact was lost and after three hours on the water the Sunderland had to abandon the attempt, taking off again with the 10 foot swell breaking over the aircraft.

The detachment returned to Dar-es-Salaam at the end of July, where the rest of the Squadron had been engaged in the regular escort and antisubmarine operations, along with transport and VIP flights, mapping, air-sea rescue, training and exercises with naval forces. The work of the adjutant, Frank Ward, was much appreciated by the CO, as also were the efforts of the NCOs, who had to shoulder considerable responsibility at the detached bases. Morale was kept up by sporting activities and it is recorded with great pride in the OR Book that the Squadron's football team won the Dar-es-Salaam 2nd Division 'Kassum' Cup by beating the King's African Rifles by three goals to two. It was also noted that Mussolini had been forced to resign and that King Victor Emmanuel had taken charge, with Marshal Badoglio as Prime Minister.

Sadly, on 20 August, EJ131/T, captained by Flight Lieutenant AD Todd, went missing on patrol from Pamanzi. It had been tasked to escort the seaplane carrier HMS *Albatross,* and HMS *Nepal* had been unable to locate them in the Mozambique Channel. Having contacted Tulear twice for bearings an SOS message was sent to the effect that the aircraft was making a forced landing; searches in the days following proved fruitless. (The detachment had recently been established at Pamanzi in the Comoro Islands to carry out antisubmarine patrols in the Mozambique Channel.)

On 25 August Wing Commander Taylor departed and newly promoted Wing Commander Bednall took over. He was concerned about the lack of forward firing armament provided for the Sunderland. Submarines had been equipped with more formidable anti-aircraft defences and were becoming much more inclined to stay and fight an attacking aircraft rather than submerge. With the enthusiastic co-operation of the Squadron's Armament Officer, he devised a modification which enabled a Sunderland to be fitted with a fixed 20mm cannon fired by the pilot and aimed by means of a simple ring and bead sight. A suitable cannon just happened to be in the Squadron stores. Unfortunately the plan was discovered by the AOC on an inspection visit, who ordered the

immediate removal of this unauthorised modification.

From September to November JM659/Q, flown by Flying Officer DW McNichol and W4021/W, Flying Officer FJ Statham, were based at Aboukir and flew special transport missions to the Dodecanese Islands. On 7 November W4021/W was struck by a motor launch at Castellorosso and an engine was badly damaged. Statham tried to take off on three engines but the aircraft struck a submerged object. He decided to scuttle the aircraft to avoid the possibility of it falling into enemy hands.

The Pamanzi detachment was ordered to move to Mombasa in late October and to carry on with the same patrol duties.

Routine duties continued with patrols and transport flights to the Seychelles, Aldabra Islands, Madagascar and others. A detachment at Kisumu flew a transport service to Khartoum and back. Many miles over land and sea were covered in this unspectacular but useful fashion. It is instructive to consider some of the distances involved; from Dar-es-Salaam to Tulear on the southwestern coast of Madagascar was over 1200 miles, to Pamanzi in the Aldabra Islands was 600 miles, to Kisumu on the shores of Lake Victoria was more than 700 miles. From Kisumu to Khartoum on the White Nile was 1000 miles and from the Aldabras to the Seychelles was 800 miles. However as the CO later wrote:

> It was always difficult keeping morale up when the Squadron's base is not threatened by the enemy; it all seems 'far from the action', added to which the operations against enemy submarines decreased. When you took off you hardly expected to see anything of the

enemy, unlike the days of 1940–43 when the Squadron was in the Mediterranean.

An incident describing the technical difficulties to which the Pegasus engine was prone in tropical climes was described many years later by former Corporal Giff Blamey of No 209 Squadron, who was travelling as a passenger on a 230 Squadron Sunderland, W6078/N, flown by WO N Porri, from Mauritius to Diego Suarez in Madagascar on 1 October 1943:

> As we approached the harbour and the pilot eased the engines back, they started to backfire. We got down all right but they had to tow us to the buoy. We were there three or four days while our two fitters and the Flight Engineer worked on the engines round the clock.

The next port of call was the Seychelles where the same process was repeated. EJ140/V, which at that time was virtually brand new, arrived at the harbour and all personnel transferred on board. Giff Blamey related the next part of the tale, "We took off in a tropical rainstorm but we got clear of it and climbed to about 8000 feet, which proved to be very, very fortunate." Having had some tea and bully beef sandwiches, Blamey retired to the bomb room for a sleep. On awakening he could smell petrol was told that this was due to 400 gallons having recently been jettisoned. The outer port engine had caught the backfiring problem and been shut down. Some time later the inner starboard engine commenced belching smoke and flames and was also shut down. Giff continues:

> We soldiered on losing height. We opened up the bomb bay and out went the guns, ammunition, freight and anything else we could find, including a ship's anchor.

*Sunderland Mk III W6078/N was based at Dar-es-Salaam when this picture was taken.*

Wg Cdr Dundas Bednall/
John Evans Collection

The captain, Flying Officer Oxley 'Ox' Watson, then announced that they were lost and requested that all hands man the portholes to search for anything familiar. In the nick of time Nyali Beach at Mombasa was sighted:

> We glided over Mombasa and we just stalled right on the water, made a beautiful landing and what motors were still there just stopped – due to the petrol having run out.

The Kisumu to Kharthoum run provided another quite similar incident recalled by David McNichol many years later. On the morning of 14 December 1943 JM659/Q was en route to Kisumu with nine passengers and 1450 lbs of freight when engine trouble was experienced with the starboard inner. McNichol decided to land on the Nile at Malakal and prepared to jettison fuel to lighten the aircraft. He was concerned about unloading too much petrol as there were bush fires raging below and he did not wish to either add to the conflagration or the thick smoke haze surrounding the aircraft. When the starboard outer began to play up he ordered the freight in the bomb room to be thrown overboard. A safe landing was made at Malakal, two BOAC launches towed the flying boat to a buoy and McNichol telephoned the Governor of the Province to inform him of the nature and position of the air-dropped cargo. The crew celebrated their safe arrival with a beer and thereby hangs a tale. Also stored in the bomb room was a crate of Australian beer (144 large bottles of Resch's Pilsener) which had been given to Flight Lieutenant McNichol by the Australian Comforts Fund in Alexandria. This was not jettisoned, being regarded as much too vital a piece of equipment to waste. On enquiry David McNichol was told by the bomb room crew that the beer had been saved as it was too heavy to lift.

Another aircraft was lost on 29 December when EJ140/V impacted on Sangalla Hill near Voi while flying in thick cloud on a calibration flight from Mombassa. Flying Officer DE Lumsden and all his crew were killed.

*The crew of Sunderland Mk III JM659/Q celebrate a safe landing at Malakal with a beer. Those standing include Pete Smith, T Hulme, Ron Schmidt, Murray Storch, David McNicol, Stan Gorman and Jock Marshall. In front are Ken McLean, Jack Jones and the (un-named) W/AG from Sunderland W.*

T Hulme

# CHAPTER 5
# 1944

At the beginning of 1944 Flying Officer Alan Deller joined the Squadron, just in time to experience the delights of being a Sunderland captain in the western Indian Ocean. He described his impressions of the islands:

> At Diego Suarez was a large lake more or less rectangular in shape and surrounded by picturesque hills covered by every kind of luxuriant green vegetation mixed with the ubiquitous palm trees. After dinner in the Army mess we sat out in the evening air, heavy with the scent of bougainvillaea, while a band of the King's African Rifles played jolly music and we drank long John Collinses. The landing area at Pamanzi was a long strip of water between steep hills which were again covered in green vegetation but also with brilliantly-coloured flowers which seemed to blaze forth and hang from every tree and shack as we drove up from the little landing stage to the rickety but friendly Mess. The experience of sitting on the small verandah in the warm scented evening air with a rather warm drink and looking down on our aeroplane moored far below was one of the most delightful I had ever enjoyed.

*Mk III Sunderland S for Sugar of No 230 Squadron RAF (Alan Deller's aircraft) at moorings at Addu Atoll, Maldive Islands. Passengers are being ferried out to the aircraft by one of the small, fast flying boat tenders – known universally as 'dinghies' – that served valiantly in every part of the British marine aircraft world.*

Imperial War Museum, London (CF 620)

*Mk III Sunderland S for Sugar about to leave the water travelling at about 95 knots (c105 mph) at Addu Atoll, Maldive Islands, Alan Deller at the controls. The four aerials on top of the hull are part of the early radar equipment.*

Imperial War Museum, London (CF 657)

*Alan Deller collecting official mail ("By safe hand of captain") from Flight Lieutenant Lancaster, Commanding Officer, Kelai advanced flying boat base, Maldive Islands. Left to right: ?, Flight Lieutenant Lancaster, Flight Sergeant Ellard, Joe Eggett, ?, Alan Deller, Sidney Moorhouse (War Correspondent, Yorkshire Post).*

Imperial War Museum, London

*Mk III Sunderland J on patrol over the Indian Ocean. Many thousands of miles would be covered on flights such as this.*

Crown copyright

The first sight of the Seychelles did not disappoint us: those rich green islands with the surrounding ocean changing from blue to dark green to light green and then crystal clarity approaching the dazzling white beaches was simply stunning. There was a limitless choice of landing area in the sea off Victoria, the capital, on the big island of Mahé. As we approached the shore in the dinghy we were met by the curious sweet-ish smell of copra, the main export of the islands. Our mess was built entirely of palm trunks and palm–frond wattle and was literally on the beach a stone's throw from the water's edge. During the day the whole atmosphere of heavily scented flowers and humid heat was enervating.

While moored off Victoria the aircraft, W6078/N, became unserviceable with ignition problems. The enforced stay meant that Deller and his crew were able to return some hospitality:

*Cocktail party aboard Alan Deller's aircraft at Mahé, Seychelles.*

Alan Deller collection

I invited a number of officers from the Army and the RAF, together with the RN officers from the shore base and the sloop, to a sundowner party aboard the aircraft: the crew had helped to get everything tidy while George Allen (the Navigator) and I collected whisky, sherry and gin and tonic and a pile of attractive snacks from shore. Sundry marine craft ferried the guests out to the aircraft and we all managed to get into the wardroom with an overflow into the galley. The wardroom table looked marvellous with all the goodies and bottles arranged – even some modest flowers.

In February the order was given for the Squadron to move again, this time to the far side of the Indian Ocean – to Koggala Lake in Ceylon where it had been instrumental in developing facilities for flying boat operations in the winter of 1939–40. Enemy activity off the coast of East Africa had declined; the surrender of the Italian Fleet in September 1943 had vastly improved the situation with regard to sending convoys to India through the Suez Canal, while Japanese and German submarines were posing a greater threat in the eastern Indian Ocean. Losses of Allied shipping in the Indian Ocean in the first quarter of 1944 came to almost 200,000 tons – heavier than any other theatre.

Wing Commander Dundas Bednall found the move a challenging experience:

> We began frantic preparations to move the whole squadron. Heavy equipment and stores, such as flying surfaces, engines, etc., were to go by sea. As much material as possible would be taken by our own aircraft. Although a squadron in wartime gets used to moving around at short notice it still demands a lot of work, especially from the NCOs who have to select, pack and list every item. The whole operation has to be finely co-ordinated so that the work of the squadron is not brought to a halt if one of our Sunderlands containing all the supply of one particular item is held up for any reason. As many men as possible were to be carried in

the flying boats leaving a rear party to wind up affairs in Dar-es-Salaam. Those travelling by sea would obviously be some weeks late arriving in Ceylon.

The main group of aircraft was led by the CO and instead of flying across the Indian Ocean, he was instructed to take it the long way round, to Kisumu on the shores of the vast, glittering expanse of Lake Victoria, then across the swamp-lands of Uganda and the plains of Sudan up the White Nile to Khartoum, over the dusty-brown and desolate mountains of northern Ethiopia and across the Red Sea to Aden. The next leg was to Masira, a sandy island off the coast of Oman at the mouth of the Persian Gulf and from there to Karachi. From Karachi the next port of call was Cochin which took about eight hours flying down the west coast of India. The final stage was a three hour 'hop' to Koggala. In all, this was a journey of some 5000 miles and in excess of 40 hours in the air. Having brought all his aircraft safely to their new base,

no doubt Dundas Bednall was anticipating a few kind words from the Station Commander but instead he was quizzed as to why he had not come on ahead first with the advance party.

He described Koggala as follows:

> A freshwater lake separated from the sea by a narrow strip of land, it lies on the southern coast of Ceylon some 75 miles from Colombo. It is surrounded on other sides by low hills and palm trees. The takeoff area was adequate as far as length goes but just about when you became airborne there was a small islet and the takeoff route turned a few degrees to starboard. You got used to it by day but it caused the odd spot of anxiety on a dark night, especially when heavily laden.

The setting was truly magnificent from a scenic point of view, with palm fringed beaches and the old town of Galle, situated within the walls of a massive fort. Officers were granted honorary membership of the Galle Club. It was also very humid, hot and damp, with the added

*The Officers Mess, Addu Atoll, Maldive Islands.*

Alan Deller collection

*Two crew members un-mooring a Sunderland at Addu Atoll, watched by the captain. Flaps have been lowered fully to help the wind to drift the aircraft astern to clear the buoy.*

Crown copyright

'attractions' of large spiders, scorpions, mosquitoes, the occasional cobra and a sixteen feet long crocodile. This last named served to concentrate the minds of the fitters perched on their little platforms over the water.

Patrol duties were commenced almost at once and advanced bases were established at Addu Atoll (now better known as Gan), Diego Garcia and Kelai for the operation of detachments. Pilot Officer John Foxon served for a time on the island of Diego Garcia as Operations Officer. It was a dot in the ocean over 1000 miles south of Ceylon. He described the conditions in a letter to his wife:

> The atoll is a horseshoe-shaped reef with a lagoon in the centre, with one outlet to the sea. The water in the lagoon is moderately calm but on the outside shores terrific breakers beat up over the coral reef. All night when everything is quiet, you can hear the breakers crashing on the shore. By day you would find the most wonderful colourings in the sea. I've had a most exciting time and worked damned hard. During the fortnight I've had only one complete night's sleep and I've done nearly thirty hours flying too.

At Addu Atoll, during 1944, Flight Lieutenant John Rankin was appointed in command of No 28 Advanced Flying Boat Base, with responsibility for the refuelling and re-arming of visiting Sunderlands and Catalinas:

> All the gas was in 5-gallon drums that were really old. They had to be bowsered out to the aircraft, hand fed to the wing top and emptied. It all had to be filtered through a felt hat – a Catalina needed 294 drums. We had contact with Koggala by radio and a radar beacon could be turned on when requested by approaching aircraft. We had a 45-feet high speed launch to travel to Gan and the RAF Station. Nothing very exciting happened during my time there but we had great sunsets and a wonderful ocean breeze swept over the Atoll.

No contact was made with the enemy by aircraft of No 230 Squadron but equally no allied ships were lost for several months.

The problems experienced with engines on the far side of the Indian Ocean began to surface again; some engines were lasting a bare twenty hours. A great deal of time and effort was expended by technical staff in trying to rectify

the problem, which was diagnosed as sticking exhaust valves but the operational capability of the Squadron was degraded. An unsung hero of the period, who was an expert in keeping the recalcitrant Pegasus engines firing on most cylinders, was Sergeant Nobby Clarke.

In order to keep up morale the CO set up a training programme practising night flying and simulating attacks on enemy shipping, using a high speed launch as the target vessel. To help with improving the performance of the aircraft by reducing weight and drag, the dorsal turret was removed and the opening faired over. Cruising speed was raised by 15 to 20 knots and fuel consumption was improved. An experiment was conducted to reduce the visibility of the Sunderland when attacking in low light conditions. One aircraft JM673/P was painted black, the only Sunderland so painted, and it became known as 'Black Peter'. Bednall also agitated for the re-equipment of

the Squadron with the latest model of the Sunderland, the Mk V, which was fitted with Pratt and Whitney engines.

In the spring of 1944 several aircraft assisted in the rescue of the crew of the SS *Fort McLeod*, a cargo vessel of 7127 gross tons, which was torpedoed on 3 March while on passage from Colombo to Durban. The 56 crew members abandoned ship and manned two lifeboats. Their position was some 200 miles from Addu Attol. The waters were less than inviting as they appeared to be infested with sharks which were longer then the lifeboats, to which they gave exploratory nudges. The mariners were first of all spotted by a Liberator and then on the afternoon of 5 March by one of the Sunderlands. The naval vessels HM Trawler *Sluna* and HM Tug *Integrity* rendezvoused with the lifeboats and embarked the survivors for Colombo, leaving behind some rather disappointed sharks.

*Sunderland Mk III JM659/Q* Gert *on Lake Indawgyi in June 1944.*

Fred Mock

On 17 May the Supreme Commander, Admiral Lord Louis Mountbatten arrived at Koggala. The Station personnel were assembled and Lord Louis gave what was later described as a spirited talk, using a packing case for a podium. Alan Deller noted that, "He looked terrific in his beautifully-tailored tropical uniform and his naval cap, dripping with 'scrambled eggs', at a jaunty angle."

Then in June 1944, just as the Second Front was being opened in Europe, the opportunity arose for a most unusual detached duty which gave two crews the chance to participate directly in the Burma Campaign. Since the Japanese invasion in January 1942 the British, Indian and Gurkha soldiers of the 14th Army had been engaged in a bitter struggle in the most difficult terrain – virtually trackless, disease-infested, jungle-clad mountains; swamped for half the year by monsoon rains – against the forces of Imperial Japan. The zenith of the Japanese advance had been achieved in May 1942 when they reached the Indian-Burmese border. The first allied counter attack was the unsuccessful Arakan offensive of 1943, which saw the blooding of the Chindits, regular forces acting as guerrillas behind the enemy lines.

The Chindits, or 77 Indian Infantry Brigade as they were more correctly, but less famously, known, were commanded by the unorthodox and charismatic Brigadier Orde Wingate. They were supplied in the jungle by air and made extensive use of wireless communications; their main task was to cut and harass the Japanese supply routes and cause chaos along the River Irrawaddy.

Another important figure took command of the 14th Army in late 1943, Lieutenant General Bill Slim, who took a demoralised army and led it to win a series of remarkable victories, which would do much to eradicate the memories of 1942 which had culminated in the fall of Singapore. The turn of the tide came with the decisive battles of Kohima and Imphal in the spring and early summer of 1944. The Chindits played their part with a much enlarged force, now 3 Indian Infantry Division, which helped stem a projected Japanese attack on the Assam–Bengal railway in India – again by attacking the enemy's lines of communication.

230 Squadron was tasked to send two aircraft to Burma to rescue hundreds of sick and wounded Chindits from behind enemy lines. Over 500 casualties were unable to march or fight their way out. The monsoon rain had swamped any possible landing grounds – the only way

to avoid the men being left to the less than tender mercies of the Japanese was to land on Lake Indawgyi and the only aircraft type that could carry out the task was the Sunderland. Squadron Leader John Middleton was appointed to command of the detachment, with Flight Lieutenant Jack Rand and Flying Officer Ted Garside as the captains of JM659/Q and DP180/O respectively. The chief navigator was Flying Officer Noel Verney.

The aircraft were based at Dibrugahr on the Brahmaputra River which made the journey to Lake Indawgyi a three and a half hour round trip. The time factor was the least of their difficulties. They had to fly across the Chin Hills, which at that time of year were always covered in thick cloud and through the Ledo Pass. The pass was at a height of 8500–9000 feet and in the prevailing conditions the Sunderlands could fly no higher then 11,000–12,000 feet, which did not leave a really comfortable margin for error. Further complications were added of not especially accurate maps and frequent thunderclouds creating heavy turbulence. On landing the aircraft were met by American DUKW amphibious vehicles with the casualties, many of whom were suffering from dysentery. About 50 were flown out on each trip. Fortunately the Japanese only strafed the area once while Jack Rand in DP180/O was awaiting his passengers. Less happily JM659/Q was wrecked at her moorings either by a particularly violent monsoon storm or according to another version, by collision with a DUKW.

Over a period of 32 days 537 serious casualties were evacuated to Dibrugahr for onward transfer to hospital in Dacca. Middleton, Verney and Rand were all awarded DFCs for their efforts, while Flight Sergeant R Webber received the DFM. The two aircraft were given a more informal but affectionate reward, being christened *Gert* (Q) and *Daisy* (O) after two well-loved stage and radio comediennes of the period, Elsie and Doris Waters ( who were the sisters of the actor Jack Warner). The mission was successfully completed by the first week in July.

Back at Koggala in July 1944 there was an increase in the activity of Japanese submarines in the waters around Ceylon. 230 Squadron did not score any victories but it was instrumental in locating 250 survivors from torpedoed P&O liner *Nellore* and the American ship *Jean Nicolet* and in transporting 70 of them to Addu Atoll from Diego Garcia in a single trip, flown by Flight Lieutenant Ingham in EJ132/X. For the next few

*Wounded Chindits are made ready to board the waiting Sunderland. Mk III JM659/Q Gert. on Lake Indawgyi in June 1944.*

Fred Mock

months duties consisted of the transport of freight and passengers to the island bases, convoy escort patrols, fighter affiliation, air firing and bombing exercises. Squadron and Station teams also participated in cricket, football and hockey tournaments. An old friend returned in August when Group Captain Geoffrey Francis became the Station Commander. In October Dundas Bednall's tour as CO came to an end; he was replaced by Wing Commander Lionel Powell.

Now and again the opportunity arose for the Station Commander to keep his hand in with some flying. On 16 November Group Captain Francis was skipper of ML868/H on a routine sweep to Addu Attol when a message was received to provide air-sea rescue cover for the last stage of a flight involving a B25 Mitchell carrying the Supreme Commander on a visit to this base. Technical problems resulted in the Mitchell having to make a forced landing at Gan. Francis was ordered to land and convey Lord Louis back to Koggala.

Sadly on 28 November 1944 'Black Peter' was lost while on an antisubmarine patrol from Koggala into the Bay of Bengal. The weather conditions were adverse; indeed the radar at base watched JM673/P's blip merge with that of a cyclone from which it did not come out. A large scale search failed to find anything of the aircraft or crew, captained by Squadron Leader KV Ingham RAAF. The OR Book noted that the intensity of the searches was a tribute to the esteem in which Ingham was held by his comrades. 230 was a happy squadron and part of the reason was this felicitous blend of personnel from United Kingdom, Canada, Australia and New Zealand.

To round off the year, on 21 December Flight Lieutenant Ken Nicholson departed from Koggala on a nine day tour of the island bases, carrying an ENSA concert party and its production of 'Fantasia'.

*Sunderland Mk III 230/S is shown here at Koggala having been hauled out of the water for servicing or maintenance.*

Crown copyright

# CHAPTER 6
# 1945

During January and February 1945 the Squadron was re-equipped with the Sunderland Mk V. This version of the aircraft was regarded by many as the best, not least because of its reliable and powerful Pratt and Whitney engines. It was also equipped with the latest Mark III ASV radar which 'painted' a map on the cathode ray tube with the aircraft in the middle, picking up ships, submarines, islands and coastlines. It was armed with a total of twelve machine-guns, four in the rear turret, two in the front, two amidships and four more mounted either side of the bow compartment to be fired by the captain.

The first to arrive at Koggala on 6 January 1945 was PP147/U, flown by Flight Lieutenant Charles Potter. Almost the entire Station turned out to watch and were duly impressed, particularly by the aircraft's climb performance. As the new machines arrived the Mk IIIs were flown to 374 MU at Korangi Creek, Karachi to be handed over to Ferry Command.

Before saying farewell to the Mk III the Squadron was tasked once again to support the 14th Army directly. In early February it was planned to open the offensive towards Mandalay. Engines and spares were required for the assault craft which would make the crossing of the Irrawaddy. The Sunderland was selected as the best aircraft for the job and Squadron Leader Alan Deller was placed in command of the detachment. He was much respected and regarded with some awe by the junior officers. He also had a unique claim to fame in that he had sat across the desk from Douglas Bader, in the service of the Shell Petroleum Company, before the war. He recalled Bader as a really fine type, very extrovert and a great charmer of the ladies.

On the morning of 2 February he took off from Koggala in ML861/K, accompanied by Flight Lieutenant Potter in ML846/W. They also carried a maintenance party of seven personnel with spares and tools, under

Sergeant Clarke. On arrival at Trombay (Bombay), Deller was briefed on the daily requirement, which was to uplift 5100 lbs of freight consisting of three marine engines, each in a large case and weighing some 1100 lbs, together with the control mechanisms and underwater gear – the parts necessary to build one entire craft except for the hull. The port bomb trolley of the aircraft was fitted with a chain operated hoist which made loading a relatively simple business. It was decided to move the maintenance party and spares across India to Bally (Calcutta) which would enable each aircraft to be thoroughly checked before flying on to the final destination of Kalewa on the Chindwin River in Central Burma.

On 5 February Squadron Leader Deller flew from Calcutta to Kalemyo by Dakota and thence by road and motorboat to inspect the landing area. He decided that it was adequate in spite of hills rising vertically to 200–300 feet at each end. A strip of water was marked out with yellow-painted oil drums, a buoy was fashioned from two 40-gallon drums painted white and the local Burmese villagers were asked to remove their fishing stakes from the immediate vicinity.

The first cargo trip was made on 8 February by Deller in ML861/K. The Chin Hills were the greatest obstacle, forcing Deller to "take the aircraft with persuasion, at full revs hanging on the props" to a height of 10,700 feet. At this stage thick cloud and considerable turbulence forced him to return to Calcutta. The first successful trip was made on 10 February, though the conditions were still challenging. There was very little probability of making a survivable forced landing en route, so the crew wore parachutes at all times, a very unusual occurrence in a flying boat.

A third Sunderland arrived to join the detachment, DD866/T flown by Flight Lieutenant Alan Pedley. This aircraft suffered a twin engine failure while making a return trip on 15 February but made it back to Calcutta

*Sepoys of No 5 Inland Water Transport Company, Royal Engineers (Commanding Officer Major Corbett, third from left) watching the unloading of a half ton marine engine from an aircraft's bomb room, using the electrically-operated bomb trolley visible top centre.*

Alan Deller collection

and "the dirty, swirling waters of the Hooghly" successfully, "losing height only quite slowly the whole way". Another aircraft, W6078/N, captained by Flight Lieutenant Dick Levy-Haarscher, arrived on 21 February. Some of the inbound trips also carried foodstuffs and on the outward leg some passengers were taken on leave and repatriation. The final sortie was flown on 9 March. Squadron Leader Deller paid tribute to the maintainers:

> The fact that ML861/K was able to four complete trips (nearly 100 hours flying) and the other aircraft the trips allocated to them redounds to the credit of Sergeant Clarke and his party; their hard work and Sergeant Clarke's advice to me on technical matters made them the mainstay of the operation, particularly in view of the fickle nature of our very old Pegasus XVIII engines, the incessant climbing with heavy loads imposed a big strain on them. Night maintenance was not resorted to; I considered it dangerous in view of the lack of marine craft and the turbulent flow of the Hooghly, into which a man, working on the narrow engine stands, might easily fall and be lost.

Deller, Pedley and Potter were subsequently awarded the DFC for their respective parts in this challenging and difficult task.

The boats were later christened HMS *Una* and HMS *Pamela* by Slim and Mountbatten, for which they received a 'rocket' from the Board of Admiralty for having the temerity to do so without prior consultation and approval!

Back at Koggala the Squadron had continued training to use the new Mk V Sunderlands in a day and night anti-shipping role. Tactics were devised – with the assistance of some Royal Navy 'Fairmile' motor launches – which required three aircraft to fly parallel search patterns. Once a target had been spotted the sighting aircraft would home the other two and all three would then circle. One aircraft would make the bombing run while the others suppressed anti-aircraft fire. Fighter affiliation exercises were also carried out with the Spitfire VIIIs of No 81 Squadron, which was based nearby at Ratamalana.

On 13 March 1945 Wing Commander Powell flew in

*Spring 1945 and Squadron personnel gather in front of a Sunderland Mk V at Koggala just before the move to Burma.*

Fred Mock collection

PP145/O along with Squadron Leader Harry Sheardown RCAF and the Station Commander at Koggala, Group Captain Francis, to Akyab on the northwest coast of Burma. Their task was to inspect the harbour in advance of an impending move by the larger part of the Squadron, which was now designated a Fully Mobile Unit. This required an increase in complement which gradually built up to a total in excess of 500. Accommodation would be in the somewhat cramped quarters provided by the SS *Manela*, a small ex-British India liner. Medical preparations were also made, with the issue of anti-malaria tablets, cholera vaccinations and the spraying of the aircraft with DDT. The first seven aircraft flew to the new base later in the month and leading the way on 16 April were the CO in PP158/T and Squadron Leader Sheardown in PP145/O. Squadron Leader Deller stayed in Koggala in command of the remainder.

Mandalay was re-captured by the 14th Army by the middle of March; the next stage was the drive towards Rangoon – 'Operation Dracula', a combined airborne

and seaborne assault. On 30 April Flying Officer Toller in ML799/W began a sequence of patrols above the invasion fleet heading south from Akyab towards the Andaman Islands. The heavy escorting ships included the French battleship *Richeleau*, HMS *Queen Elizabeth* and the battlecruiser HMS *Renown*. The following day Squadron Leader Sheardown in PP145 covered a formation of 38 DC-3s which were carrying Ghurka paratroops. It was discovered that the Japanese had already withdrawn from Rangoon, a fact confirmed by aerial reconnaissance which observed a sign painted on the roof of Rangoon gaol, "Japs Gone, RAF Here, Extract Digit." Wing Commander Powell landed near the city in ML799/W on 5 May carrying Army medical and administrative officers. Hostilities were still continuing on the west bank but the Sunderland returned to Akyab without incident. Meanwhile, in Europe, Germany surrendered unconditionally on 7 May.

A further flight to Rangoon was made on 10 May when Squadron Leader Sheardown took ML800/X with a VIP party, including the AOC, Air Marshal Sir Keith Park, General Sir Oliver Leese and Air Vice-Marshal the Earl of Bandon. A contemporary account written by the Squadron summarises its activities over this period thus:

> In conjunction with Liberator squadrons it provided the air reconnaissance of the Andaman Seas from Port Blair to Malaya for Operation Dracula – the capture of Rangoon. Not only were the Andamans kept under close observation but the Squadron participated in the Rangoon episode by leading in the airborne armada and covering the sea assault at the mouth of the Pegu.

Akyab was now too far from the scene of operations to be of use as a base, so the SS *Manela* steamed south to Rangoon, where due to sandbanks it was unable to moor closer than five miles away from the Sunderlands, which were at Syriam about nine miles up river from the city. This was a highly inconvenient arrangement, which the Squadron records describe as "most difficult and trying". The heat and humidity on board the Manela were so great that the regulation day uniform

was shorts only, with insignia of rank worn on khaki-drill wrist straps. In any case the Squadron was soon busy attacking enemy shipping, mostly small vessels – barges, schooners and sampans, all of which were shallow in draught and could creep along the islet-studded coast, too close in to be attacked by warships. Some were camouflaged with foliage to look like tree-covered islets and were usually armed with anti-aircraft guns. One barge could carry enough rice and basic supplies to feed 100 soldiers for a month.

The Sunderlands carried out air strikes over the Gulf of Tavoy on the west Burmese coast across Kra Isthmus on the border with Thailand and into the Gulf of Siam. Flying Officer Lewis Day RNZAF was the second pilot on one of these strikes made by Flight Lieutenant Levy-Haarscher and his crew in PP155/Z:

> A stationary wooden coaster was attacked from 200 feet with machine-gun fire. Two further camouflaged barges were strafed from low level. Accurate return fire damaged the Sunderland in eight places but causing

*Another painting by* **Fred Mock,** *this time of a Sunderland Mk V over the SS* Manela, *off Rangoon.*

no casualties. Later a larger coaster was unsuccessfully attacked from 50 feet, the depth charges failing to explode due to the shallow water and the bombs hanging up. Machine-gun hits were observed and the vessel was left listing to starboard. During the return flight back to Rangoon, the engineers fitted rubber bungs in the holes in the hull and broke up part of a wooden cupboard. They used the wood, wrapped in Mae Wests along areas in the hull where slits had been made. These repairs were completely successful for landing and the subsequent mooring at Rangoon after a flight of ten and a half hours.

In all over 750 tons of shipping were sunk and many other ships were damaged by Squadron aircraft being used in this role, so contributing to the blockade of Singapore. Of somewhat more debatable efficacy were the many thousands of leaflets dropped exhorting the locals to make life as awkward as possible for the Japanese. Meanwhile back at Koggala, the detachment carried on with training and transport tasks. On 16 June the Supreme Commander South East Asia Command, Admiral Lord Louis Mountbatten, reviewed a celebratory fly-past in Rangoon, the Squadron's representative being Squadron Leader Sheardown in PP145/O. The day before, Flight Lieutenant E Holstein flying PP157/S had spotted the 10,000 ton tanker *Tohu Maru* steaming northwards under escort in the Gulf of Siam. Liberator bombers from 159 and 356 Squadrons were sent off on a 2500 mile round trip to attack the target which was duly dispatched – the last enemy supply ship of any size to be sunk in the theatre.

Flight Lieutenant Alan Pedley later told of an experience that he had on 30 June while flying PP147/V:

> I was briefed to do a photoreconnaissance of Singora in the South China Sea, round about the Malay-Thailand border, so I was flying behind Jap lines. I went down the coast of Malaya, got down to the height of the palm trees and did the last 150 miles at virtually sea level, getting over Singora undetected. We flew around at 400 feet taking photographs. On the third circuit we opened up from the turrets on anything that looked Japanese but by then the Japs had found where they had hidden their guns and started firing back. I got a few holes in the back of the aircraft and lost a lump from the tailplane. Having dropped our depth charges we set off back to Rangoon. We were debriefed, turned in our photographs and about four days later in the *SEAC Times*, we saw that Bomber Command from India had done a night raid on Singora. They had blitzed the town from 5000 feet. That was the end of the story until I was coming home on the *Mauretania* in November 1945. When chatting on deck with various other aircrew, one skipper said he'd been in Bomber Command and his last trip had been a beauty. It was a night raid on Singora for which he had been provided with really high quality photo-montage, taken by some silly beggar in a Sunderland at low level.

It is interesting to reflect on the CO's comments in June 1945, made in his monthly report:

> Confidence in both the Allied cause and in the prosecution of the war remains at a high level. Our equipment being new is a cause of great satisfaction. The general outlook on service in the Far East leaves much to be desired as the feeling of being forgotten still prevails. Service in Europe has a far greater appeal for several reasons – nearness to home, out of the SUN and leave in the home country.

The next stage planned to bring the war in the Far East to a conclusion was known as 'Operation Zipper', the invasion of Malaya and the recapture of Singapore. At the end of July the Squadron left Rangoon for another new base at Red Hills Lake, near Madras, to begin training for the assault. The advance party consisted of Wing Commander Powell, his crew, Squadron Leader Deller and ten maintenance personnel in PP158/T. On 13 August a new CO arrived, Wing Commander DE Hawkins DFC. His experience as a wartime leader of the Squadron was brief, as after the dropping of the atomic bombs on Hiroshima and Nagasaki on 6 and 9 August, Japan offered to surrender on 10 August, the war coming to an end five days later. The Squadron listened to the announcement being made on the radio by the newly-elected Prime Minister, Clement Attlee. Two days holiday were granted. On 20 August Flight Lieutenant Thompson in 230/Q, Flight Lieutenant White, 230/S and Pilot Officer Wykes, 230/O flew to Madras to take part in the 'VJ' fly-past. By the end of the month the Koggala detachment was ended. The 'Zipper' landings in Malaya on 9 September became a matter of re-occupation rather then assault.

The cessation of hostilities increased rather than reduced the Squadron's commitments. All combat armament was removed by the hard-working ground crew, the turrets were taken off and safety hatches installed, so reducing weight and increasing the load carrying ability. The aircraft were adapted to carry 20 passengers and up to a dozen stretcher cases. Eight aircraft were fitted with the US navigational aid LORAN.

On 1 September 230/T and 230/O flown by Flight Lieutenant CV Brown and Pilot Officer Wykes took staff from the War Graves Commission, the Japanese Control Commission and the Military Services Commission from Red Hills Lake to Rangoon while five days later Flight Lieutenant Bill Hallisey flew PP149/R to Koggala on detachment to the Station Flight and from there on 10 September he proceeded to Seletar, with a number of VIP passengers. The purpose was to attend the official surrender by the Japanese to the C-in-C SEAC. On arrival at the Seletar Officers' Mess, Group Captain Francis was surprised to see the original letter rack still in place with his name on it – in the rank of Flight Lieutenant. On 12 September the Japanese senior officers were marched around the city at a brisk pace, between two ranks of tall Allied Forces officers. They then had to bow and lay down their swords before Lord Mountbatten at the foot of the steps of Government House. Flight Lieutenant Hallisey

was part of a ceremonial fly-past of Sunderlands led by Group Captain Francis. Hallisey was followed to Seletar by the CO the next day in 230/U, a flight which lasted nearly twelve hours from Red Hills Lake and carrying 3000 lbs of Red Cross parcels. So began a daily ferry service to Singapore to evacuate prisoners of war and fly in supplies, mail, nursing personnel and medical stores. Organisations whose members were often transported included the Red Cross and RAPWI (Relief of Allied Prisoners of War and Internees). The medical condition and the state of malnutrition of the liberated POWs was deeply shocking, as was the fact that piles of Red Cross parcels had been simply left to rot in a hangar at Seletar.

Three aircraft were also detached to Seletar for local ferry work and air-sea rescue duties. By the end of October 112 passengers and 68,429 lbs of cargo had been flown in, while 315 ex POWs and 14,830 lbs of baggage were flown out. Regular sorties were also made from Seletar to carry much needed rice to the famine stricken state of Penang. These relief supplies could not be

*Some air and ground crew members on the 'hard' at Seletar in autumn 1945, with Sunderlands in the background*

Fred Mock

brought in by sea as unswept minefields had rendered the waters too hazardous. The appearance of Sunderlands at Kuantan on the east Malay coast caused something of a local sensation, local boatmen charging 10 cents a time to have a closer look at the 'great white bird'.

The main problem faced by the crews was the weather in the Bay of Bengal, as the late autumn was the time of the monsoon, which created line squalls of connected cumulonimbus clouds which could only be flown through. Sadly on 13 October Flight Lieutenant Levy-Haarscher, the crew of NJ277/X and 15 ex POWs were lost when the aircraft crashed on a hillside northwest of Johore.

The rest of the Squadron relocated to Seletar by the end of November, with the troopship SS *Derbyshire* and the freighter SS *Stancleave* bringing the men and stores.

Another task commenced in December. Three aircraft per day departed Seletar at 0630 to fly the 484 nautical miles to Batavia, leaving for the return trip, with a full load of 60 passengers, no later than 1400. Conditions on board were a little spartan, with no eating or drinking

permitted in transit. By the end of the year, nearly 2000 Dutch women and children had been evacuated from Batavia on the island of Java in the Dutch East Indies, where they had been the prisoners of the Japanese invaders. One of the internees, Cornelia (Cory) van Gennep, was transported in PP149/V flown by Flight Lieutenant Sid Lane. The navigator was Flight Lieutenant Peter Bradford, who took a liking to Cory which was reciprocated. They lost touch briefly when the aircraft landed in Singapore but the crew were determined that the romance would flourish and a search was made which ended with a message being flashed onto a cinema screen which Cory saw, "Will Miss Gennep please come to the foyer." Peter and Cory were reunited and were married in England in June 1946.

The year closed with the addition of two other destinations – 230/T, Flight Lieutenant TBA Moonlight, travelling to Labuan in Borneo, while the first trip taking 20 passengers to Hong Kong was made in RN304/S, flown by Flight Lieutenant CV Brown.

*Sunderland Mk V RN299/P was flown by Flying Officer Graham Stevens and Flight Lieutenant Eddy Bardgett between 8 September 1945 and 15 April 1946.*

Eddy Bardgett

# CHAPTER 7
# 1946–1949

A detachment was sent on communications duties to Labuan Island. The first to arrive was Flight Lieutenant CV Brown flying RN304/S on 4 January 1946. He was joined three days later by Squadron Leader KW Nicholson in 230/X, who had been tasked to carry out a reconnaissance tour of Borneo and Celebes, photographing and observing the suitability of landing areas. One of the typical tasks was returning District Officers to their posts in Sarawak and British North Borneo to pick up the reins of an Empire on which the sun would soon be setting. Most days one aircraft would head westwards to Kuching, Miri, Marudi and Bintulu, while another flew east and then south to Lahad Dahtu, Tawau, Sandakan and Balikpapan. Other tasks included those which fell to Flight Lieutenant WG Abel in 230/Q – parachuting supplies to the crew of a Mosquito from No 110 Squadron which had force-landed in the jungle – and to Flight Lieutenant J Toller in 230/Z conveying Japanese war criminals around the coast from Kuching to Pontiniak for imprisonment, trial and, possibly, execution.

Living conditions were described as rough with food being rationed – so causing some crews having to fly without breakfast. Accommodation was in tents on the beach and was a little too close to other inhabitants such as coral snakes, sharks, crocodiles and blackfly, for comfort.

There were some compensations. Flight Lieutenant Eddy Bardgett remembers being invited to the first post-war dinner of the Anglo-Chinese Society of Sandakan, along with his skipper, Flying Officer Graham Stevens. They followed this with a visit to Sandakan's only nightclub, where they could dance with "charming, chong-sam wearing Filipino girls". Unfortunately there was only one record for the gramophone, 'The Girl in the Alice Blue Gown', which was played all night against the background noise of the chirping of jungle insects. Another perk was the ready availability of Jeeps, left behind by the Americans in a vast vehicle compound.

A 'First Squadron Reunion' was held in Singapore on 10 January 1946 to celebrate the return to Seletar and "In commemoration of those who have given all their efforts in maintaining the Squadron's finest traditions throughout the years of war and in setting a standard of which the Squadron will always be proud."

There was a certain rising tide of unrest later in the month which manifested itself when all the airmen at Seletar downed tools as a protest against the alleged slow rate of demobilisation, the poor quality of the food and overcrowded accommodation. They were paraded in the afternoon to be addressed by Air Chief Marshal Sir Keith Park but it took "a supreme effort" by all Unit Commanders to persuade the men to return to work thirty-six hours later.

Having completed his tasks in Borneo, Squadron Leader Nicholson in 230/X set out on a marathon journey on 23 January. He flew to Darwin in Australia and then to Cairns and Sydney. He left the aircraft there to depart for two months leave in Fiji. The captaincy was assumed by Flight Lieutenant Moonlight who carried on to Rathmines and then back to Cairns, Darwin, Balikapapen and Labuan, where he arrived on 5 February.

On 9 February Flight Lieutenant Bill Hallisey, in 230/N, departed from Seletar en route to Hong Kong with a party from the Birmingham Repertory Company. He was to make what the OR Book described as an outstanding flight. Strong headwinds reduced the aircraft's speed to 100 knots and it became necessary to seek a diversionary alighting spot. The nearest available was Saigon in Vietnam, on the river in a previously unknown area. The river was only a few hundred yards wide, with shifting sandbanks. Hallisey watched the track of a small coastal vessel to help him pick his spot. On mooring he discovered that no fuel was available so he took off again for a French Naval Air Station at Cat Lai a little further upriver. There was none there either, so the Second Pilot,

Flight Sergeant RS Millington, commandeered a British naval launch, which had a Japanese crew, and set off for Saigon with the actors, who were accommodated on board the French warship *Bearn*. The fuel arrived in the early hours of the next morning transported by steam tug and in 40 gallon drums. A lighter brought the drums alongside, with Mae Wests being used as makeshift fenders. Later that morning, re-united with the passengers, who had greatly enjoyed their night on the *Bearn*, where female company was most welcome, they set off for Hong Kong, having demonstrated "great initiative and resource".

Flight Lieutenant J Toller departed Labuan in 230/Z on 11 February with 16 passengers. By the time he returned on 8 March he had visited the following locations: Darwin, Cairns, Sydney, Melbourne, Adelaide, Hobart, Sydney, Brisbane, Cairns, Port Moresby and Moratai.

One of the visits to Australia was not apparently without incident, as it is believed that one pilot made something of a name for himself by flying his Sunderland under Sydney Harbour Bridge.

The CO also made a pioneering trip during the month when on 20 March 1946 he set off in 230/W for Japan with a cargo of Staff Officers. The first landfall made on the coast of Japan was just south of Nagasaki. The aircraft also overflew Hiroshima. Landings were made at Hirowan and in Tokyo Bay, with a visit being made to the seaplane base at Iwakuni on the Inland Sea. Wing Commander Hawkins was much impressed by the facilities offered on board the US seaplane tender *Greenwich Bay*, which had air conditioning and played nonstop jive music over the tannoy.

A long-serving member of the Squadron departed in February on 'Class A' release, Warrant Officer 'Nobby' Clarke MBE, who had been with No 230 since March 1938. It was recorded that:

> Without doubt he has borne the weight of infusing the Squadron 'esprit de corps' into new arrivals and maintaining the fine tradition throughout difficult times.

March brought a notable trip for Flying Officer Graham Stevens and the crew of RN304/S. They had been tasked to fly to Hong Kong with nine passengers which included three high ranking Army officers, a Group Captain and an Army Nursing Service Officer. Due to unfavourable weather conditions they had to divert to Hainan Island off the coast of China. They landed in Sama Bay to find another Sunderland from No 209 Squadron already there. That afternoon the Second Pilot, Flight Lieutenant Bardgett, went ashore in a 'J type' rubber dinghy for the purpose of augmenting the Sunderland's rations. He returned with water, eggs and bananas, supplied from a Chinese National Army post, in exchange for cigarettes. The crew cooked a meal – being pleased to note that the Group Captain was prepared to muck in and help with the chores – and settled down for the night. The stay stretched to three days, waiting for the weather to clear, for formal takeoff clearance to be given by the Chinese authorities in Canton and for the arrival of another 209 Squadron Sunderland with more fuel.

On board the flying boats personal hygiene was becoming something of a problem. Nobody really fancied a dip in the shark-infested South China Sea so facilities were arranged at the Chinese Army post. Graham Stevens recalls:

> It was very primitive, just a well in the middle of an area enclosed by huts. This was fine until the turn of final party of four came, which included the nurse. We eventually got it across to the Chinese Army officer that it was just not British for a lady to splash about with three men in the altogether. So they took her away and about 30 minutes later we all met again – feeling a lot fresher. The nurse smiled as she told us that she had been given a tin bath in one of the huts – overlooking our well.

Except for the weekly service to Borneo, Squadron aircraft ceased operational flying on 22 March to allow air and ground crews to concentrate on ensuring 100% serviceability for the homeward flight.

The Squadron returned to the UK in April 1946, being based initially at Pembroke Dock from where aircraft flew to take part in 'Victory' celebrations at Greenwich and Plymouth. A temporary move to Castle Archdale in Northern Ireland was made over the summer months and then the Squadron finally settled down at Calshot in September. At the same time a new CO, Wing Commander VHA McBratney AFC, who had served with the Squadron prewar, took over from Wing Commander Hawkins. During November 1946 one Sunderland, PP117/P, flown by Squadron Leader PWG Burgess, visited the Faroe Islands on a special mission to hand over RAF equipment to the Danish Government. Alan Deller flew to these remote North Atlantic islands during

*A view over Tokyo, taken in February 1946 from the Sunderland flown by the Commanding Officer, Wing Commander DE Hawkins.*

Eddy Bardgett

the war and described them thus:

> The first approach to the islands was astonishing: they rose straight out of the sea as vertical cliffs that were unbelievably high – to check we flew close along the cliff tops and the altimeter read two thousand feet. Even more remarkable was our approach to our destination, Vagar, at the head of a fjord that was itself about a thousand feet above the sea, its waters spilling over a sheer drop into the sea below in an impressive waterfall.

The following month two officers, Flight Lieutenants Harkness and Houtheusen, delivered four Sea Otter amphibians to Copenhagen. This is of particular interest as a Sea Otter was attached to the Squadron for the next twelve months, proving very useful for local flying and training. The Supermarine Sea Otter was an improved, tractor-engined version of the famous Walrus biplane.

The first item of note in 1947 was escort duty for the last Royal Navy battleship, HMS *Vanguard*, provided by Wing Commander McBratney in NJ264/R. In June several aircraft took part in a Home Fleet exercise, being based

at Alness near Invergordon. They also visited Stornoway and Lochboisdale in the Hebrides, Belfast and Wig Bay. In the autumn three Sunderlands, VB887/X, SZ581/Y and SZ582/O flew to Norway and Denmark on goodwill visits. This made an agreeable first deployment for the new CO, Squadron Leader GA Huxford.

The whole Squadron went to Northern Ireland for the Joint Antisubmarine School (JASS) course at HMS *Sea Eagle* in Londonderry. This centre had officially opened on 30 January 1947, its task being to run training courses – with the emphasis on combined air and sea tactics – for airmen and sailors. JASS courses normally consisted of ground school in tactics and techniques, followed by theoretical exercises and then a full-scale exercise at sea with ships, submarines and aircraft. The aim was to constantly review and improve the tactics required to combat the threat posed by the Soviet submarine fleet. Former Flight Engineer Fred Maryon recalls:

> We had lessons in classrooms and in a vast operations room with WRENs crawling around the floor moving warships, submarines and convoys over a large map of the seas around the British Isles. Regarding the WRENs, we were told that we might look but must not touch. We learnt about protecting convoys from and searching for submarines. As the course progressed we went out from

Castle Archdale on exercises with the Navy. These were known as Flag Officer Submarines' (FOSM'S) Summer War. Sometimes we took the naval boys with us, the submariners seemed particularly scared of flying. I guess I would have felt the same way in a submarine. On other days we went to sea in a frigate. The aircraft would drop a number of sonabuoys in the water to track the position of the submarine and then home the frigate to the sub's position. In war the frigate would then have dropped depth charges. As this was an exercise a hand grenade was used. We stood near the bow and watched as the ship moved into position over the submarine as directed by the Sunderland overhead. When judged to be close the weapons officer pulled the pin from the hand grenade and dropped it over the bow. We saw the resulting waterspout when the grenade exploded and seconds later the sub fired a cartridge from underwater with a Very light attached. It came up almost under the bow of the frigate. One abiding memory of that time was flying antisubmarine patrols around the Western Isles in the early hours of the morning. The time was midsummer and the sun was still evident, low on the horizon, bathing the sea and the islands in a golden light.

Similar visits to JASS were paid each year thereafter. A feature of the 1947 trip was a guided tour of captured German U-boats tied up at Lisahally on Lough Foyle.

*Back in home waters, Sunderland Mk V SZ577/Z rests on the hard standing. The date is some time in the late 1940s.*

Crown copyright

*Another picture of SZ577/Z, this time being prepared for launching.*

Crown copyright

Another enjoyable experience happened in December 1947, when the opportunity arose for some fighter affiliation exercises with Gloster Meteor jets. To finish off the year, a transit flight carrying officials to Gibraltar was combined with a navigation exercise, another activity that was to be repeated at regular intervals.

The final duty before Christmas was a flight out to the weather ship *Weather Recorder* by Flying Officer Bailey in SZ582/O to drop some containers full of seasonal cheer. On the same day, 22 December, the Sea Otter bowed out, with JM805 being taken for a local trip by the CO and Flight Lieutenant Harkness.

In 1948 the Squadron participated in several exercises, including 'Exercise Dawn' in the North Sea, with major units of the Home Fleet. SZ577/Z is noted as having been 'attacked' by Sea Hornets and 'Sea Furries' of the Fleet Air Arm. (The writer may well have meant Sea Furys!) A popular diversion was to make sorties to intercept and photograph the majestic Cunard liners, RMS *Queen Mary*

and RMS *Queen Elizabeth*. Greetings were exchanged with the Captain or Officer of the Watch over the radio and a low fly-past was always performed – to the delight of the passengers and crew. These activities were soon to be replaced by a return to operations. By this time the CO was Squadron Leader A Payn MBE, who had succeeded Squadron Leader Huxford.

A dramatic raising of tensions between Western Europe and the Soviet Union created the situation which brought the Sunderlands into the headlines. In accordance with the agreement reached at the Yalta Conference in February 1945, Berlin had been divided into four zones of occupation – British, French, American and Soviet. Access to the Western Allies' zones was allowed by means of specific corridors from Western Germany through the eastern Soviet-controlled part. Elections in Berlin and the introduction of a new currency in West Germany had caused alarm as the Soviets, quite accurately saw these as the first steps to German self-government. The result

*A Supermarine Sea Otter was attached to the Squadron in 1946-47.*　　　　　　　　　　Ray Burrows collection

was several months of uncooperative and obstructive behaviour which culminated in a road and rail blockade denying Western access to Berlin. The British Foreign Office summarised the position in June 1948:

> If the Soviet Government were to succeed in their efforts to force us out of Berlin in humiliating circumstances the effect would be extremely grave not only in Berlin but in Western Germany and in Europe at large. It might prove impossible for the Western Powers to maintain their position at all in Western Germany, if Berlin were lost to them, except by heavily reinforcing the military forces there.

The decision was made to supply Berlin by air – the only means short of a major assault of keeping two million West Berliners warm and fed and also as a political statement of the West's commitment to them.

On 2 July 1948 the Squadron had just finished taking part in FOSM's Summer War, the last sortie having landed at Castle Archdale at 10.25am, when orders were received to return to Calshot immediately for further instructions. This was accomplished by 7.45 the next morning. The news that greeted them was that they were to depart for Hamburg with all dispatch to take part

in what was to become known officially as 'Operation Plainfare' but more familiarly as the Berlin Airlift.

Remarkably, within twenty-four hours they were ready. The four aircraft were VB887/X, flown by Squadron Leader Payn; SZ582/O, Flight Lieutenant Harkness; SZ581/Y, Flight Lieutenant Bailey and SZ573/W, Flying Officer Cookson. They landed at lunchtime on 4 July on the River Elbe at Finkenwarder, where they would be working alongside aircraft from No 201 Squadron and, for the first month, No 235 Operational Conversion Unit (Heavy). The combined unit was known as Coastal Command Detachment (Finkenwarder) British Air Forces of Occupation (BAFO). It was accommodated at No 22 Heavy Workshops REME, which was situated in the former Blohm und Voss aircraft factory – "a magnificent establishment" according to Squadron Leader Payn. The OC Flying was Wing Commander JI Crosbie, who had reconnoitred the area previously and who had returned in VB887/X with Squadron Leader Payn.

Finkenwarder was a shallow tidal basin which had once been a home for the flying boats manufactured by Blohm und Voss. REME not only provided

*Sunderland flying boat VB887/X off-loading on the Havel River.*
United States Air Force Europe

accommodation and hospitality for the detachment but was also of considerable help in resolving the practical difficulties of refuelling and loading the Sunderlands. There was no slipway and long hours had to be spent on the water making the aircraft ready. Refuelling was carried out in the early part of the operation by hand pumps from 40-gallon drums, while the freight was loaded from Army amphibious DUKWs and barges.

The takeoff and alighting area on the Elbe was not without hazard, as not only was it a regular shipping channel, it was also liberally strewn with sunken wrecks, especially in the basin, not to mention the uncharted sandbanks in the river. The presence of pleasure craft on the river was an added factor guaranteed to raise stress levels until they were banned from the area. Moreover, the mooring facilities were less than ideal, consisting of large iron buoy markers, manoeuvring close to which was described by Squadron Leader Payn as, "an exciting business without reversible pitch propellers".

The first sortie to Berlin was made on the afternoon of 6 July. VB887/X was captained by Wing Commander Crosbie and made the first ever landing by flying boat on the Havelsee. The loads carried soon took on a standard pattern – tins of meat, dehydrated potatoes, dried eggs and milk, money, cigarettes, assorted tinned food and salt for gritting Berlin's runways – weighing up to 10,000 lbs. As the Sunderlands, being marine aircraft, were anti-corrosion treated, the carriage of salt became something

of a speciality. The reception that the aircraft received in Berlin was very enthusiastic, with crowds lining the shores of the lake, singing songs and paddling out in canoes to bring the crews flowers.

In August 235 OCU was ordered back to England and was replaced by the Short Hythe flying boats of Aquila Airways, chartered by the Air Ministry and with civilian crews who were mostly ex-RAF types. These converted Sunderland IIIs were G-AGEU *Hampshire*, G-AGIA *Hazlemere* and G-AHEO *Halstead*. They made 265 sorties between them.

The Squadron summary notes that, "Intelligence on Russian aircraft, road and rail movements was continuously passed to HQ 85 Wing by the detachment" and that:

> Routes in and out of Berlin were changed from time to time in order that the continuous streams of aircraft at all heights could be maintained without mishap. Weather limitations so far as flying boats were concerned, were a cloud base of 1000 feet and visibility three miles.

On a typical day six round trips would be flown with aircrews being given one day in four as rest. The time in the air to and from Berlin was about an hour each way. Now and then Russian fighters approached the stately, white painted Sunderlands cruising at 1000 feet outbound and 1500 feet on the way back. One of the three 20 mile-wide air corridors from West Germany to Berlin began just east of Hamburg and navigation was mostly achieved

by means of referring to the map and looking out of the window to spot ground features. A non-directional radar beacon at Gatow airfield helped to ensure an accurate arrival into the Berlin Zone before turning right to descend into the wood-fringed Havelsee.

The situation at base was improved by the arrival of Short Brothers mooring buoys, RAF refuellers and of the RAFV *Bridport* with marine craft and aircraft spares. Moreover, Hamburg offered more than just the notorious Reeperbahn – the Four Seasons Officers' Club overlooking the Lester near the city centre, where wining and dining in an attractive location cost a fraction of London prices, while the State Opera House offered Mozart, Beethoven, Rossini and Wagner.

The loading of cargo on the outbound flights from Berlin commenced in August with tons of documents, then in October, manufactured articles were flown out including Siemens light bulbs. The lightweight bulbs were a loadmaster's dream, thousands could be crammed into every nook and cranny without having to worry about distribution, centre of gravity or maximum load. The evacuation of under-nourished children and medically unfit adults began in November. It was recorded that:

> Little trouble was met from the children, some of whom enjoyed their first flight, even under the prevailing circumstances. The percentage of passengers who were airsick was surprisingly small.

It was also noted that the weather in November was very foggy – the worst experienced by most of the aircrews. Squadron Leader Payn also described the morale of the unit:

> Records in turn rounds at Finkenwarder and Havel were continually being broken, a great rivalry existed between the crews. In fact the enthusiasm displayed was remarkable due, no doubt, to the exuberance and high spirits of the aircrew, who realised the importance of their work, who were well looked after in the mess and whose welfare was the major concern of higher authority. At the end of November the record turn round at Havel was 12 minutes from alighting to takeoff and at Finkenwarder, 20 minutes, which included refuelling and reloading, an almost unbelievable achievement.

By the middle of December ice was forming on the waters of the river and the lake, it was becoming too dangerous for flying boats to operate. The last aircraft to be flown from Hamburg back to Calshot was PP115/V by Squadron Leader Payn and his crew on 18 December.

During the deployment, which lasted five months, Squadron aircraft flew over 5000 tons of supplies, 1113 children and many other passengers in over 1000 sorties – with not a single mishap or injury. Flight Engineer John Sayers made 114 trips between Hamburg and Berlin, mostly as part of Flying Officer Holt's crew. He felt a real sense of satisfaction in carrying out such a worthwhile job.

In February 1949 secret talks between the Allies and the Soviets began. The blockade was lifted in May, though the airlift continued until September – just in case the Russians changed their minds.

Back home normal peacetime flying continued with the first event of note being the detachment of two aircraft to Gibraltar to assist in the search for a USAAF B29, which had gone missing on a flight from West Africa to the UK. Sadly, no trace was found. On 16 February the Squadron moved base from Calshot to Pembroke Dock. It was now known as No 230/240 Squadron, an administrative measure designed to keep alive the number plate of a flying boat squadron of similar lineage to 230, which had been disbanded in 1946. The crest of No 240 squadron was presented to the OC for safekeeping by the AOC-in-C Coastal Command Air Marshal Sir JW Baker KCB, MC, DFC, when he visited Pembroke Dock on 21 July.

In the early summer a delivery programme of the aircraft to Belfast for 'High Tea' modification work was begun. Then during July and August, the Sunderlands took part in an extensive programme of visits to seaside resorts for PR and recruiting purposes. These included Margate, Broadstairs, Ramsgate, Eastbourne, Brighton, Worthing, Falmouth, Penzance, the Scilly Isles, Tenby, Bangor, Llandudno, Southport and Blackpool. One of the features of these trips was a mayoral reception and lunch with the local dignitaries – for the Captain only. The crew remained on board and entertained themselves by taking it in turn to be the Captain – as the enterprising operators of small craft brought trippers to view the flying boat for a fee, with an additional amount payable to shake the 'Captain's' hand. In September one crew was sent to the Tower of London, fortunately as the guests of the Royal Fusiliers. RN299/P, Flying Officer Comber and crew were part of the Battle of Britain Week attractions in the capital city.

*Sunderland Mk V RN270/O moored by Tower Bridge on 12 September 1950. It was open to the public during Battle of Britain Week.*

*Aeroplane Magazine*

# CHAPTER 8
# 1950–1957

Squadron Leader Payn was succeeded as CO by Squadron Leader OJ Wells in February 1950 and at the end of that month Flying Officer Holland and RN299/P visited Felixstowe, the base where the Squadron was formed, to familiarise themselves with the facilities in case of need as a diversion. In July three aircraft (plus a reserve) participated in the Farnborough Air Display, though it could be argued that in this instance that even a formation of Sunderlands was somewhat upstaged by another flying boat, the magnificent, 100 ton, ten turbo-prop Saunders-Roe Princess G-ALUN. In the autumn several crews took part in ferrying Sunderlands to the Far East Air Force at Seletar. Squadron Leader AM Campbell took over in November 1950. Bill Campbell is remembered as a big, friendly man with a liking for powerful, open-topped sports cars – which was not surprising as he was a relative of the record-breaking Donald Campbell of Bluebird fame.

A goodwill visit was paid to Norway in August 1951 by four out of the Squadron's six aircraft. They also took part in an exercise with Norwegian Navy units. A fifth Sunderland, RN299/P, participated in a very unusual and exciting activity which heralded a return to the headlines for the Squadron in 1952. On this occasion it was flown by a mixed crew, drawn from the Flying Boat Wing, to Seal Lake in Greenland. The mission was to uplift four officers and a guide who had been exploring the possibility of using an unnamed lake, 35 miles to the north of Seal Lake, for flying boat operations the following year.

In January 1952, Squadron Leader JS Higgins DFC, AFC assumed command. From 1 May the 230/240 appellation was dropped as No 240 squadron was re-formed at RAF Aldergrove, equipped with Avro Shackleton MR1s. Two aircraft, RN270/O, flown by the CO and RN290, Wing Commander Barnett, flew to Malta on detachment. This became a popular destination, along with the regular trips to Gibraltar. Usually, navigational

exercise purposes could be cited in justification of these valuable and morale-building excursions, which also helped to bond crews into teams. Fred Maryon remembers Gibraltar fondly:

> It was our first taste of 'foreign parts'. The sights and sounds of the place were so different. It was so densely populated. Main Street was about the only road that you could drive on and as there were more pedestrians than cars, the drivers were constantly using their horns or banging on the sides of their cars. It was a free port and the goods were very cheap. We could get watches, lighters and cameras; for our girlfriends there were always nylon stockings and dolls dressed as Spanish ladies. You hoped that you would not be there at the same time as the US Navy, as when the Yanks were in port, the prices were always highly inflated. It was a fascinating place but not the best location to have to land. The Rock is 1300 feet high and very close to the airport runway. Although Sunderlands always landed in the harbour, our approach was generally down the runway – a bit off-putting if you looked out of the window before touchdown.

Rather more regular and routine features of peacetime squadron life were the bombing and gunnery exercises carried out on targets on and around the beautiful Chesil Beach area in Dorset. In an interesting commentary on the post-war RAF, Peter Price, a National Service Air Gunner, recalled those days:

> Britain is supposed to be stiff and starchy, yet we had a sergeant as captain, with officers as Navigator and Engineer. In fact, for a time, the CO was Geordie Cooper's Second Pilot. I remember Geordie giving him an earful when he closed the throttle on No 4 engine when Geordie was doing a rate-five turn to port. The CO was quite crestfallen and apologised.

The driving force and inspiration behind the British North Greenland Expedition was Commander Jim Simpson RN, who had spent five years planning this

return to polar exploration – a field of operations in which the Royal Navy had excelled since the 18th century. Its objectives included giving service personnel experience of working in extreme conditions and of making topographical and geological surveys. On 21 July 1952 Sunderland RN270/O, flown by the CO and carrying Commander Simpson, left Pembroke Dock and flew to Reykjavik, en route for Greenland, where the first task would be a series of reconnaissance flights over the ice-packed seas to discover the easiest passage to Young Sound for the supply ship MV *Totten*.

Two weeks later four more Sunderlands under the command of former Battle of Britain pilot Flight Lieutenant CM Stavert in RN290/Z, with SZ581/Y, Flight Lieutenant Cassels, RN299/P, Flight Lieutenant Bowater and RN304/V, Flying Officer Beer, headed off for the icy wastes. They carried expedition members, television and newsreel cameramen, the BBC's Air Correspondent, and 8000 lbs of stores and equipment.

The first port of call in Greenland was at Young Sound, from where the personnel and materiel were air-lifted 190 miles further north to Base Camp on the shores of the newly-named Britannia Lake in Queen Louise Land. The lake had never before been used by flying boats and was indeed a remote and beautiful location well inside the Arctic Circle. Disaster was averted in the first week when a dinghy carrying Commander Simpson, Lieutenant Angus Erskine RN and 230 Squadron Flight Engineer, Sergeant Derek Shelton-Smith was overturned, tipping all three men into the icy waters. Flight Lieutenant CM Stavert taxied 230/Z close to the struggling men in a 40 knot wind and they were pulled on board by rope. A tot of rum was administered, which was particularly welcome to Lieutenant Erskine no doubt, as he had the unusual experience of passing under the hull of the Sunderland before he was rescued. In all the flying boats ferried 150 tons of stores and equipment to be unloaded at Britannia Lake, taking four tons on each of

*This picture of the support ship MV* Totten *amid the pack ice, was taken from SZ581/Y by* Fred Maryon *in 1952.*

*Sunderland Mk V SZ581/Y in Young Sound 1952.*

Fred Maryon

*Base Camp at Young Sound, North Greenland. Striding across the camp is Sgt (Flight Engineer) Fred Maryon.*

Fred Maryon

four daily trips, flying 260 hours and making 120 flights.

The conditions were particularly taxing for the 20 servicing personnel, whose working day began at 5am and continued to 10pm, loading stores and pumping by hand 600 gallons of petrol daily to each aircraft. All operations were carried out in daylight as this lasted 24 hours a day. Pontoon stagings were set up at Young Sound and an empty trader's hut was taken over as the cookhouse. A search was initiated for ten tons of coal believed to have been cached nearby. Squadron Leader

Higgins commented to the press:

> I will have to detail a party to find the hidden coal. In this direction 20 year-old Leading Aircraftman MD Roderick from South Wales, a former collier's assistant, might come in handy.

The window in the weather allowing the safe operation of aircraft onto the lake was not long. As the end of August approached the short Greenland summer terminated abruptly, huge pieces of drift ice began to form and the final air drops were made to the advance

89

*Preparations are in hand to re-fuel SZ581/Y.*                                    Fred Maryon

party, plodding through the ice cap with their teams of huskies to set up field stations. Other RAF aircraft to be involved included Hastings transports which flew dropping sorties from Thule; one of these aircraft crashed on the ice, fortunately without serious injury to those on board. The Sunderlands headed for home arriving back at Pembroke Dock on 23 August, satisfied in the knowledge that a challenging task had been well-accomplished. Once more the flying boat had proved its versatility. Considerable favourable coverage in the national and local press had also been attracted.

The new year began with the welcome news of the award to the CO of a bar to his AFC. Later in the year Flight Lieutenant Stavert was also awarded the AFC. In March two aircraft, RN290/Z and ML763/R, captained by Flight Lieutenants Stavert and Smith, escorted the Yugoslav ship *Galeb* carrying Marshal Tito on a visit to Britain. A new destination was added in April – the Spanish Air Force Marine base at Pollensa on the island of Majorca. The traditional Spanish hospitality was much appreciated by the CO and his crew in RN299/P. Three aircraft were on detached duty in Malta in May when they were tasked, at short notice, to transport personnel of 40 Royal Marine Commando to the Suez Canal Zone. The aircraft were RN299/P, Flight Lieutenant Bowater DFC, SZ581/Y, Flight Lieutenant Cassels and ML763/R, Flying Officer Beer.

On 15 July 1953 the Squadron took part in the Queen's Coronation Review at RAF Odiham and its aircraft were the only flying boats in the Royal Fly-past. Squadron Leader Higgins flew RN270/O; his Flight Engineer was the Berlin Airlift veteran John Sayers, who was on temporary attachment fulfilling his reserve commitment. The other participants were ML763/R, Squadron Leader Stavert, SZ581/Y, Squadron Leader Cassels and RN299/P, Flight Lieutenant Bowater. The rehearsals for this unique event took many hours of preparation and training during the month before.

In August of the same year Squadron aircrews assisted in the delivery of clothes and medical supplies to the earthquake stricken Ionian Islands. Flight Lieutenant Bowater in ML763/R conveyed Lord and Lady Mountbatten on a tour of the worst hit areas, visiting Argostoli, Zante and Samos. A few days later this aircraft was joined in Malta by RN270/O, flown by the CO. At the end of the year Squadron Leader Higgins was succeeded by Squadron Leader EC Bennett DFM.

Another new location was visited in February 1954 when, following a fighter affiliation exercise with the aircraft carrier HMS *Eagle* off Gibraltar, Squadron Leader Bennett in DP200/Z and Flight Lieutenant Day in RN299/P were diverted to Lisbon due to bad weather.

In the summer of 1954 the Sunderlands returned to Greenland to bring the expedition to its scheduled close and evacuate the remaining members of the team. Highly skilled airmanship was required in a region where

*Dinner time for the huskies!*
Fred Maryon

*Right:* *A/M Traill and*
*'Jock' Cassels.*
Fred Maryon

*Below, left to right:*
*Flt Lt Smith, Flying Officer*
*'Jock' Beer, 'Jock' Cassels,*
*Flt Lt 'Red' Stavert and Flt*
*Lt Alec Yates.*
Fred Maryon

meteorological assistance was almost non-existent and where fog, ice, intense cold and treacherous winds were a daily hazard. DP200/Z was flown in by Squadron Leader Bennett, followed by SZ567/P, Flight Lieutenant Stan Bowater, PP155/O, Flight Lieutenant NC Day, NL763/R, Flight Lieutenant EC Donoghue and a No 201 Squadron aircraft VB889/D, Flight Lieutenant Don Wynne. An extra task was to make an aerial photographic survey of 200 square miles of the region, which uncovered an unexpected difficulty when the aircraft's compass bearing was thrown off track by the presence of what appeared to be mountains of solid iron ore.

With the weather once more deteriorating rapidly, and giant ice floes being spotted in the vicinity, the decision was made to advance the date of final departure to 13 August. The honour of flying out the last Sunderland fell to Flight Lieutenant Bowater, a veteran of 1952, in 230/P. Before Commander Simpson hauled down the Union Flag which had flown over the base for two years, he gave Bowater and his crew a Jolly Roger which flew proudly from 230/P's masthead all the way home. The waiting crowds at Pembroke Dock gave the flying boats a rousing welcome, with particular interest being shown in the expedition's dozen huskies. After a period of quarantine these hardy dogs were shipped out to the Falkland Islands. One of the pups was retained as a Squadron mascot and named Kita.

*Flight Lieutenant Don Wynne and his navigator with Joanna in the bows of VB899/D in August 1954 prior to taking off for Pembroke Dock.*
Crown Copyright

***Below:*** *DP200/Z was one of the four aircraft which flew to Seletar on exercise in May 1955.*
Crown copyright

The Squadron was far from inactive on its return; in September three aircraft took part in Battle of Britain commemorative fly-pasts, visiting more than 50 displays in the course of a single day. Sadly the following month brought a tragic accident when, on a mission to the Faroe Islands, PP155/O broke up on alighting; the aircraft sank in deep water. Three members of the crew – Flight Lieutenant Hill, Flying Officer Howatson and Sergeant Cronk were drowned while a fourth, Flight Sergeant Davies, died later. The others, including Squadron Leader Bennett, were picked up by local fishing vessels.

There was better news to begin the following year, with the award of the OBE to Squadron Leader Bennett and the AFC to Flight Lieutenant Bowater.

A return to the Far East was made in May 1955 when four aircraft were detached to Seletar for a South East Asia Treaty Organisation (SEATO) exercise. In command was Squadron Leader CM Stavert, who had taken over in January. The other captains were Flight Lieutenants Yates and Duffield and Flying Officer Nicholas. The aircraft were SZ567/P, EJ153/R, ML817/X and DP200/Z. During their time in Singapore the aircraft took part in the Queen's Birthday Fly-past and also flew to Hong Kong.

All were back at Pembroke Dock well in time to prepare for the visit of Her Majesty to the Station on 8 August. Upon the departure of the Royal Yacht *Britannia*, eight Sunderlands flew overhead in formation, three of which were from 230 Squadron.

On 29 December 1955, Squadron Leader Stavert relinquished command to the final flying boat 'Boss', Squadron Leader PG Adams DFC, the last of a long and distinguished line stretching back to the very first flying boats of the 'War Flight' in 1917. Sadly the era of the flying boat in RAF service was drawing to its close.

During 1956 quite a few more flights then usual were made to Gibraltar and Malta, allowing the crews to have the experience of an overseas trip in a flying boat before that era was gone forever. In September Flying Officer RJK Nicholas flew SZ560/R to Felixstowe to take part in the film 'Yangtse Incident', which starred Richard Todd as Lieutenant Commander Kerans of HMS *Amethyst*. A final period was spent at Castle Archdale in October, with the last visit there being made by SZ560/R (Squadron Leader Adams) on 18 December, carrying a party of Royal Marine Commandos.

10 January 1957 brought the final tasking, a

*Eight Sunderlands in formation salute the departure of Her Majesty the Queen in the Royal Yacht* Britannia *from Pembroke Dock in August 1955.*

Crown copyright

photographic survey of all the main Transport Command airfields by Flight Lieutenant WD Lincoln in JM718/Y. The rest of the time was spent on local continuation training and air tests.

The last two home-based squadrons, Numbers 201 and 230, which made up the Sunderland Wing at Pembroke Dock, were reviewed on parade on 31 January 1957. Present at the ceremony was John Lankester Parker, Short Brothers Chief Test Pilot, who had taken the prototype on its maiden flight in 1937. The Reviewing Officer was the AOC-in-C Coastal Command, Air Marshal Sir Bryan V Reynolds. After the inspection Sir Bryan addressed the parade:

> I want you to know that I, most of my staff at Coastal Command Headquarters and, I am sure, those at the Air Ministry are rather sad today, for two reasons: firstly because the era of the flying boat ending here today in the United Kingdom and secondly because the number-plates of two of the oldest squadrons of Coastal Command, Numbers 201 and 230, are to he hung up. My staff have been working on ways to retain the numbers of your squadrons but so far have not found other operational units suitable to be called No 201 or No 230 squadrons. However, as you know from the histories of the squadrons, they are from time to time disbanded and re-established sometime later. We shall see that when numbers are re-allocated they are given to units worthy of such renowned squadron titles.

*Flight* magazine reported on the final moments in the life of 230 as a Sunderland squadron:

> It had been intended to fly one Sunderland for the last time and to have the crews standing on the wings of their aircraft while the AOC-in-C took the salute from a launch. Unfortunately, even the weather at Pembroke Dock was in a tearful mood; the rain teemed down and the wind gusted at up to 70 knots. But not to be entirely defeated, the two squadrons marched out of the hangar in which the parade had been held, crossed the windswept apron and paid a last tribute to the Sunderlands by passing in front of 201's A-Able parked by the open hangar door. The parade dismissed at the double; and the last sight of the last marine aircraft in the RAF in Britain was a line of Sunderlands – still after 21 years, looking curiously modern – riding at their buoys and obscured every now and then by flurries of wind and rain. A great and heroic epoch was ended.

All that remained was the formal disbandment date of 28 February, by which time all the five remaining Sunderlands had been flown to the Flying Boat Storage Unit at Wig Bay. The very last flight was made by Flight Lieutenant Pearson of the Flying Boat Test Flight who departed Pembroke Dock in SZ560/R at 0905 on 20 February 1957.

# CHAPTER 9
# 1958–1962

Within a few months the Squadron was to be reborn and in this connection it is worth quoting in full a letter dated 6 January 1958 from Air Marshal Sir Andrew McKee KCB, CBE, DSO, DFC, AFC, the AOC-in-C Transport Command at RAF Upavon to Group Captain RJ Oxley DSO, OBE, DFC, the Station Commander at RAF Dishforth in Yorkshire.

### Squadron Number Plates

Air Ministry have recently completed a review of all squadron number plates to decide which should be retained as the Royal Air Force decreases in size.

I have now received details of the review together with the list of squadron number plates selected for retention. Priority has been given to all squadrons which already have the Standard; the remaining squadrons have been placed on a priority list based on a points system – points being awarded for length of service, operational record and for other distinctions. It is apparent that the order of priority for number plates has been arrived at in a fair and reasonable manner.

Included in the number plates that will have to be discarded is that of No 215 Squadron, which is unfortunately very low on the priority list. In its place, however, Air Ministry proposes to allocate the number of No 230 Squadron; a brief history of this squadron is :–

Originally an RNAS Squadron, formed in 1918 for antisubmarine work; it was disbanded in 1923. In 1934 it was formed with flying boats for service in the Middle East and Far East, where it remained until 1946. It was awarded the Standard in 1956.

You will note that No 230 Squadron is a very old squadron with a good service record and I am sure that you will agree that the number plate will be a worthy successor to that of No 215 Squadron.

At this stage the Air Ministry proposals are of an advanced nature only – however as they affected No 215 Squadron I felt that you should know of the proposals. Accordingly,

no executive action should be taken until the Air Ministry announce the general policy for the re-allocation of squadron number plates.

No 215 Squadron had originally been formed on 10 March 1918 as No 15 (Naval) Squadron RNAS at Coudekerque in northern France, not far from Dunkirk. It was equipped with Handley Page O/100 heavy bombers and trained specifically for night bombing, taking part in combined air and naval operations aimed at blocking the entrances to Ostend harbour and the Zeebrugge canal. The O/100s were replaced by the improved O/400 in May, just after the Squadron had been re-designated No 215 Squadron RAF and had moved to Netheravon. It returned to France later in the summer as part of the Independent Force, commanded by Major General Sir Hugh Trenchard. This was the first aerial force in the world to be formed for the purpose of a strategic assault on the enemy, independent from the Army or Navy. It was thus the direct ancestor of what was later Bomber Command.

The Handley Page O/400 was an advanced machine for its day. It was powered by two Rolls-Royce Eagle engines, could carry 2000 lbs of bombs, had a maximum speed of 95 mph, an operational ceiling of 8500 feet and a defensive armament of up to four Lewis guns. Flying from Xaffervilliers on the Franco-German border near Nancy on the night of 25/26 August, two O/400s of 215 Squadron carried out a particularly effective attack. The Badische Anilin Works at Mannheim was badly damaged with the aircraft, flown by Captain WB Lawson and Lieutenant MC Purvis bombing and strafing from as low as 200 feet.

The Squadron was reduced to a cadre and disbanded in 1919, to be re-formed in 1935 at Worthy Down in Hampshire and equipped with the Vickers Virginia X all-metal biplane heavy bomber. These were followed by the monoplane Avro Anson and the Handley Page Harrow bomber/transport. The Vickers Wellington then

*No 215 Squadron was equipped with Handley Page O/100 heavy bombers in 1918.*      JM Bruce/GS Leslie Collection

served with the Squadron for most of the war, until it was replaced by the Consolidated Liberator in 1944. The Squadron served in India from 1942 on day and night operations – bombing missions and supply drops, then in Burma, Malaya and Hong Kong in 1945/46, when it disbanded. It was reformed for a year in 1947/48 as a Douglas Dakota transport squadron, at Kabrit on the shores of the Great Bitter Lake in Egypt.

On 3 May 1956 it was formed again at RAF Dishforth under the command of Squadron Leader JJ Woods DFC and equipped with six Scottish Aviation Pioneer CC1s. The prototype Pioneer II, which had been re-engined with a 520 hp Alvis Leonides radial, had flown from Prestwick in June 1950. Forty were supplied to the RAF between 1953 and 1957. Its primary function was intended to be light liaison and transport duties in support of the Army, giving a greater capability than the long serving Austers. The wings were fitted with full-span controlled leading-edge slats and large-area, Fowler-type trailing edge flaps – resulting in a remarkable short field performance. The Pioneer could take off in 75 yards and land within 66 yards. A party piece performed by Pioneer pilots was, when flying into a moderate wind, the aircraft could be taken off and landed within the width of a standard runway. It had a sturdy fixed undercarriage with long-travel legs and could thus operate from rough, unprepared strips. It was of high-wing configuration, giving the pilot an excellent view. Four

passengers or troops could be carried. Alternatively, the two rear seats could be removed to allow the installation of a stretcher with room for two medical attendants.

A further use was the carriage of a light cargo load. The aircraft could cruise at 100 mph, with a maximum speed of 145 mph. The stalling speed was 43 mph in still air. Its range was 280 miles with the maximum freight payload of 1000 lbs or 750 miles with maximum fuel and 470 lbs of freight. The Alvis Leonides engine was an old design but was very functional and reliable, performing well in all climates. The Coffman starting system was particularly useful when operating away from base, being a revolving container of six cartridges which fired up the engine without the need for an external trolley. Type conversion was quite an interesting experience as there were no dual controls. The instructor had to sit behind the new pilot and offer good advice – a disadvantage that will be highlighted later in this account.

The slow-speed capabilities of the Pioneer – as low as 25 mph into a headwind and sometimes backwards after takeoff – were sometimes demonstrated to great effect to motorists on the Great North Road. An aircraft would be gently cruising home from the field training area at Barnard Castle along a low level route parallel to the road and would be overtaken by the invariably startled driver of a faster moving vehicle.

On 5 September 1958 No 230 Squadron was formally

*The remarkable takeoff performance of the Pioneer is well-illustrated in this fine study by* JK Fletcher . . .

*. . . and also on the Squadron Christmas card from 1959. This card was based on an original drawing by artist* Wren *and illustrates well the Squadron's capacity to exaggerate the ability of its pilots and 'Single' Pioneer aircraft to do 'really short' takeoffs!*

reborn under the command of Squadron Leader WJ Simpson DFC, a New Zealander, who had flown Pathfinder Force Mosquitoes during the War. He had been CO of No 215 Squadron since July. During the Station Commander's monthly parade all No 215 Squadron personnel marched onto the parade ground. The Station Commander, Group Captain FM Osborn OBE, DFC, AFC, read out brief histories of both squadrons and presented

the CO with 230's Squadron Badge. 230 Squadron then led the march past.

It was not long before the Squadron was tasked to send two aircraft to West Germany to take part in 'Exercise Crossed Swords II', one of the purposes of which was to evaluate a range of light fixed-wing aircraft and helicopters in respect of their suitability as to providing support to 1 (BR) Corps in the field. Two aircraft, XL558

and XL702, crewed by the CO and Flight Lieutenants Len Sandbach and Peter Goad, made the journey to RAF Wildenrath on 11 October. Other aircraft being operated or evaluated by the newly-formed Army Air Corps were Austers, a DHC2 Beaver and an Edgar Percival EP9 as well as several types of helicopter – Skeeter, Sycamore and Alouette. The CO wrote a somewhat trenchantly phrased report in which he described the event as a farce, believing that the Army was completely disinterested in exploring the capabilities of the Pioneer.

A cure for his disgruntlement was at hand, when in November the Squadron was given five days to prepare for active duty for the first time in its new incarnation. This came without any prior notification. The destination was Cyprus. The island, which had been part of the Ottoman Empire, was annexed by Britain during the Great War and became a British Crown Colony in 1925. Four-fifths of the population was Greek and after World War Two many favoured union with Greece, 'Enosis', to which the Turkish Cypriots objected. A conflict between British Forces and the Greek Cypriot terrorist group EOKA began in 1955.

In November 1958, due to an increase in violence, it was decided to increase the number of light aircraft in Cyprus to support the Internal Security forces in anti-EOKA operations under the codename 'Thwart'.

Fortunately it had been intended that the Squadron would be fully mobile so servicing equipment, spares and special crates were held in store at RAF Dishforth.

The Squadron's aircraft were dismantled, crated and loaded into Blackburn Beverley freighters. Their arrival at RAF Nicosia on 27 November 1958 was greeted with rather more enthusiasm than accuracy by the local press. It took some time for the pilots to live down their billing as "10 Daredevil Hedgehoppers . . . flying in geese formation . . . after being given the order to 'Scramble!' by General Darling." (The Director of Operations in Cyprus was Major General KT Darling). The first aircraft, XL557, was reassembled and air tested, by the CO, within 24 hours. By 2 December all personnel, aircraft and equipment had arrived safely, apart from one box which turned up several weeks later at RAF Abingdon.

The main purpose of the Pioneers was to undertake communications flights with passengers and official mail, VIP flights, casualty evacuation, supply dropping and reconnaissance. The Squadron acted as a self-contained unit, carrying out its own servicing. In the beginning the living conditions in the two tented sites allocated to the Squadron for accommodation and offices were miserable – being unfurnished and dilapidated. It took much hard work from everyone, including pilots unused to physical labour, to render

*Above:*
**"It took much hard work from everyone . . . to render the locations habitable."**
*Here we see Jeff Chantler (with cup) and Ted Douglas (with hammer).*

Crown copyright

**Left:** *Corporal Butcher with his masterpiece – the replica of the Squadron badge – which he drew and painted entirely from memory.*

Crown copyright

the locations habitable. Morale was kept up by the production of a Squadron newsletter, *The Tiger Rag.*

Operational flying commenced almost at once. There were about a dozen airstrips with which the pilots had to familiarise themselves. These were mostly of adequate length but some were rather narrow and bordered by ditches, which made crosswind landings more interesting. To begin with the aircraft were used almost exclusively in the communications role, flying to a strict timetable on the lines of a bus service. Though this was a useful function, it was felt by the CO that it was rather a waste of their potential. Representations were made to the Director of Operations and authorisation was given to broaden the scope a little.

Travel by air proved to be very popular with the VIPs, the majority of these flights being between Nicosia and Episkopi. Over 70 reconnaissance and escort sorties were flown and a limited amount of aerial photography was carried out. Perhaps the most demanding task was supply dropping. In January 1959 operational drops were carried out in the Troodos Mountains and Karpas Peninsula. The drop zones (DZs) were in hilly, wooded country, usually to Observation Posts (OPs) on knife-edged ridges at heights of up to 4000 feet. Approach paths were usually difficult and the weather was wet and windy. Most drops were made at tree top level and at a speed no higher than 50 mph. Six Corporal tradesmen had been trained to act as dispatchers. The CO wrote in his report:

> Supply dropping was considered to be the highlight of the Cyprus detachment. Working directly with the Army in the field gave the Squadron a sense of direct participation in operations; many expressions of appreciation were received from the units concerned. The only dissatisfied customer was a Grenadier Guardsman who foolishly strayed into the undershoot of a DZ and received a personal ration delivery in the shape of a 45lb pack.

He added:

> All the Squadron pilots worked well but the greatest strain was placed on Warrant Officer CP Gilbert, the SNCOs and airmen, who worked very hard indeed under often unpleasant conditions in the open. Despite this they remained unfailingly cheerful and diligent throughout the detachment. The whole servicing team cannot be too highly praised.

By February 1959 negotiations had been concluded

which resulted in the agreement that Cyprus would become an independent republic within the Commonwealth in 1960, with Archbishop Makarios as President. It was time therefore for the Squadron to go home. The last flying task was carried out on 25 March and all the aircraft were flown back to Dishforth by the beginning of April 1959. During four months in Cyprus the Squadron flew some 800 hours, made 2084 landings, transported 1500 passengers and free dropped 12,000 lbs of supplies. It was subsequently awarded a Commendation by the AOC-in-C Transport Command.

No sooner had the Squadron returned to Yorkshire than it received orders to pack up and move south permanently. It had long been mooted that it would be more logical for an Army Support Squadron to be based rather closer to most of the Army. A spanner was thrown in the works by the AOC, who insisted that only a Transport Command airfield would do, despite the fact that there were few that were suitable or that had enough room, even for a little one. The CO rather fancied "a nice little independent billet" at Andover or Netheravon. Benson and Upavon were rejected as being inadequate to accommodate the promised Twin Pioneers. However, while in Cyprus, the Twin Pioneers were spirited away – before the Squadron even set eyes on them – for the re-formation of No 21 Squadron for duties in Kenya.

So on 1 May 1959, the move was made to "the ancient and only-just-adequate" facilities at RAF Upavon, a somewhat remote spot on top of a hilly area in Wiltshire, which in winter was occasionally cut off due to icy roads. It may be surmised that sentiment took a hand in the decision to keep operational one of the cradles of military aviation in the UK. Now was the chance to support the Army at close range, or so it was thought. Instead most of the new commitments and exercises during the year were with No 19 Infantry Brigade Group at Colchester – which was just as near to Dishforth as Upavon!

The Squadron Diary records an experience typical of this period:

> 'Exercise Black Gnat' proved to be a successful outing. It worked very well despite the best efforts of the Brigadier to snarl up the Squadron organisation to meet his requirements. On one occasion the Squadron was employed in ferrying infantry equipment from one strip to a forward strip following a light-scale night advance by the troops. In the middle of this the Brigadier laid on

*A Pioneer takes off from Alton Barnes near RAF Upavon in 1959.*

Crown copyright

a battle which demanded large ammunition supplies and casualty evacuation. The CO was in the air at the time and using his VHF set, acted as a control station to divert aircraft around the 'battle zone'. On this day some pilots did as many as 20 sorties all in a few hours. They were all short hops but the work was very tiring and much coffee was consumed at the Alton Barnes airhead. The method evolved by the Squadron of training selected Army officers from the various Brigade Group units in the techniques of choosing, marking and controlling Pioneer airstrips proved first class.

By way of a change, two aircraft took part in the Farnborough Airshow in September, displaying alongside a brace of Twin Pioneers from No 21 Squadron and in November the CO visited Sierra Leone and The Gambia for ten days to study the possible assistance the Squadron could give to the local forces and police in the event of an emergency.

A very busy year concluded with participation in 'Exercise Winged Coachman' in Northern Ireland. All six aircraft – XL555, 557, 558, 666, 702, and 703 – departed Upavon on 28 November and night-stopped at Prestwick, where they were given 'a royal welcome' by Scottish Aviation. The next day the formation proceeded across the North Channel to land at RAF Aldergrove.

The object of the exercise was to trial the movement of troops and supplies into contact with the 'enemy' quickly and efficiently. Despite rather inclement weather

conditions the Squadron acquitted itself well. Also participating were the Westland Whirlwinds of the Joint Experimental Helicopter Unit (JEHU).

The Squadron was now part of No 38 Group, the new Transport Command specialist tactical air support formation, which had been reformed on 1 January 1960. The AOC of the Group, Air Vice Marshal Peter Wykeham, took quite an interest in the Squadron's tactical mobility – to the extent that he visited camping exhibitions in the quest for superior equipment. In due course this consisted of modern Igloo tents with cabling to provide lighting for each. Part of the camping kit was a neatly fitted large box filled with Officers' Mess cutlery, crockery, glasses – everything for civilised life, bar the silver.

The New Year, soon brought another major exercise, 'Starlight One', at RAF El Adem in Libya, which took up half of February and all of March. El Adem was not only the location of an Armament Practice Camp but was also an important Transport Command staging post and had developed as a base for major Army and air support exercises.

The flight out to Libya by a formation of six aircraft, led by Squadron Leader Simpson in XL555, was made via night-stops at Bordeaux, Nice, Rome, Naples, Malta, Idris and Benghazi, with intermediate lunch and refuelling breaks in Jersey, Sicily and at Marble Arch on the North African coast. The highlight was apparently a three night 'rest' in Rome, where a friend of the CO's from Staff

*A 230 Squadron Pioneer XL666/ X flies over Nice.*

Ian Mackie

College, Colonel Pistani, was generous with regard to hospitality. Those indeed were the days! Flight Lieutenant Bill 'Chunky' Davis recalled that flying the Pioneer on long legs was, "quite hard work, as they needed a good deal of effort and some even claimed to have developed hard skin on their hands as a direct result".

Once at El Adem the hard work began, flying out and maintaining Army formations in a harsh and hostile environment. Bristol Britannias of No 99 Squadron, Handley Page Hastings of Nos 24, 36 and 114 Squadrons and Bristol Beverleys of Nos 47 and 53 Squadrons flew some 4000 troops and 130 vehicles to El Adem, then tactically-employed Beverleys lifted them to the forward air head at Tmini. Next it was the turn of the short-range, close support aircraft of No 230 Squadron and the

Westland Whirlwind helicopters of No 225 Squadron (as JEHU had been redesignated) to keep the Guards Brigade Group logistically supplied to operate in the field, as well as evacuating 'casualties'. The Beverleys, Pioneers (Single and Twin) and Whirlwinds worked along with the Royal Army Service Corps to provide an efficient battlefield support system.

The work was intensive with aircraft being available for tasking from 6.00am to 11.59pm, leaving the remaining six hours for maintenance. It was found that journeys of under 50 miles were the best suited for the helicopters, with longer sorties being the province of the fixed-wing types. Strong winds and dust storms added to the difficulty but the aircraft stood up well to the requirement. The OR Book also records the Squadron's

*Libya 1960. These jerry cans were all ferried into the 'front line' area by Twin Pioneer, but not all in the one load!*

Crown copyright

*Above:* *The Twin Pioneers are marshalled into their allotted spaces.*

Crown copyright

*Left:* *Two Pioneers await loading. Note the Canberras in the background.*

Crown copyright

successful involvement in a search operation for a soldier lost in the desert 50 miles from El Adem. The 25 flying hours devoted to this task were also useful training in desert navigation as the terrain was featureless and the maps virtually useless. The Squadron was augmented by the long-promised arrival of its first two Scottish Aviation Twin Pioneer CC Mk 1s, XL996 and XM370. The crews for these aircraft had been trained at RAF Benson in February and they were pressed into action soon after arriving at El Adem in the middle of March.

The Twin Pioneer, or 'Twin Pin', first flew on 25 June 1955 as a 16-passenger civil transport. Its potential was recognised by the RAF, with 32 CC Mk 1s and seven CC

Mk 2s being ordered. Deliveries began early in 1958. The 'Twin Pin' had the same short takeoff and landing (STOL) characteristics as the Pioneer and was equally rugged. It was equipped to carry out similar tasks but offered greater capacity and speed. It could carry either 11 fully-armed troops, nine parachutists, nine stretcher cases or up to 3000 lbs of freight. There was even provision for up to 2000 lbs of bombs fitted on carriers under the wings.

A new arrival to the Squadron at this time was Flying Officer Ian Mackie, and he recalls with pleasure the period he spent in the desert:

> My main memory of that sojourn was that the CO took off one of the two doors on an aircraft and

commandeered Flight Sergeant Scaife of the RAF Regiment (who was armed with a .303 rifle). They flew off towards the nearest oasis in search of food. F/S Scaife shot a gazelle and Squadron Leader Simpson landed on an old track, still littered with debris from the Desert War, to collect the kill. The Squadron chef played his part and produced one of the finest curries that I have ever had. Sitting around the camp fire, under the desert stars, eating curried gazelle and singing risqué songs is a memory I shall always treasure.

On return to Upavon in April a new activity was commenced – using the Twin Pioneers for paratroop training with the SAS Regiment, which was to become a regular tasking at home and in Germany. Ian Mackie suffered an unfortunate crash in Pioneer XL555, when simulating a forced landing:

> Climbing away at 17 knots on the short field takeoff profile, I felt the hand of the Training Officer, Flight Lieutenant John Wallace, on my shoulder – signifying that I should initiate the landing. I closed the throttle but my height was insufficient to accelerate to our minimum gliding speed of 60 knots. Wallace leant forward to open the throttle but it was too late. The aircraft was a write-off and we both ended up in hospital with fractured lumbars. The first man on the scene was the AOC, Air Marshal 'Square' McKee.

Flight Lieutenant Davis flew up to 14 Maintenance Unit (14 MU) at Carlisle in May to test the practicability of using the MU's internal roads as runways, in order to collect spares for keeping the V-Bomber Force operational in the event of a major war. This was followed at the end of May with another change of location – to RAF Odiham in Hampshire, where the Squadron was co-located with Headquarters No 38 Group as well as the Whirlwind and Sycamore helicopters of No 225 Squadron. On 30 June Squadron Leader Simpson came to the end of an eventful tour and was succeeded by Squadron Leader HJ West DSO, DFC. The new CO had been a bomber pilot and was awarded an immediate DSO during the war, as having been wounded on his way to the target, he pressed on and bombed successfully.

Preparation began for another overseas deployment and the Squadron was divided into two flights. 'A' Flight was tasked to undertake 'Operation Hopscotch' in the Southern Cameroons in West Africa. The former German Protectorate of Cameroon had been divided into French and British Mandates as part of the Treaty of Versailles

settlement in 1919. France had granted independence to its section in January 1960. The purpose was to assist the Army during the period of a plebiscite which would decide the future of the British administered territory.

The long journey to Africa began on 10 September when the Twin Pioneers XM940, flown by the CO, XL996, Flight Lieutenant Ross and XM966 (with a ferry crew en route for Eastleigh in Kenya), departed for Bordeaux. The next day they reached Elmas in Sardinia, staying in the Jolly Hotel – which was "very good" and from there proceeded to Idris in Libya, where the food was "below average". After a three day stay at Idris for servicing, the crews were briefed on the next leg south to Sebha. A Michelin map was provided showing the roads and the landing strips used by oil companies. The Sebha Palace received a favourable mention but it was noted that the Rate 1 allowance was insufficient to cover costs.

On the next leg an Avro Shackleton from No 38 Squadron in Malta was provided as escort. This was the most difficult part of the trip – more than 650 miles of mainly un-mapped desert, with scanty radio navigational aids. The most striking topographical feature was the Tibetsi mountain range, which rose to more than 12,000 feet and was reminiscent in parts of the Grand Canyon, with sheer buttresses and precipices of 2000 feet. The flight to Faya Largeau in Chad took six hours. This was a lonely but "most hospitable" French Air Force base situated in an oasis where the shade temperature was 125 degrees Fahrenheit; in the sun it was 40 degrees higher. The ferry crew parted company for Nairobi and the two remaining 'Twin Pins' flew on to Fort Lamy, near the Nigerian border, where once more the French Air Force Officers' Mess did the honours. The penultimate stop was at Kano in northern Nigeria and the final stage to Mamfe was completed on 24 September. Squadron Leader West assumed command of RAF Mamfe. His force was augmented by the arrival of a third Twin Pioneer, XM961, ferried from Eastleigh.

The detachment started work almost at once and was soon operating what amounted to a scheduled service between Mamfe, Bali and Tiko, carrying supplies, essential passengers and medical cases. The weather was extremely wet with frequent thunderstorms; all flying had to be done in the morning, as by noon the regular thunderstorms were building up to be followed in mid-afternoon by steady rain. Early morning fog was an additional hazard. The country over which the aircraft

*This air-to-air shot, taken somewhere between Derna and Tmini in Libya, shows the difficult terrain in which the Twin Pioneers operated.*

Crown copyright

*Members of 230 Squadron pose in front of a Twin Pioneer 'somewhere in Libya'. Flying Officer Ian Mackie is seated on the last chair to the right on the front row.*

Ian Mackie

operated was quite varied – from the palm and banana plantations at Tiko, to the more mountainous region on the way to Bali, following a route up a valley between 8000 feet high peaks, to thick jungle in the lower lying ground to the south. A pleasant change from routine occurred in November when an aircraft flew to Port Harcourt, where Twin Pioneers were also being operated on survey work by Fisons Ltd.

Meanwhile, back at Odiham, Flight Lieutenant RH Burgess had assumed command of the six Pioneers and a solitary Twin Pioneer, which now constituted 'B' Flight. The normal round of training and exercises continued. The Squadron's performance during 'Exercise New Year' produced a warm letter of appreciation from Brigadier DW Jackson, the Commander of 19 Infantry Brigade Group. In his report on this exercise the acting CO recommended that the Pioneers and the Squadron transport should be camouflaged to reduce their visibility in field conditions.

The festive season was duly celebrated at RAF Mamfe in traditional fashion, with the Officers and SNCOs serving the Corporals and airmen their Christmas lunch, with all the trimmings. Squadron Leader West noted that *"only* 290 cans of beer were consumed" – surely not a bad effort for 78 Corporals and airmen! Sport also generated considerable enthusiasm, with facilities being available for cricket, football, rugby, badminton, basketball, volleyball, softball, canoeing and fishing. The local wildlife was studied with interest – hippos, monkeys,

snakes, exotic birds and lizards all being spotted. Jungle treks also became a popular diversion during which valuable training was given in the techniques of survival in this difficult environment.

In the New Year work began at Odiham to respray the Pioneers in standard grey/green camouflage. However a more exciting development was at hand, as orders were received to deploy a Pioneer to the Northern Cameroons. XL558 was dismantled and loaded aboard a Beverley, while a Hastings took the motor transport and the rest of the equipment. Night stops were made at Idris and Kano. Both aircraft arrived at Maiduguri in Nigeria on the morning of 6 February 1961. In command of the detachment was Flight Lieutenant Roy Burgess, who then flew the reassembled Pioneer the 150 miles to Mubi, while Flight Lieutenant Bill Hughes went ahead in the Beverley. Once established in position the aircraft was made available to the Resident, Mr DJ Muffett, from dawn until an hour before sunset each day. To allay the fears of the locals that the aircraft was French, several Union Flags were provided, one of which was tied to the underside of the fuselage to general approval.

The plebiscite took place on 11 February. Polling was orderly with no trouble reported. The Southern Cameroons voted for unification with the Cameroun Republic, while the Northern Cameroons opted to become part of Nigeria.

The Pioneer detachment was flown home at the

**Left:** *In 1961 work began to respray the aircraft in standard grey/green camouflage.*
Crown copyright

**Opposite:** *XL558 is readied for being loaded into a Beverley freighter en route for West Africa in 1961.*
Crown copyright

end of February and a letter of thanks was sent from the Administrator, Northern Cameroons to the Station Commander at RAF Odiham:

> The arrival of the Beverley at Mubi and the landing of the Pioneer on the roads of the district had a tremendous steadying effect on rising political temperature while the behaviour of all ranks was in the best traditions of the Service. The visit of the RAF here will long be remembered with affection. Could you please pass on to Burgess, Hughes, Sergeant Hibberd and all the others our best thanks and good wishes. We were most sorry to see them go.

April brought another unusual detachment. Two Pioneers, flown by Flying Officers Inward and Newall, were sent to RAF Kinloss. From there they flew on behalf of the Ministry of Science, taking gravity readings at

Kinloss, Benbecula, Stornoway, Wick, Kirkwall, Fair Isle and Sumburgh. The landing on Fair Isle, on 16 April, was the first aircraft to visit this bird watcher's paradise since 1946. Another Pioneer, XL664, was modified to fire Nord SS 11 guided missiles but unfortunately it crashed near Kidderminster on 6 June while en route from Prestwick to Boscombe Down for trials. No Squadron personnel were involved but an intriguing extra role for the aircraft was shelved. Flight Lieutenants Davis and Mackie were particularly disappointed as, earlier that year, they had attended a three week Instructors' course in Paris, which had featured not only some very interesting training but also several excellent lunches. Interestingly, during the period they were being instructed at the French military air base, Villacoublay, an assassination attempt was

*Left:* XL558 in Northern Cameroon. It suffered a bent prop but was flying three days later.

Crown copyright

*Below:* XL558 with the bent prop clearly visible.

Crown copyright

made on General De Gaulle en route from the airfield to the Elysee Palace. This was the incident that inspired Frederick Forsyth to write *The Day of the Jackal*.

Back at Mamfe some reconnaissance missions were flown during April and May which were of great assistance in countering terrorist activity. Squadron Leader West returned to the UK and was replaced as detachment commander by Squadron Leader HM Rice. Relief personnel were by now being rotated through on a regular basis, as well as one replacement aircraft, XM285 being swopped for XM961. The tropical monsoon period in July made the conditions gruelling, though it certainly proved the worth of air assets as the roads were practically impassable. A liaison visit was also made to Yaounde in the Cameroun Republic.

Yet another new destination for the Squadron was visited in July when a VIP flight conveyed the AOC-in-C Transport Command and the AOC No 19 Group Coastal Command to the Isles of Scilly in a Twin Pioneer. In the same month Flight Lieutenant Capewell represented the Squadron at the ceremony to mark the unveiling of the statue of Lord Trenchard in front of the Air Ministry. A third flight was added to the Squadron in August, specifically for Twin Pioneer conversion.

In September two aircraft, a Twin Pioneer flown by Flight Lieutenants Campbell and Hobday and a Pioneer, Flight Lieutenant Davis and Flying Officer Inward, were part of a 38 Group demonstration at the Farnborough Air Show, showing the aircraft, weapons and techniques employed by the Army and the RAF in limited war.

By the beginning of October all three Twin Pioneers, XM940, XM285 and XL996, had returned from Cameroon. This time they flew around the coast of West Africa to Gibraltar, along the Portugese coast, across France and so to Odiham. Coinciding with the last arrival, four Pioneers and a 'Twin Pin' left Odiham to take part in 'Exercise Spearpoint' in West Germany.

A further operational deployment arose in November when two Pioneers were tasked with assisting the security forces in Northern Ireland. The IRA 'Border Campaign', which had begun in 1956, had another year to run. The Bristol Sycamores of No 118 Squadron at RAF Aldergrove had proved a useful asset but only one was serviceable and it was being sent to Kenya for flood relief operations. Therefore the Pioneers had to fill in for a month. A Twin Pioneer escorted the two aircraft

to Aldergrove and shepherded the Sycamore back to Odiham. Several low level reconnaissance missions were flown along the border carrying Army and RUC personnel. During the brief period of detachment, the IRA was active, killing one policemen, burning three vehicles on lonely roads and blowing up a bridge.

A very busy year concluded with the Squadron reunited at Odiham.

1962 saw some very bad weather towards the end of February, which allowed time for officers not engaged on other duties to carry out a very important task – building the coffee bar in the Pilots' Crew Room. When completed it was much admired for its tiger decor. The CO thanked all concerned but especially Flight Lieutenants Ken Johnston and Bill Easterbrook.

Three of the Pioneers, XL558, XL665 and XL516 were withdrawn from use in April, preparatory to being crated and sent to No 209 Squadron in the Far East Air Force. Sadly a further reduction to only two aircraft occurred in May when XL667 suffered heavy damage while landing near RNAS Lossiemouth during 'Exercise Spring Flight'. In the same month the shape of things to come arrived at Odiham – the first two Whirlwind helicopters, XP362 and XP363. As the CO commented, "The Squadron looks forward to receiving some helicopter trained pilots so that these aircraft may be flown."

Flight Lieutenant Ian Mackie took part in an air display at Liverpool Airport, still known as Speke in those pre-Beatles days. His cargo of parachutists left the aircraft successfully but an unexpected gust of wind deposited them in the Mersey rather than on the airfield. This seemed to amuse some of the VIP guests – Bessie Braddock, Barbara Castle and Harold Wilson being among these – who mentioned it repeatedly but less than tactfully at the cocktail party held in the wonderful art-deco terminal building later.

A Helicopter Training Flight was formed by the end of June, with Flight Lieutenant HH Thompson as the Qualified Helicopter Instructor (QHI). The conversion of two pilots, Flight Lieutenants Easterbrook and Larkin, to rotary-wing flying began at the same time. The fixed-wing aircraft amalgamated into the Pioneer Operational and Twin Pioneer Conversion Flights and the probability of a move to RAF Germany in the New Year became a topic of conversation. More Whirlwinds arrived in July (XP395, XP396, XP397, XP399) and September (XP401,

*HRH The Duke of Gloucester salutes the Squadron Standard at the presentation ceremony held at RAF Odiham on 26 October 1962. Also pictured are Group Captain Sheen and Flying Officer Probert.*

MT Stubbs

XP402). Examples of each of the three types serving with the Squadron took part in the Battle Of Britain Day display at RAF Benson on 15 September. Work then began in earnest with regard to cleaning, painting and polishing in preparation for the presentation of the Squadron Standard. The new CO, Squadron Leader DH Thomas, who was a former wartime fighter pilot, remarked that it was fortunate that the Station did not have a coal dump and an excess of white paint!

26 October 1962 was a "great and memorable" day in the history of the Squadron when Marshal of the Royal Air Force HRH The Duke of Gloucester KG, KT, KP, GCB, GCMG, GCVO presented the Standard and addressed the parade:

> Squadron Leader Thomas, Officers and Men of No 230 Squadron: I am proud to have been asked to come here today to present you with your Standard and am glad also to have this opportunity of paying my tribute to Transport Command and to your Squadron in particular. Although a Standard had largely ceased to be a rallying point in battle before the birth of the Royal Air Force, it still remains a symbol of honour in peace; all of you must indeed be proud of those honours embroidered on your own standard. Since its formation, No 230 Squadron has always carried out its varied roles in an outstanding manner and I am certain that those now serving will continue to uphold the high standards and traditions of their predecessors. I congratulate you on your smartness of turnout on parade and wish the Squadron continued success and a happy tour of duty in Germany. In handing over this Standard, I am confident that it will be in safe keeping in your hands.

The weather was cold and wet but this did not deter about 250 guests from watching the parade. A souvenir programme outlined the history of the Squadron and was illustrated with finely drawn sketches of Squadron aircraft types.

Whirlwind taskings began in November, giving troops helicopter experience at Tidworth and Colchester. The final fixed-wing sorties were flown in December and the Pioneers became part of an independent Conversion Flight at Odiham. Also in December another Whirlwind, XR456, was delivered bringing the Squadron strength up to 11.

So closed the third phase of the life of the Squadron, with the end of fixed-wing flying. The Scottish Aviation Pioneer and Twin Pioneer era had been only a few years in duration but much incident had been packed into that time. Many lessons had been learned about supporting the Army in the field and the efficacy of airpower as a flexible means of response in the internal security role had once again been demonstrated. Little of this would have been achieved, however, without the efficient and supportive ground crew, whose untiring efforts were much appreciated by the pilots.

# CHAPTER 10
# 1963–1966

The Westland Whirlwind HAR Mk 10 was developed from the original Sikorsky S-55, the prototype of which had first flown in 1949. The early Whirlwinds were powered by piston engines, whereas the Mk 10 benefited from a Bristol Siddeley Gnome turboshaft. The engine incorporated an electronic control system which considerably reduced the pilot's workload. It was faster, had a longer range and could carry a greater payload than earlier versions. The fuselage was basically a large box mounted on four landing wheels, with a slender tail boom attached. The engine was in the nose and connected to the rotor head by a drive shaft which ran diagonally between the two pilots, who sat above the cabin and the engine. This design was revolutionary for its time and solved centre of gravity problems which had plagued previous early helicopters. Many consider that the S-55/Whirlwind was the first truly practical operational helicopter.

The Squadron's move to Germany was delayed because of heavy snow over southern England – which actually began to fall the same day that the Beverleys arrived at Odiham to start loading up. Six Whirlwinds, under the command of Flight Lieutenant JPS Dixon, were detached to RAF Chivenor in Devon on New Year's Day to assist No 22 Squadron in relief work. The tasks included fodder dropping, casualty evacuation and the delivery of food, medical supplies and fuel oil. The weather throughout was dreadful with continuous heavy snow, freezing rain and very poor visibility. The temperature was at all times below freezing, the helicopters' engines experienced difficulty with snow clogging the nose intakes and the pilots had to face the visibility problem of white out. Over the course of eight days 124 sorties were flown, delivering 56,000 lbs of supplies.

With the arrival of the twelfth and last Whirlwind, XR457, and the return of the detachment, the Squadron proceeded with the move to RAF Gutersloh. Six

*A Whirlwind lifts an underslung load.*

Crown copyright

helicopters departed Odiham on 16 January and six more three days later. The journey was made via Manston, Brussels and Wildenrath. A signal – "Move Complete"– was dispatched by the Adjutant to Transport Command and HQ RAF Germany at 11.55am on 19 January.

*A 230 Squadron Whirlwind in the Cairngorms in the early 1960s.*  Crown copyright

*A crewman looks out from a 230 Squadron Whirlwind during relief work in North Devon in January 1963.*  *Daily Sketch*

At that time the Cold War was very chilly indeed, the Berlin Wall having been erected in August 1961, the Cuban Missile Crisis only just being resolved in October/ November 1962 and with President Kennedy's "Ich bin ein Berliner" speech to come in June 1963. The RAF maintained a very substantial presence in West Germany, fulfilling not only a NATO commitment but also the requirement to police the airspace over a sector of the country as defined by the Potsdam Agreement of 1945. RAF Germany had its Headquarters at Rheindahlen, with five operational stations – Gutersloh, Laarbruch, Bruggen, Wildenrath and Geilenkirchen. The three main types of fixed-wing aircraft were English Electric Canberras, Gloster Javelins and Hawker Hunters.

230 Squadron was in a slightly different category being NATO-earmarked but not NATO-assigned. It was the first tactical helicopter squadron in RAF Germany and to that extent it was writing the book with regard to operational control and its relationship with the Army. Its primary responsibility was to First British Army Corps (1(BR) Corps), in whose area it was to reside. To begin with its first function was to teach the soldiers basic techniques for operating with helicopters and familiarising Army units – infantry, engineers and artillery – with its capabilities. These included troop and supply airlifts, casualty evacuation, mine-laying, bridge-building and demolition work. Standard Operating Procedures were drawn up so that any unit would know how to marshal and load a Whirlwind, as well as being able to get in and out safely. Bearing in mind that there were no less than 55,000 British troops in Germany this was quite a job.

The Squadron also had a nuclear role. In the event of war, an Atomic Demolition Munition (ADM) and its accompanying US officer, equipped with the necessary key, would be flown to several 'choke points' – with the aim of disrupting the advancing Soviet tanks.

(It is interesting to note that the bush telegraph in 1963 was predicting the Whirlwinds would soon be replaced by the larger Westland Wessex HC Mk 2.)

The first field exercise in which the Squadron took part was in June. The local population was won over very rapidly when a large cow was lifted by the CO, as an underslung load, from a peat bog, in which it had become stuck. (A letter from the then Squadron Adjutant, Flying Officer Michael Stubbs, to the author has revealed that the cows were in fact startled into a stampede by a low-flying helicopter suddenly swooping over the brow of a hill towards them!)

A regular pattern of training and exercises developed over the course of the year. The Adjutant made all the necessary arrangements while in the field, ably assisted by his staff, giving the pilots time to concentrate on their flying. Michael Stubbs continued:

> It was also lucky that I had a lot of experience as a scouter and enjoyed living under canvas.
>
> Conditions could be challenging while camping on the North German Plain; in January 1964 it was so cold that the fuel froze. A good wood fire was kept going and the local inn provided us with suitable internal antifreeze.

*January 1964 saw the Squadron on exercise on the North German Plain and experiencing the 'delights' of living under canvas.*

MT Stubbs

*Right:* *"It was so cold that the fuel froze."*

MT Stubbs

*Below:* *A Whirlwind on exercise over a cold north Germany.*

MT Stubbs

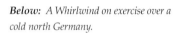

February 1964 saw a considerable reduction in the number of aircraft available in Germany, with two Whirlwinds being detached back to the UK for a month and four more being sent to Cyprus at short notice.

Relationships between the Greek and Turkish Cypriot communities had deteriorated to such an extent that the threat of war between Greek and Turkey loomed. It was decided that a United Nations force should be introduced to attempt to keep the peace. To begin with the Whirlwinds were amalgamated with the Sycamores of No 1563 Flight to form a Nicosia helicopter squadron, in which the latter retained SAR responsibility. March, however, saw the start of a pattern which was destined to last. The Whirlwind flight in Nicosia became part of the United Nations force, the aircraft being painted with UN insignia and the personnel supplied blue berets, scarves and UN badges, while No 1563 Flight moved into the recently constructed airfield at Akrotiri and re-equipped with Whirlwinds. The operational roles for the UN-assigned helicopters included troop carrying, casualty evacuation, VIP flights, resupply, landing patrols in mountain villages and reconnaissance. In addition to these day-to-day tasks, support was also given to several operations in which heavy fighting took place. Aircrew

and ground personnel were rotated on two month tours of duty between Gutersloh and Nicosia.

One particular incident received very favourable coverage in the local press, when a badly injured Swedish officer was airlifted to hospital in difficult circumstances. It was late afternoon and the light was poor. The helicopter had to land in a saucer-shaped bowl in a ravine 1500 feet below the surrounding hills in the Troodos area, where the land was steeply sloping and heavily forested.

In the meantime the rest of the Squadron back at Gutersloh carried on with the normal round of exercises and training. The CO and the Wing Commander Flying had a lucky escape on 17 August when XP397 suffered an almost complete loss of control. The tail assembly was broken away, the centre fuselage structure fractured and the undercarriage crushed. Squadron Leader Thomas and Wing Commander Conway were fortunate not to suffer major injury.

A special task on 19 September 1964 was the airlifting, as an underslung load, of a wooden cross, weighing 800 lbs, by Flight Lieutenant SR Lilley. It was put in position on a hill overlooking the village of Bruchausen and was given some coverage by German television. On 19 November operations in Germany

*Whirlwinds over Cyprus near Kyrenia in 1964.*

RO Hepburn

*Above:* Re-fuelling on exercise in Scotland in the 1960s.

Crown copyright

*Left:* Exercising with the Army in the 1960s.

Crown copyright

*Opposite:* 230 Squadron helicopters were transported by HMS Bulwark *from Singapore to Borneo in 1965.*

Crown copyright

ceased to allow the Squadron to concentrate its efforts on getting ready for a move back to the UK. The helicopters were ferried back to Odiham and one pilot, Flying Officer Ronald Hepburn, reported flying into a 50 knot headwind and being overtaken by a tram near Ostend!

The Cyprus detachment was withdrawn on 9 January 1965 and returned to Gutersloh in time for the whole Squadron to return to RAF Odiham and prepare for service in Borneo as part of the Far East Air Force (FEAF). This included fitting the pilot seats with armour plate and providing Bren gun mountings for the doorways.

Nine Whirlwinds were embarked on the aircraft carrier HMS *Triumph* on 29 January 1965, collecting, in passing, four more from Cyprus and replacing them with three Wessex from No 18 Squadron, also making use of the carrier transit. The Squadron air and ground crews were flown to Singapore in a Douglas DC-7c of Caledonian Airways on 19 February, ready to

meet *Triumph* and fly their aircraft to Seletar. Here the opportunity was taken to pay a visit to the Tiger Brewery, where Flying Officer Anthony Barnetson distinguished himself by consuming a glass boot of beer, containing four and a half pints, within a stipulated 20 minutes. He was presented with a shirt embroidered with a tiger's head and a certificate. The CO returned the honours by giving the brewery a Squadron Badge to display in the Tiger Tavern. One of the pilots, Flight Lieutenant J Webster AFC, was on his second tour with the Squadron – he had flown Sunderlands up to the time of the disbandment in 1957.

After a few days local training, the entire unit embarked on another aircraft carrier, HMS *Bulwark*, arriving at Labuan on 10 March. Operations commenced almost immediately. The first sortie was flown that afternoon by Squadron Leader Thomas in XP363, taking the Director of Operations, Major General WC Walker CB,

*The Officers' Mess at Labuan.*
Crown copyright

CBE, DSO, to Muara and conveying four troops and 200 lbs of freight from Brunei to Labuan. Labuan, which was part of Sabah, was a small but pleasant island 20 miles off the coast of Brunei.

The policy of 'Confrontation' instigated by President Sukarno of Indonesia had begun following the establishment of the independent Federation of Malaysia in September 1963. Two of the constituent parts of the island of Borneo, which lies 400 miles east of Singapore – British North Borneo (Sabah) and Sarawak – had joined the Federation as East Malaysia. Sandwiched between these was the independent Sultanate of Brunei. The bulk of the island, Kalimantan, was part of the Republic of Indonesia, which deeply resented the establishment of East Malaysia. A frontier of nearly 1000 miles stretched between the four territories, with ground heights up to 8000 feet, few roads and an abundance of featureless primary jungle.

The trouble started late in 1962 with an internal revolt in Brunei, which was rapidly suppressed with the assistance of the Special Air Service. Thereafter the offensive activity by the Indonesians chiefly consisted of incursions along the border, which amounted to an undeclared war. The Army was deployed all along the Kalimantan border in a chain of forward bases from which patrols were made. Helicopter landing points were constructed every thousand yards or so for the purposes of resupply, troop movements and casualty evacuation. As roads were virtually non-existent, the importance of the helicopter can hardly be overemphasised. Food, water, kerosene and ammunition were supplied to the bases daily and troops could be airlifted rapidly to border crossing points where incursions had occurred. Flexibility

in response to fast developing local situations and central tactical control of the bigger picture were the key factors in utilising aviation resources efficiently.

The weather was an important factor in dictating the level and intensity of flying activity. Morning mist and low cloud were frequent and tenacious, the afternoon thunderstorms were widespread, regular and heavy. A further factor to be considered was balancing fuel against payload, as refuelling was available at the jungle clearing bases in cases of emergency only.

The Squadron established two detachments, one at Tawau and another at Sepulot. The main task was the resupply and reinforcement of forward patrols along a 120 mile sector of the border. At this stage the troops being supported were 42 Commando Royal Marines and 2/7 Ghurkas.

In April, Flight Lieutenant Bill McEachern in XP396, with Sergeant G Ashall acting as crewman, carried out a very difficult rescue operation on Mount Kinabalu. He landed on a ledge at 8300 feet and waited there for nine hours in less than ideal weather conditions, while two injured civilians were brought down 5000 feet from the peak. (McEachern had completed a wartime tour on Lancasters for which he had been awarded the DFC. After the war he returned from Australia and re-enlisted as an NCO. He then won a DFM flying helicopters in Malaysia.)

During that first full month nearly 200 sorties were flown, as the CO noted, "Comment is superfluous, the facts speak for themselves, I am very satisfied with the Squadron's achievement." A month later he was less happy:

> This Squadron has now been operational in this theatre
> for eleven and a half weeks during which time it has

*Borneo 1 – 'The Chaps'*

*Left to right:  Sgt House, Cpl Blythe, Cpl McGarry and Cpl Spooner.*

All Crown copyright

***Above:*** *Borneo 2 – The Longhouse.*

*In the distance is the Squadron longhouse; it accommodated SNCOs and aircrew, with all mod cons.*

***Left:*** *Borneo 3 – Detachment at Nanga Gaat.*

flown 1510 hours. As a new unit in Borneo it was considered advisable to fly whatever hours were demanded by the tasking authority as it was assumed that the spares situation in the Command was fully appreciated and that consistent over-tasking might settle down when we had been absorbed into the normal pattern. Three months have shown no reduction in task but considerable reduction in spares. This can be accepted on a short term basis but it must be appreciated that continuation of this policy may well result in a lower serviceability rate at a time when maximum effort may be an urgent operational necessity. Training hours are down to an absolute minimum. In future this Squadron will not exceed its established task unless specifically ordered by higher authority.

The tasks performed by the Squadron were many and varied to go along with the regular commitments.

The next month brought a 'hearts and minds' round trip taking a medical team to immunise local village children and, in contrast, the extraction of SAS troopers from a dangerously isolated position. The SAS were Australians, and fearsome warriors, but they tended to smell less than wholesome after a month in the jungle. It was common for the pilots to fly the return journey with their heads out the cockpit windows to avoid the aroma wafting up from the cabin!

A decision was made to add a black pentagon to the Squadron's tactical badge on the cabin doors. This was an Indonesian Satanic Sign and was intended to frighten those with hostile intent. In July, XR402, flown by Flight Lieutenant AJ Atkinson, was lost when it suffered a complete engine failure and crashed into the sea. Luckily it was hovering at low level while holding to take part in a display at Labuan Red Cross Fete. No lives were lost though three crew members suffered compression fractures to the spine. Later that month the Tawau detachment received a distress call from a hovercraft which had jammed in reverse gear and had accordingly been forced to anchor. Flight Lieutenant Trevor Wood in XP400 flew overhead and winched down mineral drinks to the crew and passengers, who were suffering in the midday heat. A tug was then summoned which towed the hovercraft back to base. Another maritime rescue saw XP390 and Flight Lieutenant MG Hall towing the Station Sub Aqua Club's dive boat six miles to harbour, when its outboard failed.

Squadron Leader Thomas came to the end of his tour in August 1965 and was replaced by Squadron Leader Keith Cawdron.

Flight Lieutenant Wood, Flying Officer Dickie Holmes and Flight Sergeant A Hood were involved in a dramatic and dangerous rescue in October. Wood was operating a troop lift in XK986 when he received a message that three RAF Regiment personnel were drifting down the Talankai River on an air drop container. The container, which was full of rations and beer, had been swept into the swollen waters of the river along with the men. He quickly returned to Sepulot to off-load the soldiers and pick up Holmes and Hood. Soon Jock Hood was dangling over the rushing waters while Wood manoeuvred the helicopter as close to the overhanging trees as he dared; the rotor blades were actually chopping at the foliage. The first man was rescued then Hood returned to pick up a second man but disappeared underwater, entangled with the parachute and the panicky survivor. With some difficulty he freed himself and gestured to Dick Holmes, who was acting as winchman, that the helicopter should tow them 200 yards to the bank. Trevor Wood landed and took both exhausted men on board. The third man was saved by a Wessex of 848 Naval Air Squadron.

The New Year 1966 brought a visit by the Leader of the Opposition, Edward Heath MP, Anthony Barber MP and Christopher Chataway MP, along with a posse of radio and newspaper reporters. The award of a Queen's Commendation for Valuable Service in the Air to Flight Sergeant Hood was, perhaps, greeted with more enthusiasm.

The Squadron's complement was undergoing considerable change as many aircrew and technicians were coming to the end of their tours. Experienced pilots were being replaced by newcomers straight out of basic training. The last member to have been with the Squadron in Germany, the Engineering Officer, Flight Lieutenant RN Smith, departed for home in March. In the same month a year's service in theatre was completed. The CO noted that the Squadron had flown 5742.45 hours out of a task of 5160 hours, carried 2,036,968 lbs of freight, 25,539 passengers and 295 casualties.

In April it was decided that as the weather had been very good for a week, it would be a good idea to have a Squadron barbecue. Naturally this brought on the rain but Pilot Officer D Bailey had more luck when he bartered 100 nails for a pig. The pig's fate was "to supplement the not over-abundant rations".

As the year wore on rumours of an end to the 'Confrontation' began to grow. The flying task continued except for the movement of fighting patrols into the combat areas on the border, which had diminished in line with the decrease in Indonesian incursions. The Minister of Defence for Air, Lord Shackleton, arrived in June and he was taken to see Mount Murud, which he had climbed in 1932.

The detachments at Sepulot and Tawau were brought to an end in July but the Whirlwinds were soon in action from Bario. In conjunction with No 110 Squadron they were tasked in connection with the last operations to sweep up the Indonesians involved in the fighting in the Long Semado area in Sarawak. Sukarno had lost power to Suharto in an anti-communist Army coup and a peace treaty with Malaysia was imminent. By the end of August the undeclared war was over.

Plans began to be formalised for the Squadron's move back to the UK. Three of the brand new Short Belfast freighters of No 53 Squadron were used for the 10,000 mile trip – XR367 *Heracles*, XR368 *Theseus* and XR369

*Spartacus*. A maximum of three Whirlwinds could be loaded into the giant aircraft; the first Belfast departed on 13 October. Squadron Leader Cawdron left a few days later; a fly-past of five Whirlwinds flew over as he walked to his aircraft, the formation leader carrying the Squadron Commander's pennant in his honour. The last operational task, a trooping trip to Brunei and back, was flown by Flying Officer M Catlow in XP396 on 21 October.

The final figures for the Squadron in Borneo were 8558 hours, 3,311,000 lbs of freight, 39,779 passengers and 414 casualties – a truly remarkable achievement.

The new CO, Squadron Leader DE Todd, took command on 19 November 1966. All the helicopters were back at RAF Odiham by the end of the month and the Squadron was declared non-operational until 5 January 1967. The training bill to meet this date was immense as most of the pilots had not previously operated helicopters in the UK. Instrument flying, night flying and formal categorisation were the main priorities.

*230 Squadron prepares to return to the UK in October 1966 aboard Short Belfast freighters of No 53 Squadron.*

Crown copyright

121

**Left:** *Whirlwind XP357 is loaded into the Shorts Belfast freighter* Spartacus. *Note the Twin Pioneer in the lower right background.*

Crown copyright

**Below:** *The Squadron, now back at RAF Odiham, receives a visit from a US Chinook in 1967 – shades of things to come for the Royal Air Force and Odiham in particular.*

Crown copyright

# CHAPTER 11
# 1967–1971

With the resumption of operational status in January 1967, the Squadron was soon involved in numerous exercises, which required three to five day detachments. The first major one of these was 'Stardust'. Otherwise, the normal routine was Army co-operation flying – practising emplaning and deplaning, aircraft marshalling in the field, hooking up underslung loads and casualty procedure. In March two aircraft were detached to RAF St Mawgan to be available to assist in the fight against oil pollution of the beaches of Devon and Cornwall following the grounding, and subsequent sinking, of the tanker *Torrey Canyon*; 'Operation Mop-Up' continued into June. The *Reading Evening News* described the typical tasks:

The helicopters of No 72 and No 230 Squadrons have two missions – to fly detergent all round the threatened coastline and to take VIPs and experts out to examine the situation. The Odiham machines have already made scores of trips, taking barrels onto the beaches, which can only otherwise be reached by precipitous paths. They are also dumping the barrels at low-water level so that troops and firemen don't have to carry the heavy loads distances of up to half a mile over the sands. Flight Lieutenant Ron A 'Chunky' Lord is the detachment commander of 230 Squadron – this is their first task since returning to the UK from Borneo.

In all 361 hours were flown – 3539 sorties, carrying 1,500,000 lbs of freight, 530 passengers and one casualty.

*A visit is made to RFA* Sir Bedivere *in August 1967.*
Crown copyright

*Above:* *Whirlwind XP329 overflies*
*Stonehenge during an exercise in 1967.*
Crown copyright

*Left:* *The Whirlwinds were seen in a*
*starring role at numerous carnivals,*
*fetes and displays. Here XR453*
*performs for an appreciative audience.*
Crown copyright

June brought participation in numerous carnivals, fetes and air displays, the versatility of a helicopter being such that it could take part in a major display or become the star attraction at a smaller event. A good example of the latter was the display given at Tundry Pond, Dogmersfield, not far from Odiham. Pilot Officer Chris Billings paddled a dinghy into the middle of the pond and was 'rescued' by Flight Lieutenant Lord and his crew, Sergeants John Smalley and Tom Hepple. As an encore, a little dog called

Susie was winched down and up again. In July training sorties were made to Battersea Heliport on the Thames in London. These provided valuable experience of flying in tightly controlled airspace. September was spent preparing for 'Exercise Overdale' in Germany, in which eight aircraft took part in October. Flying was restricted later in the year by the onset of the foot and mouth epidemic.

1968 brought about a major structural reorganisation of the RAF – Bomber Command and Fighter Command

*A Squadron helicopter, XP330, lands at Battersea Heliport on the Thames.*
Crown copyright

***Above and below:*** *Cyprus once more on United Nations duties in 1968.*
*Note the combined 230 Squadron/UN sign.*

Crown copyright

merged to become Strike Command, which a few months later absorbed Coastal Command. Previously, Transport Command had already been renamed Air Support Command, to which were added Hawker Hunter ground attack aircraft.

The United Nations in Cyprus (UNFICYP) peacekeeping task was still ongoing and was shared with the Wessex helicopters of Nos 18 and 72 Squadrons. The existing establishment of ten Whirlwinds was insufficient to allow 230 Squadron to participate fully and still carry out UK-based tasks. It was therefore increased to 13 aircraft which resulted in four aircraft being deployed to Cyprus in March. They were fitted with long-range tanks for the 2200 nautical mile journey and flew via Orleans-Bricy, Lyons, Nice, Pisa, Rome, Brindisi, Andravida, Athens and Rhodes. Squadron Leader David Todd described the trip as "Great fun". The handover was marked by a special fly-past of three each of Sioux, Wessex and Whirlwinds from the AAC, 72 and 230 Squadrons respectively.

In April the Squadron received a visit from Wing Commander PR Woodward RAF (Retd), who had served with 230 during the war in the Mediterranean. He presented the Squadron with the Visitors Book from his aircraft, in which he had transported numerous VIPs.

Flying Officer Roger Barnes and Sergeant Andy Aldridge were involved in a nasty incident in June 1968, while giving an air experience flight to seven Air Training

*VIP flying was a regular Squadron duty.*

Crown copyright

*In 1969 the Harriers of No 233 OCU joined 230 Squadron at RAF Wittering.*

Crown copyright

Corps cadets. The Whirlwind suffered engine failure at 100 feet and auto-rotated to the ground, breaking up on landing. Luckily the impact had been cushioned by the trees of Nutley Wood. There were no serious injuries and each of the cadets later received a special scroll from the Ministry of Defence. In the same month, four aircraft were detached to RAF Brize Norton for VIP flying duties in connection with the Royal Air Force's 50th Anniversary Review at RAF Abingdon. A new CO , Squadron Leader Trevor Jones AFC, took over in November 1968.

The Cyprus detachment came to an end in February 1969, just in time for a change of base from Odiham to RAF Wittering in Lincolnshire. The Squadron made a fine sight, arriving in formation, pennant flying from the lead helicopter, to be welcomed by the Station Commander, Group Captain GK Williams. Wittering was to be the base for co-location of two types of 38 Group tactical support aircraft, allowing the Wessex of Nos 18 and 72 Squadrons

to concentrate at RAF Odiham. Soon to arrive were the first Hawker Siddeley Harriers, which would enter service with No 233 Operational Conversion Unit at Wittering on 1 April. A visit was made to Denmark in September, for 'Exercise Green Express'.

In February 1970 the Squadron again took over the UNFICYP task, with XR330, XK986 and XL110 being flown out by Belfast freighter. The helicopters' main role was the resupply of UN observation posts, many of them high up in the jagged peaks of the Kyrenia Mountains. Troops from Finland, Denmark, Sweden and Canada formed part of the peacekeeping force at that time. The Squadron served there until the end of 1971, when the practice of rotating detachments was replaced by the permanent presence of No 84 Squadron, which was formed in Cyprus early in 1972.

Back at Wittering, on 25 February 1970, two Whirlwinds were scrambled when the crew of a US

*In September 1971 the Squadron Crest from the Officers' Mess at Seletar was returned to the Squadron. It remains a treasured memento and hangs in a place of honour. Flight Lieutenant Martin Coales, of No 205 Squadron, is pictured handing the Crest to Squadron Leader John Black.*

Crown copyright

Phantom had to eject over the Wash. One survivor was winched to safety. In April, the CO visited the Isle of Skye to assist the Royal Engineers in dismantling a bridge located in a highly inaccessible position. Another unusual duty involved photographing Phantoms, on training sorties, carrying out live firing of SNEB rockets at ground targets. In August two aircraft working along with troops, police and tracker dogs, acted as the hunter force in an escape and evasion exercise with 22 Squadron SAS. In 1971, much time was devoted to parachute dropping, both free fall and static. Some variety came in March with the provision of ship to shore transport for survey teams in the Scottish Islands and during May, several aircraft took part in filming scenes for the long-running BBC police series 'Softly, Softly'. One of the stars of the show, Stratford Johns (who played Chief Superintendent Charlie Barlow), was an enthusiastic passenger.

In September the local press reported the return from RAF Seletar of a Squadron Crest, beautifully carved in teak, which had hung in the hall of the Officers' Mess there since 1938, when it had been presented to the Squadron by Group Captain Wilfred Dunn (who reached the rank of Air Commodore before he retired in 1944). Remarkably it survived the wartime Japanese occupation intact.

The time given over to para-dropping culminated in October with the first ever free-fall, night descent by the RAF Falcons parachute team. This, the final year with the

Whirlwind, was also spent giving hovering experience to the new Harrier pilots and preparing to become a Puma squadron at Odiham. One of the final duties for the Whirlwind was a brief visit to Northern Ireland in December for photographic tasks.

A Puma conversion unit had been set up at RAF Odiham in late 1970 and in October 1971 No 230 Squadron (Puma Echelon) was formed. This consisted of four pilots, three crewmen, a ground liaison officer and four ground crew. The Whirlwinds left Wittering in December 1971 and the delivery of new aircraft to the Squadron at Odiham commenced, the first two being XW219 and XW220. The AOC No 38 Group sent a valedictory signal:

> No 230 Whirlwind helicopters completed their final operational task in the UK since the Squadron returned to 38 Group from Borneo in 1966. It has completed many hundreds of operational and exercise sorties in a most commendable manner and in so doing has enhanced the image of the Group and the RAF as a whole. Please extend my thanks and appreciation for a job well done to all Squadron personnel.

Squadron Leader PJ Maitland AFC handed over command to Wing Commander PDA Austin AFC, who had flown Belvederes in the Far East and who rejoiced naturally in the nickname of 'Bunny'. He was an excellent pilot (Support Helicopter A Category – exceptional) and proved a very popular boss.

# CHAPTER 12
# 1972–1979

On 7 January 1972, in a brief handover ceremony at RAF Wittering, the Squadron Standard and the original painting of the Squadron Badge, signed by King George VI, were passed on for carriage to the new Squadron HQ at Odiham.

The Helicopter Sub Group of the Anglo French Aircraft Working Group had been considering collaborative projects since the mid-1960s. The chosen type as a medium-lift helicopter was the SA-330. The Westland/Aerospatiale Puma SA-330E originated in 1963 with a French requirement for a tactical helicopter. The prototype, F-ZWWN, flew on 15 April 1965 at Sud Aviation's Marignane plant. The Anglo-French helicopter agreement gave Westland licences to assemble Pumas and Gazelles in return for a French share in, and purchase of, the Lynx. The first British-built Puma flew at Yeovil on 25 November 1970. Rolls-Royce and Turbomeca shared the manufacture of the engine. The Puma was designed to replace Whirlwinds and Belvederes in a tactical support role and entered service as the HC Mk 1 in June 1971 with No 33 Squadron at RAF Odiham.

The Puma was powered by two Turbomeca Turmo IIIC4 turboshaft engines, each of 1328 shp, giving a maximum cruising speed of 139 knots, a service ceiling of 15,750 feet, a maximum rate of climb of 1200 ft/min and a maximum range of 341 miles. Sixteen fully armed troops could be carried. The initial buy was 40 followed by a top up purchase of eight to SA330L standard. The RAF had originally bid for 68 to provide three squadrons of thirteen, giving the capability to lift three companies. Over 1000 of the Puma family were produced in all. The French name Puma was retained by the RAF but others were considered by the Air Force Board – Normandy, Consort, Brigand, Carosse, Gauntlet, Warrior, Atlas, Machete and Mistral being some of the alternatives.

One of the pilots to fly the Puma in its early years with the Squadron was Flight Lieutenant Duncan Donaldson.

He recalled the period 1971–72:

> It was great fun during the formation period as we had no formal tasking but we had plenty of aircraft and plenty of flying, such as school and PR visits which the RAF loved. I took a Puma back to my old school at Gourock, Scotland and on my way back collected a load of kippers from Machrihanish.

The roles assigned to the Squadron were logistic support – principally the internal and external carriage of freight, troop movements, aeromedical evacuation and training in all Support Helicopter functions. The first exercise in which the Squadron was able to try out its new aircraft was 'Frozen Tiger' in February 1972. Training visits were made to Germany and two aircraft flew to RAF Ternhill in May to allow Prince Philip to gain some experience of the helicopter. Later in the summer 'Exercise Sky Warrior' at Otterburn, allowed the Squadron, which had been declared operational on 1 June (one month ahead of schedule), to gain some useful experience of low level navigation and concealment in the field. Once both 33 and 230 Squadrons were operational one aircraft from each was selected for intensive flying with a view to checking the wear on the main components such as the gearboxes and engines. The aim was to extend the service life of these and so reduce costs. Duncan Donaldson commented:

> It sounds fun but in fact the pressure to keep two aircraft flying at least 100 hours per month resulted in a lot of unnecessary weekend work and a lot of unrepresentative flying, for example hovering around the airfield in fog.

The two squadrons also developed slightly differing operational principles. 230 Squadron operated on a captain, copilot and crewman basis, whereas 33 Squadron made do with a pilot and a crewman. As both squadrons were manned at only 1.5 pilots per aircraft this made life on 230 rather busier then on 33. It also meant that 230's pilots only got half of the flying time with their

*Above: This striking portrait of a 230 Squadron Puma shows the rugged lines of this aircraft to good effect.*

*Below: Troop movements are a speciality of the Puma.*

Both Crown copyright

hands actually on the controls. The basis for the different procedure was that 230's CO believed that the increased cruise speed of the Puma as compared to a Whirlwind, combined with the Army's requirements for ultra low level operations, necessitated a cockpit crew of two. Subsequent experience in Northern Ireland tended to underline this point and eventually the manning was sorted out to enable Pumas to operate more comfortably with two pilots.

The chance to show off the aircraft to the public came in September with the Odiham Families Day and the Battle of Britain Day displays. In October aircraft deployed to Denmark and to Italy, which though enjoyable experiences, served also to highlight the need for the installation of better navigational aids. The first year with the Puma concluded with three aircraft being sent in the capacious hold of Belfast freighters, under the command of Squadron Leader I Wines, to the Bahamas to exercise with 40 Commando. One particularly worthwhile result of this trip was assisting the local authorities in the seizure of £500,000 worth of smuggled drugs.

1973 began with a strong rumour that aircraft were going to be detached even further afield, to Nepal. Plans were formulated but in the event the requirement was cancelled. In March the lifting capacity of the Puma was tested by an operation near Chester which involved the carriage of a cabin containing a dialysis machine and weighing a total of 4150 lbs. On Sunday 15 April the Squadron marked the 60th Anniversary of its earliest antecedents at Felixstowe in 1913 by a church service at which the Standard was paraded. Additionally some 18,500 philatelic first day covers were produced. On 17 April 17,500 of them were flown by Squadron Leader WH McEachern DFC, DFM, Flight Lieutenant AW Jones and MALM JD Sankey from Odiham to Yeovil, Leavesden,

Battersea and back to base. This was the Squadron Leader's final flight in a service career of 29 years with the RAAF and RAF. The remaining 1000 envelopes were flown to Paris by the CO.

A portent of duties to come was heralded at the end of April by the first detachment in support of the security forces in Northern Ireland. (The first Pumas to have served in the Province were four operated by No 33 Squadron, which were deployed in December 1972.) In the first instance one crew was rotated fortnightly through Aldergrove to gain some experience of the conditions. 1972 had been a dreadful year in the Province – Bloody Friday, the Abercorn Restaurant bomb, sectarian murders, 'Operation Motorman' and the downfall of the government at Stormont. 1973 did not start encouragingly, either. It was a difficult and dangerous time.

Other tasks during the year were rather more

*A 230 Squadron Puma hovers over a typical urban landscape in Northern Ireland.*

Crown copyright

agreeable and included the CO flying a very special VIP – King Hussein of Jordan – from London to Brize Norton, navigational exercises to France, Germany, Italy and Denmark, as well as a longer stay for four aircraft and crews in Canada in the month of August. They were flown across to CFB Edmonton by Belfast freighter for 'Exercise Pond Jump West' and from there to Wainwright Training Area in Alberta. The chief function was to provide long-range troop deployment capability for the Territorial Army, to Calgary and to Kananaskis Provincial Park survival training area in the Rocky Mountains. Some Squadron members soon had first hand experience of this rugged type of training when the CO, Wing Commander Austin, 'volunteered' three aircrew to spend a weekend with the TA walking up and down the Rockies. One of this group, Flight Lieutenant Duncan Donaldson, has fond memories of a particular incident:

> Towards the end of the deployment, which had been both successful and enjoyable, the TA put on a no expense spared lunch in the Officers' Mess at Wainwright. This was a marquee with three sides rolled up and the food beautifully laid out on self-service tables to the front. The bar was to the rear of the tent.
>
> The marquee was in a shallow hollow, with soldiers sitting on the surrounding high ground watching the proceedings with obvious interest. The CO, myself and Flight Lieutenant Dick Langworthy were invited to the lunch, which coincided with a small resupply task to an area near the Army Base. 'Bunny' decided that he would fly the task himself, drop Dick and myself at the lunch and return later, which was all typically 'Bunny' and sounded well in theory. Unfortunately 'Bunny' was a natural showman and could not stop himself from landing close to the front of the Mess Tent and surrounding audience. The landing went OK and Dick and myself jumped out onto the grass, crouching down under the downdraft, while the Puma took off and flew straight over the marquee. As we started to look up the marquee was lifting in slow motion, causing the food tables to topple their contents on the grass and roll under the canvas. Dick and I watched in awe as the tent completely dismantled and settled down on top of most of the officer contingent, most of whom had been at the bar to the rear of the tent. For a few seconds there was an absolute silence before the surrounding soldiers erupted into raucous laughter and shouts. Dick and I stood paralysed not knowing whether to cry, laugh or run.

> Anyway, we slowly approached the scene of chaos which by then was reminiscent of a enormous tarpaulin with large bugs crawling around underneath. One of the first to surface was a small and still very dapper looking TA Captain (in real life a Yorkshire lawyer) who walked directly over to Dick and I with an absolutely straight face and said, "Gentlemen, can I get you a drink?"

> Eventually things were sorted out and sufficient food and drink were recovered to let the party recommence. The Army was less than happy, however, and wanted to know when 'Bunny' would be arriving. For the first few hours after the incident I think they would have lynched him. He wisely did not appear until the early evening by which time the party was in full swing and the Army was starting to see the funny side of things. 'Bunny' arrived in an excellent disguise, as the RAF Padre, and was not recognised until he started to lead the bawdy song brigade. In a theatrical climax, which could not have been equalled, he sang solo on top of a table to a most appreciative audience, before pulling off his dog collar and declaring, "Gentlemen, it was me who blew your tent over." Of course he got away with it and it was a memorable conclusion to the exercise.

In September four aircraft were detached to Aldergrove to support night flying trials in respect of passive night vision goggles (NVG). Later in the year the Squadron aircraft came to specialise in assisting the Royal Engineers in the closure of 'unapproved' roads. The twisting and tortuous 303 mile border between Northern Ireland and the Irish Republic is crossed by many lanes and roads which paid no heed to political niceties. Much used for smuggling in the past, by the early 1970s they were an ideal means of incursion for terrorists. The Pumas carried concrete blocks, weighing more than two tons, as underslung loads and gently lowered them into position, thereby barring the roads to vehicular traffic. The possibility of attack from SA7 heat-seeking missiles was a real threat and this forced a rethink of flying tactics.

The year closed with the national energy crisis and fuel shortage which resulted in severe limitations being imposed on all flying, except in Northern Ireland. This continued into the New Year, 1974, though it did not prevent Flight Lieutenant RU Langworthy becoming the first RAF pilot to complete 1000 hours on the Puma. His valuable contribution to the introduction of the type into service was later recognised by the award of the AFC.

In Ulster the bombings, shootings and armed robberies continued. In south Armagh, the base at Crossmaglen became almost completely dependant on air support for all its daily needs. Placing more road blocks, border patrols and the insertion of personnel at vehicle check points (VCPs) were part of the routine. The establishment of refuelling points at Castle Dillon and St Angelo in March greatly assisted operational efficiency and time on task. Aircraft were also detached to Omagh and to Bessbrook. The burden was shared with the Pumas

of No 33 Squadron, also based at Odiham. Tensions were heightened by the Ulster Workers Council strike in May, which brought down the power-sharing administration, and a Puma came under fire near Newry.

A new and more effective method of blocking border crossings was devised. Large steel tanks were lowered into position over holes dug in the ground. Concrete was then poured in, not only filling the receptacle but also effectively securing it to the ground with concrete plugs. In June a dawn cordon and search out of Bessbrook resulted in the

capture of five IRA men, while later in the month Army Sioux helicopters which had broken down were recovered by air from Omagh and Long Kesh to Aldergrove.

The normal detachment period for an individual pilot was between four and six weeks, which allowed for between 80 and 100 hours per month of good operational flying. The job itself was satisfying but the frequency of rotation through the Province, and the family separation involved, caused quite a few domestic problems. Another problem was the poor serviceability of the Puma in its early years while design faults were ironed out.

Attention was diverted from Northern Ireland for a time in July, following an attempted coup d'état in Cyprus and the invasion of the northern part of the island by Turkish forces. Together with No 33 Squadron a joint detachment was rapidly assembled and sent there. Back in Ulster, a riot at HMP Maze required aerial support and trials of Nitesun equipment to illuminate landing areas at night were also carried out. On a lighter note, a prize bull was pulled out of a bog in August.

A welcome diversion came in September 1974 with a joint deployment of ten Pumas to Denmark for 'Exercise Bold Guard' just over the border in northern Germany. The daily round in Ulster – troop movements, VCPs and resupply tasks – was broken by more riots at the Maze

in October and the escape of 33 prisoners by means of a tunnel in November.

Wing Commander Austin was succeeded as CO by another well-liked boss, Wing Commander 'Chunky' Horrocks. He took over a busy squadron – the commitment in Cyprus continued, then in December the Provisional IRA declared a cease-fire which was to last for six months (more or less, depending upon one's definition of the word 'cease-fire'). December brought the first 'Treviso Trainer' a popular route training trip to Italy, which would be repeated throughout the following year, along with visits to Germany, Denmark and France.

In Cyprus the northern part of the island was declared to be a Turkish Federated State in February 1975, forcing Greek Cypriot families to flee and effectively partitioning the country. Back at Odiham some of the Squadron was able to benefit from fighter evasion training with the Hawker Hunters of 846 Naval Air Squadron. A heavy landing at Whitecross in south Armagh on 22 May resulted in extensive damage to XW215. Fortunately only minor injuries were suffered. A visit was made to the Paris Airshow in June and a training opportunity with a difference arose in July, when six personnel qualified as door gunners, the first since the Squadron re-equipped with Pumas. Another first happened on 5 September – a

*An Army Air Corps Sioux is pictured being recovered to RAF Aldergrove by Puma XW217.*

KA Boyd

deck landing on HMS *Bulwark* by Flight Lieutenant R Hayward, with a delivery of Harrier pilots.

Early in 1976 considerable aid was given to the civil community when thousands of sandbags were conveyed to Great Yarmouth to strengthen the sea defences following severe storms. On 27 January XW230 was delivered to the Squadron by the CO, Wing Commander DO Crwys-Williams, landing at exactly 2.30pm. Life at Aldergrove was rendered a little more lively by car bomb and mortar attacks at the co-located civil airport. Murders by the IRA and the 'Shankill Butchers' continued with such ferocity that elements of the SAS were sent to the Province. It was now time for 230 Squadron to have a break and to swop duties with No 33 Squadron who had been maintaining the commitment to Belize.

Until 1973 this Central American country, which is about the size of Wales, was known as British Honduras. Guatemala, its larger neighbour to the south and west, claimed the land as a residual legacy from the old Spanish Empire. British influence in Belize had its origins in the 17th century and a Scottish pirate, Captain Peter Wallace. A settlement, Belize City, was built, and the richer inhabitants lived on St George's Cay, an island eight miles off the coast. The chief business became the felling and selling of mahogany to make fine furniture. In 1862 Belize was formally adopted as the Crown Colony of British Honduras.

All was relatively peaceful until the Guatemalans began sabre rattling in the 1970s. The first RAF Harriers and Pumas were sent to Belize in November 1975. The helicopter task was shared between Nos 33 and 230 Squadrons, with officers and airmen spending the tour of duty as part of No 1563 Flight, located at Belize International Airport. Most aircrew were sent to Belize once or twice during the course of a normal tour. It was on 8 June 1976 that Squadron Leader KW Cartlidge assumed command of 230 Squadron's first Belize tour, with the Ulster detachment ending two days later.

Squadron Leader Nigel 'Smokey' Furness of 230 Squadron later described life in Belize:

> The detachments are very hard work for both air and ground crews. Aircrews average about 30 to 40 flying hours a month and because of the effects of the humid climate, many maintenance tasks have to be carried out at more frequent intervals than at home. The heat is very fatiguing to everyone when they arrive. The temperatures also reduce the load carrying capacity of the Puma but without it some of the Army posts would be completely cut off. Because of the humidity wounds and ailments do not heal well in the jungle, so casualty evacuation is a priority. The flying task itself is very exacting. Flying standards have to be high therefore, so only combat ready crews are posted here. Because of the jungle you can't see the contours of the land, which makes map reading difficult. You have to gain local knowledge quickly and learn to recognise salient features like rivers and hills. At some places we have to land in jungle clearings surrounded by 200 foot trees or perch on the side of a mountain.

The helicopters' main task was the insertion and extraction of troops from their jungle clearing outposts on the Guatemalan border. There was also a daily resupply 'milk run' to Union Camp, Cadenas OP and No Name Rebro carrying mail, foodstuffs and other consumable items. The landing sites were often a small square of pierced steel planking (PSP), just large enough to hold a Puma. They were usually situated at the top of a rocky outcrop which gave the added complication of altitude to the humid conditions. The hovering capability of the aircraft was severely reduced by the degradation of throttle response times. To increase the Pumas' range, fuel was stockpiled in Air Portable Fuel Cells (APFC) at the larger bases – the replacement of which being, of course, another task.

In the deep southwest of the country the Army had a jungle training school, which was also supported by the helicopters not only in respect of supply but also with regard to participation in Army adventurous training exercises. Another task was the provision of a standby element for disaster relief and SAR. More mundane but no less valuable aid to the civil community concerned the transport of road accident victims to Belize City Hospital.

This first experience of Belize was marred by a tragic accident on 27 October 1976 when XW230 crashed shortly after takeoff from Salamanca on a night training exercise. All eight personnel on board were killed, including Flight Lieutenant RP Lang, Flight Lieutenant RJL Whiteley, MALM CA Bolam, Sergeant NR Storey and SAC C Egen.

As 1976 drew to a close it was time to swap roles with No 33 Squadron again and return to Ulster. The facilities and accommodation at Aldergrove were being modernised and improved as it was becoming apparent that the commitment of the Forces to the Province was

*Puma XW225 is seen here on
resupply duties in Belize.*

Crown copyright

*This view shows the ramp
at RAF Belize, with a pair of
Pumas awaiting their next
turns of duty. XW204 is in the
foreground.*

Crown copyright

likely to continue at a significant level for many years. A major task occupying the Pumas in the early months of 1977 was the uplifting of 100 tons of building material from Bessbrook to Crossmaglen to provide mortar-proof living quarters for the troops stationed there. More sombre was the maximum effort required in May in respect of the fruitless search for Captain Robert Nairac,

who disappeared, and was probably murdered, while working undercover.

In June the deployments in Northern Ireland and Belize were once more exchanged with No 33 Squadron. Four aircraft, four pilots and four crewmen were the requirement.

*Two Pumas (XW 228 nearer the camera) and a Wessex pass over the control tower and fire station at RAF Aldergrove.*

Crown copyright

1977 saw the Squadron's first participation in NATO Tiger Meets. These began in 1961 as an informal fraternity of NATO fighter units which had tigers as part of their squadron badge. The constant aim has been to encourage professional relationships and to foster solidarity between allies. The opportunity is given to take part in training exercises in new environments and to learn more about other nations' operating techniques, methods and aircraft. An annual Tiger Meet is hosted, at its home base, by one of the Tiger Squadron units and other Tiger squadrons are invited to send one or more aircraft to take part in daytime flying training exercises, sporting activities and evening social events. A strong element of competition is an important component of the Tiger spirit and a trophy is awarded each year to the most successful participant.

The 17th NATO Tiger Meet was held at RAF Greenham Common in June 1977. It was combined with the Silver Jubilee International Air Tattoo. The organisers had requested the allocation of two RAF helicopters for standby aeromedical duties. As 230 had the Tiger badge, it was thought appropriate by HQ 38 Group at RAF Upavon that the Squadron should be tasked. During the event the crews, who were led by the CO, Wing Commander David Crwys-Williams, were invited to join the social programme of the Tiger Meet. This was so successful that it was proposed that the Squadron should be invited to the next Tiger Meet as an honorary member.

In July three Pumas took part in the Silver Jubilee Royal Review at RAF Finningley. Other items of note that year were visits to Germany, Italy, Bergen in Norway, to the Danish Zealand Islands for 'Exercise Arrow Express' and to Cambrai in France for a mini Tiger Meet to celebrate the 25th Anniversary of the Escadron de Chasse 1/12, which was in process of replacing its Dassault

Mysteres with Mirage F1s. Six Squadron personnel went to Cambrai under the leadership of Squadron Leader DA Spilsbury, who reported on a magnificent dinner dance laid on by the Escadron.

The detachment in Belize was not forgotten, as they were visited in December by a BBC team who were making a documentary. In the New Year, 1978, the Belize and Northern Ireland duties were again rotated with No 33 Squadron. At Odiham the year began with relief operations in coastal districts in Essex and Norfolk, as atrocious weather conditions were experienced. In Ulster the year began badly with the dreadful La Mon Hotel bombing.

By May it was time to exchange the Belize and Ulster duties again and in June two Pumas took part in 'Exercise Whirlygig' in Germany, when they were tasked to simulate Russian Hind attack profiles. On 23 June two helicopters flew to Kleine Brogel, the home of 31 Squadron Belgian Air Force, for the 18th Tiger Meet. XW223, flown by Squadron Leader Spilsbury and Flight Lieutenant MacLaine, was specially painted in a tiger stripe colour scheme. Although unable to take part in the flying competitions, the aircraft put on spirited flying displays and performed most usefully in a communications role, setting up the weapons and low level navigation sorties. The crews also took a full and active part in the social events and managed to win third place in the Tiger Games. As a result of this wholehearted approach the Squadron was unanimously awarded the annual Spirit of the Tiger Trophy. At the dining-in night it was announced that the Squadron had been elected to full membership. This honour was proudly accepted by the CO, Wing Commander Noel Parker-Ashley. It was the first time that a helicopter squadron had been accepted as a full participating member of what was essentially a fighter squadrons' organisation.

Meanwhile in Belize, a Guatemalan gunboat had come too close to the shore and had run aground. The somewhat protracted operations to refloat and salvage the vessel were closely monitored from the air. In September the entire detachment deployed for a fortnight to Cuidad del Carmen and Ixtepec airbase in Mexico to avoid the attentions of Hurricane Greta.

The Squadron Diary noted a remarkable happening early in 1979. It was possible to take a photograph of the entire Squadron as, for once, all personnel and helicopters were located in the same place at the same time, this being Odiham. Participation in a Tiger Meet was again thoroughly enjoyed in June at Cambrai. A detachment was sent to Belize in the autumn, where it was to remain for the next 18 months. In December five pilots, four crewmen and two RAF Regiment personnel joined a detachment, chiefly provided by No 33 Squadron, which was dispatched to Rhodesia for 'Operation Agila'.

In April 1979 an election had been held in Rhodesia; the state of UDI which had existed since 1965 came to an end and Bishop Abel Muzorewa became the Prime Minister. British and Commonwealth forces were sent to monitor and supervise the cease-fire, under the new Governor, Lord Soames. Tragedy soon struck the RAF as a Puma, XW228, crashed after hitting low wires near Salisbury, killing Flight Lieutenant M Smith and MALM R Hodges of 230 Squadron and Flying Officer A Cook of 33 Squadron.

# CHAPTER 13
# 1980–1990

A further election was held in Rhodesia in March 1980. Robert Mugabe emerged the winner, the name of the country was swiftly changed to Zimbabwe and the Union Jack was lowered for the last time from Government House on 18 April.

Meanwhile, back at Odiham, the Squadron welcomed a quartet of very distinguished former Squadron members in March – Group Captain Geoffrey Francis, Wing Commander Dundas Bednall, Wing Commander Pat Alington and Wing Commander Alan Lywood. A further enjoyable social occasion was the visit to the Tiger Meet held in July at Cameri in Italy, the base of the F-104 Starfighters of 21 Squadron. As Autumn began preparations were put in hand for a major move. The last Odiham-based tasking was on 27 September, a flying display at the RAF Halton Old Boys' Day.

In October 1980 the Squadron returned to Germany, based again at RAF Gutersloh and under the command of Wing Commander BA Wright. It replaced No 18 Squadron, which had been fulfilling the Support Helicopter (SH) role in Germany since 1970. By the end of that decade the importance of the NATO Central Region task meant that an enhanced capability was required.

The role of RAF Germany had not changed that much since the Squadron's last tour in the 1960s. Within NATO it was part of the Second Allied Tactical Air Force, along with units from the USAF and the German, Belgian and Netherlands Air Forces. Its area of responsibility stretched over 60,000 square miles from the borders of the Federal Republic of Germany in the east to the Danish border in the north, out over the North Sea, south along the Franco-Belgian border to the northern tip of Luxembourg and then north of a straight line running northeast to Kassel and Gottingen. The RAF contributed air defence Phantom FGR2s, strike attack Buccaneer S2Bs, Jaguar GR1s and Harrier GR3s. Venerable Hunters and Pembrokes still served in training and communications roles respectively. Gutersloh was the only operational RAF airfield east of the Rhine and was approximately 80 miles or ten minutes flying time by fast jet from the border with East Germany (the Inner German Border or IGB). In the early 1980s the nearest MiG-23 Flogger base was only a quarter of an hour away. Also located at Gutersloh were the Harriers of Nos 3 and 4 Squadrons.

The 16 Pumas were accommodated in Nos 6 and 7 Hangars, which had been built for the Luftwaffe in the late 1930s. The quality of the facilities was excellent with all the necessary offices, stores, crew rooms, planning

*230 Squadron Open Day at RAF Gutersloh in 1985 with three Squadron Pumas visible in the foreground.*

Wg Cdr RE Turner

and briefing rooms located in close proximity. The
Squadron was divided into three flights, HQ Flight's OC
was the Deputy Squadron Commander (2 i/c). He was
responsible for training and operations and had under
his command the two Qualified Helicopter Instructors
(QHIs), the Crewman Leader (the only commissioned
crewman on the unit), pilot and crewman examiners,
the four Squadron navigators and the operations clerks.
The 24 Squadron pilots were allocated to either 'A' or 'B'
Flight, as were the 16 crewmen. Often, many of the pilots
were on their first tour; by contrast the crewmen were
all senior NCOs and most were very experienced in both
fixed-wing roles and SH operations.

The Pumas' main task was once more to support
1 (BR) Corps. In combat this would have meant the
movement of stores, troop redeployment (including
anti-tank teams) and casualty evacuation. The helicopters
were equipped with TANS (tactical air navigation
system) and image intensifying goggles which much
improved their ability to operate at night. As with the
Harriers, much training time was devoted to operating
from dispersed locations.

The Squadron was equipped and trained to be
highly mobile and self-sufficient in the field, when it
would often be required to operate from unprepared
sites. It was established with a much wider spectrum
of tradesmen than a squadron based in the UK. The
Squadron Engineering Officer (SEngO), his assistant, the
Junior Engineering Officer (JEngO) and the Squadron

***Above and right:*** *In the autumn of 1980
230 Squadron returned to Germany where
it provided aircraft to 1 (BR) Corps for
use on routine day-to-day tasks and also
on periodic exercises. The routine tasks
included familiarising troops with helicopter
operations including, as illustrated here, the
preparation and dispatch of underslung loads
and the safe and efficient embarkation and
disembarkation of a helicopter.*

Wg Cdr RE Turner

Warrant Officer had a mammoth task. Not only were they responsible for the usual requirement to produce serviceable aircraft on the flight line every morning for task and training flying but they also had to plan the organising of men, materials and equipment for the many detachments of aircraft away from base. The normal strength of about 175 personnel covered first line servicing and rectification teams, armourers, safety equipment tradesmen, vehicle mechanics, a Ground Liaison Officer (GLO) (an Army Major whose role was to assist in all matters relating to the Army support task) and an RAF Regiment section. This consisted of a SNCO in charge, four corporals and twelve gunners. Their role was primarily the defence of the Squadron when in the field but they fulfilled many other useful tasks, not least of which was as specialist vehicle drivers.

The possibility of an attack by Warsaw Pact forces was taken very seriously and the training carried out was by way of an intensive preparation for this keenly felt threat. There was a distinct difference of atmosphere about a front line RAF air base in Germany during that period, when compared to that experienced in the UK. Perhaps it was the anti-aircraft 'Bloodhound' and 'Rapier' missiles near the runway thresholds or possibly it was the anticipation of a sudden 'no notice' practice alert – which could occur at any time of the day or night.

The task itself contributed to the pressure felt by all personnel. The rapid deployment by helicopter of troops and stores was intended to slow down an enemy advance, so in the event of hostilities the Squadron would have been in the thick of the action at a very early stage.

The day to day operational task revolved around familiarising soldiers with loading, boarding and disembarking – safely and rapidly. They also had to be completely at home with the preparation and dispatch of underslung loads and with travelling by helicopter at high speed and low level by day or night, under any weather conditions.

The size of the task was enormous and many more aircraft would have been needed in an ideal world to do the job thoroughly. The Squadron provided eight aircraft a day to 1 (BR) Corps, for use as directed by the Corps' tasking cell, which was manned by a mix of Army and RAF personnel. In addition to this basic daily tasking, most units ran periodic exercises which needed SH assistance for some of their phases, so it was

common for detachments of one, two or four Pumas to be deployed to the exercise location – which could be in West Germany or Denmark – in sole support of the Army unit concerned. The most popular of these included a stay in a local hotel or 'gasthof' but more often the crews were accommodated in barracks or tents.

One particularly enjoyable location was Bad Tolz, a tiny airstrip close to the Swiss border in Bavaria. The purpose was to refamiliarise crews with winter mountain flying techniques and to provide helicopter support for the RAF Winter Survival School, which was situated nearby at Bad Kohlgrub. The spectacular, snow-covered, mountainous terrain, with peaks up to 10,000 feet, provided not only challenging flying but also wonderful scenic beauty.

The Squadron had no direct involvement in 'Operation Corporate', the Falkland Islands campaign in the Spring of 1982 but one former member, Squadron Leader Dick Langworthy, performed heroically and was awarded the DFC to add to the AFC which he already held. He was the captain of ZA718/BN, the only Chinook HC1 to survive the sinking of *Atlantic Conveyor*. On 29 May, attempting to take elements of 42 Commando to Mount Kent, the Chinook ran into a storm and touched down inadvertently in the water. It lost a wheel and a door but made it back to Port San Carlos. One of the more remarkable feats was transporting 81 fully armed paratroopers in a single lift from Goose Green to Fitzroy on 2 June. BN flew for 109 hours without servicing, carrying 2150 troops, 550 prisoners and 550 tons of freight – with neither engineering documentation, tools or spares. Sadly Dick Langworthy collapsed and died 18 months later while on routine garrison duty in the Falklands. He was an almost legendary figure and his funeral at Odiham was attended by a vast number of friends from the Support Helicopter world. This sowed the seeds for the series of SH reunions that are now an established tradition.

By the summer of 1982 the CO was Wing Commander David Hamilton-Rump and so it was his happy duty to welcome the participants in the 22nd International Tiger Meet to RAF Gutersloh, hosted by the Squadron from 26 – 30 August. Some 40 visiting aircraft took part, with 140 representatives of 15 squadrons from ten nations. A full and varied programme of events incorporated the Station Fete and Squadron Open Day on Saturday 28 August. The Tiger Organisation had grown from just three countries in 1961 – the UK, USA and France – to 13, the additional members being West Germany, Italy, Belgium, Turkey, Portugal, Greece, Norway, Canada, Australia and Switzerland. Most of the aircraft types were fast jets – F104s, Mirage F1s, F5s, G91s, F15s, F111s, Alpha Jets, Super Etendards, A7s and F4s but helicopters included Royal Navy Sea Kings as well as the Pumas, while fixed-wing maritime aviation was represented by the Grumman Trackers of the Royal Australian Navy and the Lockheed Orions of the US Navy. Another special event of note took place in July of the following year, 1983, when an Open Day was held to celebrate the 70th Anniversary of the Squadron's earliest antecedents.

Returning to the day-to-day activities, the most realistic training was provided by major exercises of which there were two main types. First there were the 'no notice' alerts, which could occur at any time of the day or night; several of these were called at irregular intervals throughout the year. These could be generated either by the Station Commander or by the NATO Tactical Evaluation (TACEVAL) team. They were primarily designed to test the Squadron's ability to survive a sudden Soviet attack, which it was thought would quickly render Gutersloh unusable. Therefore it was essential to be able to deploy rapidly to field locations. This war scenario would result in the immediate recall of personnel and the swift deployment of prepacked material. The Squadron's field equipment, which included everything from fuel for aircraft and vehicles, spares and ammunition to tents, tables, chairs, lamps, generators, radios and a host of other items, was kept in a high state of readiness. Over 100 vehicles of 16 types, including Land Rovers, trailers, water bowsers, 4-ton trucks, refuelling bowsers and specialist trucks equipped with cranes for aircraft servicing were parked beside 7 Hangar. It did not take long to form them up into road convoys ready to proceed to the dispersal locations. There were about 20 of these, usually on farmland, within a 25 mile radius of Gutersloh and the actual ones selected for a particular exercise were revealed at short notice in order not to compromise security and also to make matters as realistic as possible.

The Squadron was also reorganised immediately into five flights. 'A', 'B' and 'C' were the main flying elements, each with four or five aircraft, 30 to 35 air and ground crew, including all the supporting tradesmen

required, cooks, technical supply personnel, an RAF Regiment section and an operations clerk. OCs 'A' and 'B' commanded their own flights; C Flight was composed of aircrew from the training section, augmented from the other two flights and commanded by the senior training officer. HQ Flight comprised the CO and his operations staff, including the 2 i/c, the Squadron navigators, the GLO and a team of Army signallers from 21 (Air Support) Signals Regiment, who provided the radio communications to the tasking authority – usually the Forward Air Operations Centre (FAOC) at the field Corps HQ – and from the Squadron to the dispersed flights. The fifth flight was normally located nearby. The Support Flight was commanded by the SEngO and was equipped with all the expertise, manpower, tools, spares and specialist engineering equipment needed to carry out almost any conceivable task; this might involve a team being sent out to a flight location to rectify an engine, gearbox or rotor blade. Battle damage on exercise was normally limited to that created by the over-enthusiastic soldier – possibly poking a hole in the side of the Puma with his rifle. The Squadron strength was also augmented by more than 130 station personnel – additional aircraft tradesmen, a doctor and medical orderlies, administrative staff and a padre.

The Squadron was very proud of its ability to move out, deploy into field locations and become operational within the space of four or five hours from the initial alert. In the field the Pumas relied on camouflage and continual movements to protect them from air attack. The vehicles were also concealed with a liberal use of camouflage netting. Rapid movement from site to site was also required if the battle scenario demanded it. Usually some notice was given but the possibility of a 'crash-out' departure being suddenly sprung upon them had to form part of the contingency plan. Life on exercise was rough and ready, with barns often being used for sleeping, cooking and messing. Flying activity was intensive, with little time for planning – so improvisation and initiative were highly important qualities. The ground crew were kept very busy – refuelling, servicing and rectifying faults, often in the most unpleasant of weather conditions. Nor was the administrative task any less taxing – the peacetime paperwork had to be completed, flying and crew duty time could not exceed the specified limits but the tasks had still to be achieved.

Culinary matters were also deemed to be of great importance, with each flight's cooks competing against the others to produce a 'gourmet' standard of catering. Indeed as the CO in the mid-1980s, Wing Commander Bob Turner, recalled:

> The Squadron was visited in the field in May 1984 by no less than Egon Ronay and his 1985 Good Food Guide gave 230 an excellent report.

Some aspects of field life were less welcome, including the necessity to dig gun pits and trenches to create a defensive perimeter. The ground crew had to take their turn with the small number of RAF Regiment gunners in manning the GPMGs. On most exercises mock attacks were made by 'hostile' forces, often initiated with a bursts of (blank) gunfire or a thunderflash being lobbed onto the site. All personnel then had to repel the invaders, not a lot of fun on a freezing cold night after an exhausting day's work.

Other exercises were planned well in advance. Three in particular were generated by the Squadron – 'Frozen Tiger', 'Spring Tiger' and 'Summer Tiger'. These were devised and controlled by the CO and helped to develop the skills necessary for Corps generated tasks. They were particularly useful in training new members of the Squadron in how to cope with the demands that would soon be placed upon them. Unlike the fast jet pilot whose mission began and ended on a major airfield, the young SH pilot frequently left base for a day's flying (or even several days) totally out of contact with his unit. All decisions including weather assessment, task organisation and the authorisation of flights were placed on his shoulders. One of the common pressures, which often had to be resisted, would be from an enthusiastic Army unit commander who did not fully appreciate either the capabilities or, even more importantly, the limitations of the helicopter. In such a case the pilot would have to explain as tactfully as possible, that safety had to be a major consideration and that he alone was the judge of that.

A major Corps exercise was held each autumn. These usually involved most of the war deployment plan being practised and sometimes included reinforcements from the UK. For the Squadron this would mean the addition of four Pumas and crews from No 240 Operational Conversion Unit (OCU) from RAF Odiham, which became D Flight. Extra RAF Regiment personnel in the form of 100 members of the Queen's Colour Squadron

(QCS) from RAF Uxbridge, greatly enhanced ground defence capability on the field sites. Territorial Army officers also took part, as GLOs for each flight. This type of exercise could last from ten days to a fortnight, the biggest was 'Exercise Lionheart' in 1984, which kept the Squadron in the field for three weeks.

The worst threat envisaged was that of chemical or biological attack. The use of respirators and NBC (nuclear, biological and chemical) suits had to be practised regularly. They were hot and uncomfortable to wear and also made operating the aircraft much more difficult. For flying, a special rubber hood, the Aircrew Respirator Mk 5, colloquially the AR5, had been devised and was worn under the normal flying helmet. It included an air filtration unit which was carried out to the aircraft by hand, whilst connected to the helmet by a tube – the encumbered aircrew by then bearing a distinct resemblance to Apollo astronauts. The flying task in Germany was challenging enough without the addition of the NBC equipment.

All helicopter flying was undertaken at low level, always below 250 feet, to de-conflict with fast jets, and often as low as 50 feet. As well as all the work with the Army, each pilot and crewman had to complete mandatory flights every month for general handling, instrument flying, tactical training and night flying in order to maintain their 'combat ready' qualification. As previously mentioned, one piece of kit which did improve the Squadron's capability was the introduction of night vision goggles (NVG) in the mid-1980s. It was one of the first front-line units to use these sophisticated image intensifying devices, which vastly extended the scope and feasibility of operations by night.

In 1984 a commitment was re-established which was to last until the end of the decade, rotating one pilot and two crewmen for detachment in Belize. In Germany participation in air displays included the German Grand Prix and later extended to events in Austria and Switzerland. A mini Tiger Meet was held at Gutersloh to mark the re-formation of No 74 (F) Squadron, equipped with McDonnell Douglas Phantom F-4Js and welcome its return to the Tiger community.

Wing Commander Bob Turner remembers a particularly interesting development during his time with the Squadron:

**Right:** *This snowy setting may have been appropriate for 'Exercise Frozen Tiger'.*
Wg Cdr RE Turner

**Below:** *NBC suits were hot and uncomfortable to wear.*
Wg Cdr RE Turner

In 1985, 6 Armoured Brigade was given a new anti-tank infantry role to enable it to conduct an Airmobile Brigade trial. The formation consisted of the 1st Battalion the Gordon Highlanders (1 GH) and 1st Battalion Light Infantry (1 LI) armed with MILAN anti–tank missiles and supporting elements, including some artillery. The air component of the trial comprised Nos 230 and 18 Squadrons, the latter having been re-equipped with the Boeing Chinook heavy lift helicopter, as well as a squadron of TOW anti-tank missile armed Lynx and spotter Gazelle helicopters from 4 Regiment Army Air Corps at Detmold. For the next year a great deal of intensive work was done with these Army units and a very close rapport developed between us. Complex procedures were devised and practised during numerous exercises to prove and evaluate the concept. The flying involved was different to that used for most SH tasks and quite often required 30 to 35 aircraft in a closely co-ordinated and rapidly mounted airlift of up to 1000 men and their associated weapons and equipment over large distances to forward positions in just a few hours. The trial period was deemed to be a great success and the subsequent comprehensive report provided the basis on which the now well-established 16 Air Assault Brigade was created.

The links forged with 1 GH brought some unexpected additional benefits to the Squadron. When the battalion was sent to Portugal for training it was accompanied to the Lisbon area (via Belgium, France and Spain) by four Pumas and two Chinooks. Moreover, when formal Squadron Dinner Nights were held in the Officers' Mess at Gutersloh they were enhanced by the music of the Gordons' pipers and regimental band.

In March 1987 four aircraft, XW218, 219, 227 and 229, took part in the rescue and relief operation arising from the tragic sinking of the roll on/roll off passenger car ferry *Herald of Free Enterprise* at Zeebrugge. On the evening of 6 March the ferry left harbour en route for Dover with its bow doors open. Such was the onrush of water that it took only 90 seconds for the ship to capsize, ending up on her side, half-submerged in shallow water. 188 passengers and crew lost their lives and many others were injured. It was the worst death toll, in peacetime, for a British vessel since the sinking of the *Titanic* in 1912. Key personnel and stores were airlifted into position by the helicopters thus avoiding the traffic jams created on approach roads to the harbour by ghoulish sightseers.

A much happier event took place shortly afterwards with the creation of the Squadron Association. The four founder members visited the Squadron and the 2 i/c, Squadron Leader David Waring, subsequently attended the first reunion at RAF Hendon, where he was presented with a silver-plated Sunderland to grace the table on dining-in nights. Another pleasant happening was the award of a well-merited AFC to Flight Lieutenant Raymond St George 'Chips' Carpenter. He had been the Puma display pilot for several years and, as a very senior and experienced Puma pilot, was also the pilot examiner. Many a young pilot of that era still recalls Chips' annual checks as daunting and exacting but very worthwhile.

In the autumn a further commitment was added with the detachment of two aircraft and three crews to Northern Ireland. By the late 1980s the 'Troubles' had reached a plateau of tit-for-tat provocation and incidents and the public had become hardened to a daily diet of violence. Terrorist activity could only grab the headlines with 'spectacular' attacks and the Security Forces hit back with 'supergrass' information and arms finds. The capture of the gun-running ship, the MV *Eksund*, containing some 20 SAM 7s, 1000 AK47s, 600 grenades, ten heavy machine-guns, 50 tons of ammunition and two tons of Semtex was a particularly important coup. The worst atrocity was the bombing of the Enniskillen Remembrance Parade in November 1987, which left 11 dead and 63 injured. Even amidst such a diet of awfulness, the Squadron records note the medevac of an Army sniffer dog as being one of the highlights of this tour, which lasted until March 1988.

The link with the Squadron Association was further strengthened by another visit to Gutersloh and a reciprocal one to Pembroke Dock for the reunion. Wing Commander Roger Wedge flew to RAF Brawdy and thence to 'PD', where he was presented with a silver-plated Puma.

Another detachment to Aldergrove commenced in September, this time of six pilots, three crewmen and eleven engineers. On 21 December one aircraft from the NI detachment was flown by Flight Lieutenant Rich Holmes to Lockerbie in Scotland to assist in the search of the crash site of Pan Am flight 103, the Boeing 747 destroyed in flight by an explosive device. A bomb placed on board at Frankfurt had detonated at 31,000 feet over the little Scottish town, killing all 259 passengers and crew, as well as 11 local residents. Rich later described

*Wing Commander Roger Wedge, closely observed by Kita.*

the task as one of direct support to the Scottish police. He assisted by moving teams about the area to help find casualties and areas of wreckage. The expanse of debris was very wide and flying was difficult, restricted to daylight and very harrowing. Perhaps the most memorable image of this detachment was the television footage of a Puma lifting the nose section of the 747 onto a lorry for transport.

Back at Gutersloh, earlier in the month, on 9 December, Wing Commander Wedge handed over command to Wing Commander Mike Trace in the air at 2.30pm – over the Mohne Dam.

1989 brought two events of particular note. These were the first exchange visit with the Fiat G91s of No 301 Squadron, Portugese Air Force at Montijo and 'Exercise Key Flight' in September. This was the first work-up to validation of 24 Airmobile Brigade, which saw the entire formation deployed by helicopter – Pumas, Chinooks, Lynx and Gazelles.

The 'Operation Country' commitment in Northern Ireland was terminated in March 1990; this had provided excellent flying opportunities but was also a drain on resources, as it had to be achieved within existing constraints, along with the Belize crew and the established task in support of RAF Germany. However it did prove possible to send two crews to the International Helimeet at AAC Middle Wallop in July. The detachment

led by Squadron Leader Charles Gillow entered two teams for the competition. The first comprised Flight Lieutenant Guy van den Berg, Flying Officer Andy Turner, Sergeant James Harwood and Flight Lieutenant Neil Bartlett, while the second team was Flight Lieutenant Wayne Gregory, Flight Lieutenant Simon Roberts, MALM Howie Jones and Corporal Ramsey. Both teams did extraordinarily well and came 3rd and 4th places of 44 contestants overall. Individually, the first team won the Best Navigation trophy and the Aerial Recce trophy. Together the teams were only pipped at the post for the Best Spirit trophy by No 3 (New Zealand) Squadron, who had arrived with 10 tons of Steinlager beer to sweet talk the judges – though it is possible that Andy Turner may be slightly biased in making this final judgement.

At this stage it was the intention to present the Squadron with a new Squadron Standard in February 1991. Plans were made and XW224 was adorned with a most magnificent Tiger colour scheme, credit for which must go to Mrs Lesley Palmer (the wife of Flying Officer 'Harry' Palmer), Flight Lieutenant Simon Roberts and Flying Officer Andy Turner. Indeed the effect was so striking and unusual that the AOC-in-C, Air Marshal Sir Andrew Wilson KCB, AFC was rendered speechless, a tribute indeed. As events turned out, XW224 could not stay in this livery for long.

*Puma XW224 in its magnificent Tiger colour scheme.*

Flt Lt 'Harry' Palmer

# CHAPTER 14
# 1991–2004

With the extraordinarily rapid demise of the Soviet Union, the collapse of the Iron Curtain, the Warsaw Pact and the Berlin Wall, as well as the re-unification of Germany in the late 1980s and early 1990s, which brought about the end of the Cold War, the Squadron's role in Germany swiftly diminished. A period of reduced activity levels followed with few field exercises and very much more routine Army tasking. The 'next fixture', which was feared to be the start of World War III in Europe, was indefinitely postponed.

Politicians looked to reduce the size of the armed forces as the major part of a 'peace dividend'. This euphoric and somewhat unrealistic assessment concerning the blossoming of global peace and love was dramatically interrupted on 2 August 1990 when Iraqi forces invaded Kuwait with startling speed and efficiency. Within twenty-four hours the country was occupied and Iraqi troops were starting to mass on the northern borders of Saudi Arabia. The United Nations responded swiftly to stabilise the situation and to buy time. A powerful force, the bulk of which was provided by the United States, was deployed in the region as a deterrent against further aggression. Planning was initiated, again with the USA to the fore, to remove the invader by force if diplomacy failed. On 5 October a Support Helicopter (SH) force of 15 Pumas was earmarked. A reconnaissance team arrived in Saudi Arabia later that month and negotiated some space within the vast encampment occupied by the US Marines at the Saudi Arabian naval base of Al Jubayl. The feeling amongst the aircrew and groundcrew at Gutersloh was very much that they didn't want to be left behind, everyone wanted to be part of the team effort.

No 230 Squadron commanded by Wing Commander Mike Trace, deployed to Saudi Arabia courtesy of the Lockheed C-5 Galaxies of the USAF, Heavylift AN-124s, RAF Tristars and VC-10s on 'Operation Desert Shield' (US) / 'Granby' (British) at the beginning of November 1990.

Initially it was under the command of 7 Armoured Brigade Group and later 1 (BR) Armoured Division. All personnel were proud to wear the desert rat insignia. The Squadron deployed with a flight of No 33 Squadron under command and was called the Puma (ME) Squadron.

The first sight of the US marines hardware was overwhelming evidence of the sheer scale of the military might involved; there were over 300 helicopters – Sikorsky CH-53Es and Bell Twin Hueys. The first eight weeks were spent working out of a complex set up in a car park at Ras-al-Ghar which was part of the Al Jubayl base. Squadron personnel lived in the Rezayatt which was a collection of chalets much like those found in a holiday camp and intended to house foreign workers. Training was conducted in the casualty evacuation (casevac) role, converting to Night Vision Goggle (NVG) operation and other exercises. One of the principal problems encountered concerned erosion caused by the ingestion of sand into the engines until the filters on the intakes, fitted some ten years previously to prevent similar problems with ice, were resealed and made more effective. The aircrews had to learn how to operate in the featureless desert where, under camouflage nets, all units looked the same. Satellite navigation systems were not initially available in more than a few aircraft. Navigation was by map and stopwatch with some assistance from the Doppler. The helicopters' downwash also caused problems; recirculating sand or 'brown-outs' often made landings, takeoffs and hovering difficult. Some manoeuvres, especially at night, proved impossible because of the loss of visual clues. The SH force was augmented by four more Pumas, 12 Chinooks and 12 Royal Navy Sea Kings, with a total complement of more than 1500 personnel, most of whom crammed into the Rezayatt accommodation.

On 15 January 1991 the UN deadline for an Iraqi withdrawal from Kuwait expired at midnight GMT and the following day the first phase of hostile operations began. This was the 'Air War', which was to last for just over five weeks. Its aims were to achieve overall air supremacy, damage Iraqi strategic capabilities, isolate and incapacitate the command structure, suppress all its surface-to-air defensive systems in theatre and destroy fighting equipment on the ground.

The Squadron spent the early days of the war moving to a new site at King Khaled Military City (KKMC), which Crewman Leader, Flying Officer Andrew 'Harry' Palmer later described as being the size of Aldershot in the middle of nowhere. The Division as a whole, now subordinated to VII (US) Corps, moved to its new concentration area at Wadi al Bahtin and by the beginning of February it was declared operational. The chief threat at this stage came from Iraqi Scud missiles. During one attack a Scud was intercepted by Patriot missiles overhead the Pumas' base, which was showered with the resultant debris. 'Harry' Palmer will never forget the sight of the four Patriots streaking into the sky, one of which malfunctioned and flew horizontally before self-destructing. When the NBC all clear was given he examined some of the chunks of metal from the Scud, which were covered in a green, steaming material – rocket fuel!

Conditions at KKMC were not luxurious. Everyone was accommodated in tents, washing facilities were limited to tipping a bowl over one's head as a shower, an oil drum served as a latrine and the weather conditions ranged from sandstorms to mud reminiscent of the Somme. Heavy frost was not uncommon in the mornings. The sand caused heavy wear and tear on the engines. The Pumas ranged back to Al Jubayl daily – a round trip of 700 miles – to collect supplies of food and bottled water, as well as delivering the mail. Dumps of aviation fuel had been placed at strategic intervals all along the main supply route between KKMC and Al Jubayl, a massive undertaking. Driving along this route was a hazardous occupation, it was a narrow, congested road, with tank transporters thundering in the opposite direction. The ever-present threat of chemical or biological attack added to the tension so most of the journey was done in full NBC kit, with respirators being donned when a driver was spotted coming the other way wearing his. 'Harry' Palmer recalled flying above the Tap Line Road, alongside which ran an oil pipeline, in radio silence at a height of 50 feet. Below him he could see hundreds of tanks, trucks and other vehicles. For the groundcrew this was a 20 hour drive nose to tail all the way. The Pumas also supplied an air-taxi service for VIPs and essential spares.

The resealed sand filters on the Pumas worked very well. Sand recirculation was reduced by the extensive use of plastic membrane landing sites. Life for the engineers was tough, however, with rotors, engines and gearboxes having to be changed in all weathers. They worked day and night to maintain serviceability, which, in the circumstances was exceptionally good.

*Back to World War I as Squadron members dig trenches for self protection.*
Flt Lt 'Harry' Palmer

*Conditions at KKMC were not luxurious!*
    Flt Lt 'Harry' Palmer

*Travelling the main supply route by day wasn't easy; by night it was worse!*
    Flt Lt 'Harry' Palmer

    Training at KKMC concentrated on flying at very low level – down to 25 feet by day, which was half the normal limit; this was possible due to the very flat terrain. At night sorties were flown down to 100 feet. Flights wearing AR5 respirators were conducted by day and night. Night flying in the desert even with NVG was particularly challenging due to the almost complete lack of features and light sources on the ground. It was important to practise flying as low as possible to avoid possible confliction with fixed-wing traffic. Training for the casevac role also included very close liaison with the combat medical technicians of the Royal Army Medical Corps from Collecting Troop, 24 Airmobile Field Ambulance. In effect the medics became the fourth member of the Puma's crew. An extra pair of eyes looking out from the cabin was very useful and the medical technicians were also trained in the operation of the helicopter's defensive systems. With casualties on board the medic could then give the pilot expert advice on their condition, which would influence the way the aircraft would be handled on the return to base – smooth and straight for cases in traction but as fast as possible if a patient's condition was critical. The Pumas were fundamental to the medical plans in a hostile environment with limited road systems. The thought of speedy relief and evacuation for immediate field hospital attention if required was a very useful morale booster to the ground troops.

On 14 February 1991 the Division began its march to the forward assembly area, 100 miles closer to the Iraqi border. By this time 7 Corps comprised five divisions – 130,000 men and 1500 main battle tanks. The Force HQ, the Pumas and the Sea Kings moved from KKMC with the Division, while the Chinooks moved forward with a SH stockpile of 45,000 litre pillow tanks. In the end there were seven different fuel sites with a total of over 5,000,000 pounds of fuel, all in pillow tanks or in road tankers. Major land operations began on 16 February and the 'Land War' major assault on 24 February. The British Division crossed into Iraq on 25 February. The Squadron's Forward Operating Base (FOB), some 65 miles from the Division's Start Line, was in operation from 24 February until after the cease-fire.

As the Division advanced, the lines of communication extended and Puma operations were conducted from a Forward Operating Location at Objective Platinum inside Iraq. The advance made its way eastwards into Kuwait. With the support tail moving slowly across the desert, resupply by helicopter was essential. By the time the cease-fire came into force on 28 February the Division had covered nearly 200 miles of desert in 66 hours and in the process completed the destruction of three Iraqi divisions. A total of 7024 prisoners were taken, including two Syrians captured by one of the Puma crews. Indeed, this event must not go without further mention.

The sister squadron under command (No 33 Squadron) had a flight dedicated to NATO rapid response and was known as the ACE Mobile Force (AMF) Flight. The Flight Commander and his team – Squadron Leader Alex Smyth, Flight Lieutenant Chris Ramsden and MALM Dave Combes – were crewed together. Given the speed of collapse and surrender of the Iraqi forces, taking prisoners became something of a novelty and, in their rush to be 'blooded', the AMF crew (hereafter known as Arrest More Friendlies) took prisoner, at gun point, two senior members of Coalition Forces (a Syrian Battalion Commander and his 2I/C). Later the Syrians were invited to tea with their captors in the POW complex as a palliative to the understandable ill-feeling the event had caused.

The Squadron flew over 1200 sorties during the deployment, of which 20% were at night, totalling 2207.40 flying hours, without major mishap. The CO, Wing Commander Mike Trace, was later awarded the MBE for his part in 'Operation Granby'. Approximately 3000 troops, 59 VIPs, 100 tons of supplies, 900 simulated casualties and 350 real casualties (Allied and Iraqi) were carried, in addition to several thousand prisoners of war. The POWs were often in a sorry state, in danger of dying of exposure and needing emergency supplies of food and water before transfer to a properly equipped stockade. The POWs were packed on to the cabin floor of the Pumas, 14 to 17 at a time. They ranged in age from 14 to 84, often painfully thin, worn out, demoralised by the bombing – these were conscripts and not Republican Guards. Following the liberation of Kuwait, 'Harry' Palmer recalled overflying the road to Basra. He was shocked by the sight of thousands of wrecked vehicles and could smell the stench of war. The smoke from burning oil wells, set on fire by the retreating Iraqis, hung in a thick pall, a stream of pollution 25–30 miles wide.

So ended the UK's largest operation since the end of World War Two and in which the RAF and the Squadron could be very proud of the part that they had played.

After four and a half months away from home, the Squadron returned to Gutersloh in April 1991. On 21 June XW226, flown by Squadron Leader McGeown and Flight Lieutenant Wright took part in the Victory Fly-past over the City of London. A few days later, on 24 June, two Squadron members, Flight Lieutenant G Duncan and Flight Sergeant Evans, along with Flight Lieutenant Ged Sheppeck of No 18 Squadron, had a very lucky escape when XW215 ditched in the English Channel, 20 miles east of Manston. It had suffered a tail rotor failure. The crew were picked up by a Sea King after 30 minutes in the water.

In July an appearance was made at the International Air Tattoo at Fairford. Soon after this airshow command of the Squadron changed and the new CO, Wing Commander Chris Williams, took the helm. His first challenge was to lead an exchange visit to No 753 Squadron of the Portugese Air Force at Montijo. The highlights of this trip were largely social and nocturnal and included a valiant effort by the Squadron speed skating team in the hotel bathroom to keep everyone awake in the wee small hours.

In September training was conducted at Gutersloh with the RAF Falcons parachute display team, which included free fall jumps from up to 10,000 feet. In the New Year came the decision that the Squadron would re-locate to RAF Aldergrove.

Unfortunately, whilst on another detachment to Belize, 'Chips' Carpenter demonstrated that he, too, was fallible by taxying Puma XW210 into a hangar at a remote airfield, while he was flying a VIP around the territory. The incident brought much commiseration and not a little mirth from his friends.

There was time for a final Tiger Fly-in at Gutersloh

*Aldergrove-bound 'Puma 5' XW237, crewed by Flt Lts Tilda Woodard and Phil Collyer, with Loadmaster Sgt Andy Lyes, formates on its oncoming twin over Devenish Island, just north of Enniskillen.*

KA Boyd

(attended by the Belgian, Dutch and German Air Forces) and for a last visit to Denmark to exercise with the Danish and Norwegian Jaegerkorps. On 20 April 1992, the Squadron was transferred from RAF Germany to 1 Group Strike Command. The Squadron Standard was handed over in a parade at Gutersloh, the Reviewing Officer being C-in-C RAFG, Air Marshal Sir Andrew Wilson. The new CO, Wing Commander IR McCluskie received the Standard, ready for the move to Aldergrove on 4 May 1992. Officially the event recorded that a new Puma HC1 squadron was established for service in Northern Ireland and allocated the 230 Squadron numberplate. The nine Pumas in Germany were handed over to No 18 Squadron at Gutersloh, augmenting the latter's fleet of eleven Chinooks. The Puma Force Northern Ireland (PFNI) had been established in October 1991 from 'D' Flight of No 72 Squadron, now in turn, it was subsumed within the 'new' squadron.

The security situation in the Province at that time was not good. It was a year which saw many atrocities committed by terrorists on both sides while on the mainland there was also the devastating Baltic Exchange bomb in the City of London.

A major task, 'Operation Christo', was undertaken almost at once, and involved seven Pumas, two Chinooks and six Wessex supporting the Army and the Royal Ulster Constabulary in Crossmaglen, south Armagh, where they were investigating a smuggling racket. On 9 May a barbecue was held to celebrate the Squadron's arrival and included a four Puma fly-past as part of the festivities. To commemorate the end of No 72 Squadron's domination of RAF helicopter activity in Ulster, a three ship formation of Wessex, Puma and Chinook flew around Lough Neagh.

The Squadron's accommodation at Aldergrove, a purpose-built, prefabricated structure on a previously empty site across the road from the Squadron hangar, was opened by Air Vice Marshal RE Johns, the AOC No 1 Group, on 19 May 1992. For his work in bringing this project to fruition and much else besides, the 'D' Flight Commander, and latterly the Squadron 2I/C, Squadron Leader Karl Dixon, was awarded the MBE.

Seven regular task lines had been established for the Squadron's twelve Pumas: day and night duties in the west of the Province in County Fermanagh, flying from a site on the airfield at St Angelo, similar tasks in south Armagh, operating from Bessbrook Mill and

Province-wide tasking as required by JATOC (the Joint Air Tasking Operations Cell).

On 20 June 1992 XW216 arrived painted in the new twin-tone green camouflage scheme which was in process of replacing the standard grey-green colours. Other less official painting activities had been started too. On the night of 27 April 1992 the RAF Aldergrove water tower top was rebranded in a rather dashing tiger stripe colour scheme. The enthusiastic artists (Flight Lieutenants Steve Partridge, John Taylor, Andy Turner and Flying Officers Dave Dudman and Phil Gilling) were interrupted by a young RAF Police corporal who enquired what they were doing 100 feet above the ground at one o'clock in the morning. The facetious but accurate and truthful answer, "Oh we're just painting" did not go down too well. Later that night the subsequent displeasure of 'The Boss' was compounded by a mishap to Flying Officer Dudman – who decided to leap between two buildings. The result was a broken leg and a one-sided interview!

The second painting party consisted of Flight Lieutenant Turner (again!), Flying Officer Mark Day and Flight Sergeant 'Mitch' Mitchell who decided on the night of 28 September to smarten up and rebrand the Army Air Corps' landing spot at Bessbrook by the addition of a magnificent 22 foot pentagon and a tiger's head (the Squadron's tactical badge).

In July, Squadron Leader Phil Pynegar and his crew had a very lucky escape in XW209. They were approaching a hilltop base when the helicopter suffered a tail rotor drive shaft failure. As the CO later remarked, this was almost the worst case scenario – a major mechanical failure, at night, in a geographically and operationally hostile environment. He praised the pilot's airmanship in minimising the potential damage and injury by turning a crash into a very heavy landing. Squadron Leader Pynegar was later awarded the AFC.

Aircraft were displayed at the RAF Aldergrove Families Day and the Ulster Air Show in the summer

*With Devenish again forming the backdrop, the on-going Puma 5, XW231, escorts XW237 for a few miles of the latter's return from Enniskillen. The photographer had travelled to Fermanagh on this aircraft which was piloted by Flt Lt Ade Parkinson, with Navigator Flt Lt AJ Smith and Loadmaster Sgt Aaron Lorimer. Note the duct-tape – an effective method of weather-proofing the electronics behind the inspection panel.*

KA Boyd

and on 15 August Squadron Leader Pynegar flew XW198 the short distance to Langford Lodge to make the Squadron's debut with the Ulster Aviation Society at its newly opened Heritage Centre on the airfield. A visit was also made to the mini-Tiger Meet at RAF Wattisham in September. Pilots and crewmen were also detached on a regular basis to the Helikopter Service Super Puma simulator at Stavangar in Norway.

A new Squadron Standard was presented by the Duke of Gloucester (whose father had presented the original Standard in 1962) in a ceremony at Aldergrove on 27 October 1992. Three former COs of the Squadron were able to attend – Air Vice Marshal DO Crwys-Williams CB, Air Commodore DJ Hamilton-Rump and Wing Commander RE Turner. The new standard was adorned with three previously omitted battle honours for

Egypt and Libya, Greece and Malta. This was due to the research and persuasive powers of another former CO, Wing Commander Dundas Bednall. The official opening of a new joint operations complex for Nos 72 and 230 Squadrons was also carried out and a Guest Night was held that evening.

In November a strictly amateur rock band composed of personnel from both squadrons raised money for BBC Children in Need with a concert marathon. Travelling by Puma, they performed at Aldergrove, Leuchars, Cottesmore and St Athan – Northern Ireland, Scotland, England and Wales – all within 24 hours.

Northern Ireland's, and indeed Europe's, busiest heliport – Bessbrook Mill, near Newry – was the focal point of the security forces' operations in south Armagh and along the border with the Irish Republic. RAF and AAC

*A happy group of Ulster schoolchildren meet some Squadron members.*

Crown copyright

*A good relationship with the local community is always important to the Squadron. In this case, near Ardglass, the Squadron assisted with the erection of a marker light.*                    Crown copyright

Gazelle crash-landed close by. The two Gazelle crewmen escaped with serious injuries but all four personnel on board the Puma were killed – Squadron Leader M Haverson, Flight Lieutenant SMJ Roberts, Flight Sergeant JR Pewtress and an Army officer, Major J Barr, who was on a familiarisation sortie. This was the first tragedy of this nature at Bessbrook in over 20 years of operations.

Squadron Leader Haverson's funeral was held at Aldergrove on 2 December. He had served previously with the AAC and with 230 Squadron in Germany. Three aircraft – a Puma (XW216 flown by Squadron Leader Howard Nash), a Scout and a Gazelle – flew past in farewell salute. Flight Sergeant Pewtress was buried in Peterborough the next day, with the service for Flight Lieutenant Roberts being held in Lincoln on 4 December. Much of the Northern Ireland tasking was taken over by No 72 Squadron for those two days to allow as many Squadron members as possible to attend. The fly-pasts at both were performed by Flight Lieutenant Neil Taylor in XW198. The CO summed up the feelings of all when he stated that it had been a sad, emotional but proud and dignified time.

The Squadron was now organised into three flights – 'A' to cover Armagh, 'B' to cover Fermanagh while 'C' handled training and tactics. The carriage of VIPs to meetings in the fast, smooth and relatively comfortable Puma was a regular task. On 7 December 1992 two aircraft flew to Dublin, the first visit of Squadron aircraft to the Irish Republic. XW204, crewed by Squadron Leader Wayne Gregory, Squadron Leader Roger Townend and Flight Sergeant Gary Tucker conveyed the Prime Minister, John Major, from Baldonnel air base to the Royal Hospital at Kilmainham for a meeting with his Irish counterpart, the Taoiseach, Albert Reynolds.

1993 began with a spell of weather that was more reminiscent of Norway then Northern Ireland, with dry, blowing snow and the wind gusting to 66 knots. In February a visit was made to RAF Upper Heyford, the home of the F-111s of the USAF's 79th Tactical Fighter Squadron, for a Tiger Meet. In the same month Squadron Leader Howard Nash flew ZA939 down to Baldonnel again, from Lisburn, carrying the British Ambassador to the Irish Republic. In March Wing Commander Ian McCluskie and several others represented the Squadron at the RAF's 75th Anniversary celebrations at RAF Marham. Sadly the planned fly-past on 1 April had

helicopters amassed over 600 flights a week in and out of Bessbrook – on average one every eight minutes during daylight hours and as many as 15,000 passengers a month. A dreadful accident involving a Squadron helicopter happened at Bessbrook on the night of 26/27 November 1992. As Gazelle ZB681 of 665 Squadron AAC was taking off, it collided with an incoming Puma, XW233. The Puma impacted into the perimeter security fence, while the

*This Puma is seen with rotors running on full power during a ground test following routine maintenance at Drumadd FOB in April 2002. Note the black duct-tape again. Initiated by 72 Squadron's engineers as a weather-proofing fix for the inspection panel on the nose during that unit's operation of the type, the practice has carried over with their transfer to 230.*                                                                                                   KA Boyd

to be cancelled owing to very poor weather. Over the same period a Royal Navy Sea King HC4 from 707 NAS was attached to the Squadron at Aldergrove for a few days to carry out a feasibility trial for the resumption of RN deployments to the Province, which indeed began again later in the year. In the course of a busy few days, Squadron Leader Gregory also represented the Squadron, this time at RAF Gutersloh, for the ceremony prior to its closure as a Royal Air Force base and handover to the Army Air Corps. In April RAF Aldergrove was awarded the Freedom of Newtownabbey and in May 'A' Flight visited the Isle of Man for training.

However in the midst of these activities, the security situation was giving cause for concern. The collapse

of further talks and continued successes against the terrorists from both camps had little effect on the ongoing Provisional IRA campaign on the mainland, with bombs in the City of London and Warrington. Sectarian violence further poisoned the atmosphere. Speculation was mounting that an anti-helicopter 'spectacular' was being planned and it very nearly came off. On 6 June 1993, as a Puma was lifting off from Crossmaglen and just starting to transit across the town square, mortar fire from a vehicle disguised as a baker's van hit the helipad. It was a very lucky escape.

Later in the month a visit was made by Puma to Pembroke Dock for a Squadron Association reunion. Pleasure flights around Pembroke Dock were taken by most of those that could stand the morning after the dinner. Amongst those somewhat the worse for wear was a young crewman, Rob Carr, who was 'ambushed' at the dinner by several old and bold members. The event saw the coining of a new verb – to be 'associationed' – which broadly meant to learn a lot about life, to be overwhelmed by stories of genuine gallantry and adventure and, perhaps principally, to drink a huge amount while doing the former.

Later that summer a party of Association members visited Aldergrove for the Squadron's 75th Anniversary celebrations and Station Open Day and were taken by Puma to visit old haunts from flying boat days in the late 1940s and 1950s – Castle Archdale and St Angelo. The little souvenir programme which was produced featured on its cover attractive and carefully drawn pictures of three Singapores in formation, a Sunderland, a Pioneer climbing at a very steep angle of attack and a Puma

scurrying along below. The songs listed at the back may not be described as suitable for a family audience.

More social diversions followed with airshow appearances at Laarbruch, Valley, Church Fenton, Newtownards, Fairford, Alconbury and Florennes in Belgium. On 11 September, another visit was made to the Ulster Aviation Society at Langford Lodge, by Flight Lieutenant Geoff Young in ZA939.

In the meantime administration and parenting of the regular Chinook attachment from No 7 Squadron was handed over from No 72 Squadron.

Grim reality returned later in the month when a Puma leaving Crossmaglen, crewed by Flight Lieutenant Paul 'Sticky' Newman, Flight Lieutenant Phil Gilling and Sergeant Phil Waddingham, came under heavy and sustained fire from five different points, two of which were heavy machine-guns mounted on flatbed lorries. As one of the vehicles moved off, an AAC Lynx gave chase

*On 5 December 1993 the Squadron assisted the pupils of Belfast Royal Academy in removing scrap vehicles from a scenic area in the beautiful Mountains of Mourne.*

John Reilly

and the door gunner returned fire when the target was clear of the surrounding houses. Two more Lynx arrived and the vehicles were abandoned on a farm complex. The perpetrators managed to evade capture but eventually several vehicles, a number of weapons and hundreds of rounds of ammunition were captured. The Puma, ZA940, suffered bullet damage to its port fuel jettison pump. The leak was not discovered until the aircraft returned to Bessbrook for more troops. A large area around the rear of the aircraft was covered in fuel, which was dripping onto the hot infrared jammer.

On 3/4 December, John Major visited Dublin again, two Pumas being used, XW221 and XW209 flown by Squadron Leaders Gregory and Townend respectively. This was followed by the Downing Street Declaration which stated that the Irish people on both sides of the border had a right to decide their own future and that the British Government had no "selfish, strategic, or economic interest in Northern Ireland", which was either encouraging or depressing, depending upon your point of view.

Time was found for some unusual aid to the civil community on 5 December 1993, when along with the Army, help was given to the pupils of Belfast Royal Academy in removing seven scrap cars from Castle Bog amid the scenic splendour of the Mountains of Mourne. The Puma air-lifted the cars as an underslung load, one at a time, down to waiting lorries provided by local fuel merchant, Cawoods. Much favourable press coverage ensued and the Squadron was subsequently presented with the Queen Mother's Award for Environmental Improvement.

There was some effect on the ground early in 1994 with the cessation of daylight army patrols in Belfast. In south Armagh, however, life went on much as before, with helicopters being needed to support searches, arrests, vehicle check points (VCPs) and resupply task. A particularly major task was named 'Operation Rectify', the complete rebuild of the Crossmaglen RUC and Army base. This was the biggest air-mobile operation ever attempted in the area. 1300 troops and 20 tons of stores were moved in ten hours, six of which were at night, by three Pumas and two Chinooks. In all the equivalent of a complete brigade was airlifted on three occasions into and out of disparate field locations by the time the operation was

*Another atmospheric view of Drumadd where 'Puma 3', XW213, sits under a fresh coat of snow on 16 February 2000.*

KA Boyd

concluded over the course of a couple of months.

There was also time for a very pleasant social occasion in February, the Heli-Wing dinner in the Officers' Mess, which was attended by several members of the Irish Air Corps, as well as representatives of the Royal Marines Commando Helicopter Force, the Army Air Corps and the RAF Support Helicopter world. A new CO, Wing Commander PH Rosentall, arrived in May, and he was soon involved in training to fly in formation wearing NVGs. June brought attendance at airshows in Denmark and France but also a very tragic event. On 2 June 1994 a Chinook HC2, ZD576, departed Aldergrove with a party of senior police and security services personnel, en route for a conference in Scotland. It crashed on a hillside at Beinn na Lice on the Mull of Kintyre, with the loss of all on board. The four crew members were Flight Lieutenants John Tapper and Rich Cook, MALM Graham Forbes and Flight Sergeant Kev Hardie. Though they were not members of 230 Squadron, their loss was keenly felt as the Chinook detachment from 7 Squadron was, as mentioned earlier, administered by 230 when in Northern Ireland and all the crew were very familiar faces in the crewroom.

On 12 July 1994 Puma XW225/FE was brought down by IRA mortar fire at Newtownhamilton as it was departing the base. Damage to the tail started a fire and resulted in the loss of control to the tail rotor drive. It force landed on a football field and turned on its side. The crew, Flight Lieutenants Gavin Dobson (who had been Squadron Leader Pynegar's copilot on the night in July 1992 when XW209 crashed) and 'Jenx' Jenkins, Sergeant Steve Kilbane and twelve passengers evacuated hastily with little more than bruises. For his skill in minimising injury or damage to personnel, civilians, civilian property or the aircraft the aircraft captain was awarded the DFC. The aircraft was recovered by a Chinook, repaired and was flying again before the end of the year.

August brought news of a "complete cessation of military operations" by the Provisional IRA. One of the most significant effects for the SH force was the restriction henceforth placed on low flying.

In October several members of the Squadron travelled to Odiham for the service at All Saints church when the old Squadron Standard was laid up.

1995 began with a much reduced level of operational activity. Sadly a search for missing cavers in Fermanagh was unsuccessful in that they were not recovered alive. Training sorties were made to Lossiemouth and Leuchars in connection with NVG training. In May a joint parade was held with No 72 Squadron through Belfast to mark the 50th Anniversary of the end of wartime RAF operations. A four aircraft fly-past was headed by Puma XW208, flown by Squadron Leader Gavin Davey and Flight Lieutenant Jenkins. As the summer wore on much time was devoted to training in connection with the deployment of crews to the Balkans – though there was time to mark the 50th Anniversary of VJ Day appropriately with fly-pasts. Flight Lieutenant Ian Cahill took XW226 to Pembroke Dock on 13 August, while Squadron Leader Nigel Hunt and Flight Lieutenant Higgins in XW237 and XW200 participated in the Belfast commemorations.

Following the death of Marshal Tito in 1980 the old racial and religious squabbles endemic in the Balkans began to flare up again. The collapse of the Soviet Union and the Warsaw Pact brought further instability. As the Serbs strived for supremacy, they encountered bitter opposition, which turned, in 1991, into a bloody civil war. As the fighting intensified, first the European Community and then the United Nations tried to intervene but failed to make any real impact keeping the peace where no peace existed. Outgunned and without support the UN called for help from NATO. In the summer of 1995 the UN's abandonment of a 'safe haven' to the tender mercies of the Bosnian Serbs and the subsequent massacres induced NATO to begin a sustained air and artillery offensive to impose a settlement.

The UK's contribution was substantial. The first member of 230 Squadron to leave for Bosnia was Squadron Leader Davey. He was joined by two crews who flew in the theatre around such localities as Ploce, Sarajevo, Gorny Vacuf and Mostar – names which became familiar on the evening news. Tactical flying skills were well tested, including evading a SA-6 missile which had locked on. The eventual result was that Slovenia, Croatia, Bosnia & Herzegovina and Macedonia became independent states and the greater destabilisation of Europe was avoided.

On 30 November 1995 the US President and First Lady, Bill and Hillary Clinton, arrived in Northern Ireland to add their weight to the peace process. Air Force One VC-25A 29000 (an executive conversion of the Boeing 747) arrived at Aldergrove, accompanied by a

*A very busy period at Bessbrook, as evidenced by the conspicuous absence of any other aircraft in this view of 230 Squadron's 'Puma 1', ZA936 preparing to lift one of the many loads on the helipad that day.*

KA Boyd

considerable collection of other first time visitors to the Province, bearing security staff, limousines, helicopters, the Presidential entourage and a large media contingent. These included the back-up VC-25A, two C-137s (military 707s), three massive C-5 Galaxy transporters, the press corps 747 of Tower Air and four helicopters – two VH-60 Seahawks, one MH-53 Sea Dragon and a CH-53 Super Stallion. The sight and thunderous sound of the helicopter formations crossing Belfast Lough and passing through the Glengormley Gap was a particular memory of an important few days. However, not even the presentational skills and media savvy of the US President could paper over the cracks in the faltering 'Peace Process'.

In February 1996 the Provisional IRA planted and detonated a huge bomb at Canary Wharf in the Docklands area of London. The cease-fire was over and for the Squadron tasking increased once again. It was also announced that the Armed Forces were to be reduced considerably in number over the next few years. However morale received a bit of a boost in the case of some of the crews who were deployed to 'Exercise Purple Star' in North Carolina and to Beja in Portugal for a Tiger Meet.

In May, Wing Commander Gordon Evans assumed

command. Duties in the summer focused on what was to become a depressingly annual event, the stand-off between members of the Orange Order and the security forces at Drumcree Church. Even more familiar were the haunts resumed in September when the Squadron began operating in south Armagh again.

More Pumas came to the Province in January 1997 with the arrival of five from No 18 Squadron, led by Squadron Leader Nick Laird, to form 'B' Flight of No 72 Squadron. The year also brought more violence, a bomb at HQNI Lisburn and the killing of Lance Bombardier Stephen Restorick by a sniper's bullet. A new Labour government assumed power in May and in July the IRA cease-fire was resumed. Meanwhile, in June the Squadron was given the task of conveying Her Majesty the Queen and Prince Philip between Hillsborough and Aldergrove.

1998 brought the Good Friday Agreement in April but also the Omagh bombing in October. Helicopters from 72 and 230 Squadrons, as well as a Sea King HC4 of 846 NAS, ferried casualties to hospitals in Enniskillen, Londonderry and Belfast. Twenty-nine people were killed and 399 injured. The CO, Wing Commander Ian Bell commented:

It was a very harrowing day, particularly for the young and inexperienced pilots who were involved in the operation. They coped extremely well and their response was a tremendous justification of the RAF's training system as a whole. I was very proud of them all.

A mini-Tiger Meet was held at Aldergrove over the weekend of 6–8 November. This also celebrated the Squadron's 80th Anniversary. The German and Italian Air Forces were represented by two Tornados apiece, RAF aircraft included Hawks and a Dominie but the undoubted star was a Czech Air Force Mi-24V Hind from its own Tiger Squadron, No 331. Tragically the four crew were killed when the aircraft crashed near its home base of Prevov on the return journey.

February 1999 brought what was, perhaps, a welcome break for two aircraft and their crews which flew via Valkenburg and Bruggen to Landsberg in Bavaria for 'Exercise Mountain Tiger'. The aim was to practise snow landings, mountain flying and navigation, tactical formations and operations in foreign airspace. Time was also set aside for skiing at Oberammergau and Garmisch.

NATO air forces became operationally involved in the Balkans once more in March 1999 with the commencement of a bombing campaign directed against Yugoslav/Serb military targets. The aim was to force Belgrade to desist from the offensive activity which its forces had been carrying out in Kosovo, where the Kosovars of Albanian ethnicity were being oppressed by the Serbs.

Six Pumas and eight Chinooks were deployed in Macedonia in June following the agreement by the Serbs to leave Kosovo. The helicopters' task was to provide air mobility for personnel and equipment within Kosovo and to assist the international peacekeeping force. 230 Squadron personnel took part but the deployment was under the auspices of No 33 Squadron. Thirty technicians worked a shift system of 24 hours on and 24 hours off. The work was intensive but the teamwork and camaraderie made it a worthwhile and enjoyable experience. Aircrew and technicians bonded closely together. They were based in Pristina in converted maxi-containers – known as the Trenchard Lines – protected by Russian guards.

The year 2000 brought another change of command, Wing Commander Bell being succeeded by Wing Commander Howard Nash. An unusual visitor to the Ulster Aviation Society centre at Langford Lodge airfield on 2 September was ex-230 Squadron member,

Warwick Creighton, who flew in with his 'Tiger Yak', a Yak-18 in a very distinctive Tiger colour scheme. In July 2001 it was the turn of the Squadron to feature on the front page of the *Ulster Airmail*, a colour shot of ZA939 in a very cleverly designed Tiger paint scheme – all on removable panels to facilitate a quick change. Another mini-Tiger Meet was held at Aldergrove in October 2001, featuring German and Italian Tornados, French Alpha Jets, Norwegian and Belgian F-16s and a pair of Spanish Mirages. By all accounts this was a very successful weekend, with some lively social activities.

2002 began with a very unfortunate incident on 21 January. XW234 was in process of making a landing at Ballykelly in Co Londonderry when it lost height rapidly, struck the ground hard and rolled onto its side. None of the four crew members suffered serious injury. This was followed on 16 March by an accident in south Armagh. XW227 was transporting military and civilian workers to a watchtower at Foughill Mountain, near the village of Jonesborough and close to the border with the Irish Republic, when, according to eyewitness reports, control appeared to be lost. The Puma entered a spin and descended very quickly. In the crash that followed the tailboom was snapped off and all main rotor and tail rotor blades were lost, with the helicopter coming to rest on its side on the hilltop. Several of those on board were seriously injured and were airlifted to Daisy Hill hospital in Newry for treatment. Two men were trapped in the wreckage for over two hours before being cut free.

These accidents could not really have happened at a worse time as No 72 Squadron was in process of departing the Province prior to its disbandment as a Wessex and Puma squadron. However, as a parting gift No 72 donated its CO, Wing Commander Andy McAuley who took over command of 230 Squadron in April. 'The Swift Retreat', which had been the 72 Squadron bar for many years, was refurbished and became 'The Tigers' Lair'. Drumcree time in July was spent mostly in south Armagh to allow the Sea Kings of 846 Naval Air Squadron detachment to concentrate in and around the now famous church.

Other activities in 2002 included a deployment to Portugal to participate in a NATO exercise, 'Exercise Daring Eagle', European and mainland trainers (which involved not only visits to Norway, Denmark and Holland but also a stop for refuelling on a North Sea gas rig en route) and a self-generated tactical exercise 'Cornish Tiger', which involved field deployment in and around RAF St Mawgan. 'Exercise Swifthawk' in August, at Kirkcudbright Training Area, saw the Squadron's aircraft practising their skills of Mutual Support with Army Air Corps Lynx and Gazelles. A Puma was sent to the Weston-super-Mare 'Heli-day' in July and another attended the RAF Leuchars airshow in September. Later in the same month the Squadron received a visit from the Support Helicopter Standards and Evaluation Flight. A team of four examiners put the aircrew through their paces in the air and on the ground. 'Exercise Yorkshire Tiger' in October was held at the Catterick Training Area. Two aircraft deployed for a programme of tactical flying which was badly affected by poor weather. This allowed the aircrew plenty of time to practise digging shell-scrape trenches and erecting tents. November brought the first wave of national fire strikes.

Royal flights in Northern Ireland were quite a regular feature, transporting not only Her Majesty the Queen

and Prince Philip, but also The Princess Royal and The Duke of York. Otherwise, the normal routine went on at the Forward Operating Bases (FOBs) in south Armagh, Omagh and Enniskillen each supporting an aircraft on a 72 hour tour of duty. During the daily on-call period of 14 hours, some five to eight hours may be spent in the air – moving men and supplies at the behest of the Army and the PSNI, VCPs, insertion and recovery of patrols and underslung loads being the regular tasks. Tasking is prioritised at the FOB by 'Buzzard', the Army liaison officer, usually a SNCO or Warrant Officer. 'Buzzard' has been likened to a taxi controller, with the Pumas as the cabs. For the most part the job is fairly repetitive, with Sunday morning usually being rather dull. The Puma is a good machine for going from A to B; it thrives on work but doesn't really like a lot of short hops.

A less visible security forces presence on the ground and fewer troops available has increased the value of the SH force. In the current jargon it is a force multiplier, allowing fewer troops to cover the same area, giving the

*230 Squadron Puma XW213, guided by MALM Tom Docherty in the doorway, hovers over RIR Despatcher Gordon Crozier as he earths the lifting gear before attaching the underslung strop. The other members of the Puma crew were Flt Lts Simon Gaskill and Matt Aspinall and a second loadmaster, Flt Sgt Rick Cooke. In the background, Sqn Ldr Paul Cunningham, OC Ops Flt, and Flt Lt Ben Ratcliffe's 72 Squadron Wessex XR498 'X' replens under the supervision of loadmaster Sgt 'Schuey' Thompson and the TSW refueller. Both aircraft were involved in this tasking at Drumadd FOB.*     KA Boyd

Army flexibility and mobility. Despite the much reduced terrorist violence in terms of bombings of towns and shootings of police and Army, there has still been plenty of activity for the security forces. As well as the aircraft at the FOBs, others are available for Province-wide tasks, day and night, others on one hour's notice. Aircraft are also dedicated to training tasks and undergo routine maintenance. 'B' Flight carries out the requirement for the vertical replenishment of naval vessels.

The Squadron has a very limited SAR capacity; a winch can be fitted but the crews are not trained as specialists in this role. It takes about six to nine months to train a new aircrew member – pilot, navigator or crewman – to become 'combat ready' and a tour in the Province normally lasts from 24 to 30 months. During the course of its first year and more as the only RAF helicopter unit at Aldergrove, the Squadron assumed its greater responsibility with professionalism and dedication to the task. Postings have ensured a good blend of youth and maturity in both the aircrew and groundcrew.

Over the years the Puma has been the subject of various modifications, the most extensive of which was the Puma Navigation Update (PNU) of 1995 which retrofitted the cockpit with much improved (and much needed) navigational equipment including GPS and NVG lighting. A rationalisation was attempted regarding items that had been 'bolted on' over the course of time. The display of information for the crew was enhanced by the provision of a multi-function display screen for each pilot, including VOR, ILS, TACAN, GPS, a hovermeter, compass card and homing advice for the location of rescue beacons. An audio voice alert system was also provided. Previously new equipment had included radar warning receivers from 1986 onwards (which were themselves refined with new digital technology), a missile approach warning system, a flare pack to decoy heat seeking weapons for the Gulf War and the distinctive polyvalent intake protection system, which had been fitted while the Squadron was at Gutersloh, to give sand and icing protection to the engines.

It is still quite a fast helicopter and is comfortable for passenger carrying; the cabin is reasonably spacious and the tilted gearbox allows a level flight attitude to be maintained rather than the more characteristic nose down attitude of a Wessex. In comparison with this older design it is faster, can carry more and can go further. It

is manoeuvrable in a tactical battlefield situation, it is agile at low level and can hide from enemy radar in the ground clutter. It has been described variously as an aerial 4x4, Transit Van or 4-tonne truck. It is a very good point to point aircraft and thrives on hard work, the more it flies the more reliable it becomes. It has been described as a limousine rather than a bus. For its day it was an advanced machine but it is over thirty years old and is rather thirsty as regards fuel consumption. The decision made, when purchasing the original batch to delete some of the fuel provision was not necessarily a good one.

Throughout the period covered by this account, some 90 years in total, the often unsung heroes of the Squadron have been the groundcrew. It is appropriate therefore to describe how the maintenance task is performed today. There is no doubt that the engineer officers and tradesmen of the Squadron have built up an enormous amount of expertise on the subject of looking after Pumas and keeping them flying over the past thirty years or so. As described previously, the basic aircraft has been updated several times in respect of systems and the fleet has been lavished with the utmost care and attention.

The Squadron's engineering section comprises 120 technical staff under the command of the Senior Engineering Officer (SEngO), a Squadron Leader, who has the ultimate responsibility for the airworthiness of the 15 Pumas. The Warrant Officer Engineer handles orders and procedures, as well as quality control. The other permanent day staff are the four Trade Managers (Airframe, Propulsion, Electrical and Avionics) who are Chief Techs; the Training Cell which carries out the induction of new arrivals and any refresher training required; the Squadron Mobility Officer who is concerned with all the transport arrangements for exercises etc; the Documents Control Office (both paper and computerised) and the Primary Star Servicing Team which undertakes one 250 hours service on a helicopter each month – up to a maximum of 15 per year.

Next there are the three shifts 'A', 'B' and 'C', to which staff from each of the four trades are allocated. Each of the shifts has a Junior Engineering Officer (JEngO) in charge, in two cases this is a Flight Lieutenant and in the other, a Flight Sergeant. There are between 30 and 35 people on each shift. The day shift works from 8am to 5pm, the night shift from 5pm until all necessary work is completed. A 21 day cycle per shift is worked – ten

*Flt Lt Gordon Evans watches the camera as XW231 is refuelled at Bessbrook prior to loading stores and troops for transit to the border OPs.*

KA Boyd

*The Squadron engineers have to be prepared to work in all conditions.*

Crown copyright

nights, one day off, ten days and then nine days off. There are therefore twelve complete cycles a year.

The daily task may be divided between corrective work – repairing faults and preventative maintenance – and servicing. The key aim is to provide the Squadron with 90% availability, though in reality 80% is a good achievement. Generally speaking about 60% of the work is scheduled and predictable, with 40% unscheduled and therefore rather less easy to predict. This is on a good day; there are peaks and troughs so it pays to be flexible. Unscheduled maintenance has to be fitted in on a case by case basis. Tasks have to be prioritised hourly. An average of 1.37 hours is spent per day per aircraft, totalling 7500 hours a year.

The hierarchy of scheduled work on an individual Puma is as follows:

Calendar Based:

Daily – checking and topping up oils and fluids, checking for visible damage, cleaning and general husbandry.

Weekly – each trade examines the helicopter from the viewpoint of its own specialisation.

Fortnightly – a good wash and clean, more general husbandry (akin to a Sunday afternoon 'car wash').

Flying hours based:

25 hours – 50 hours – 125 hours – 250 hours, all these can be accomplished at Aldergrove.

500 hours – 1000 hours – 2000 hours – 4000 hours, for these the aircraft must go to RAF Benson.

The Puma is well-liked by the technicians. It is less robust than the Wessex but it is quite clean to work on and most things are fairly easy to reach. However, it is an old airframe (the fleet leader XW199 has more than 12,000 hours on the clock) and is steadily becoming more maintenance intensive. More electrical problems are emerging. The PNU of 1995 had the effect of considerably increasing the complexity of what had been a relatively simple aircraft. The most tricky and demanding jobs on a Puma are a tail boom change (the wiring is simple

*A fine study of a Puma in flight over Ulster's lakeland.*

Crown copyright

enough but it is crammed into a confined space), a main rotor head change and a head and gearbox change.

It is also French in concept and design. As the owner of a Renault or Citroen will testify, some quirky Gallic features can result. Looking at UK service helicopters on a sliding scale of least to most technically advanced it falls in the middle: the line would be Gazelle – Lynx – Puma/Sea King – Chinook – Merlin.

During the course of 2003 the Squadron's work continued in support of operations in Northern Ireland, though four aircraft and crews were earmarked to be available for service out of Province should the need arise. Early in the New Year a crew was sent to No 33 Squadron's detachment in Bosnia, to remain there until the Merlins of No 28 Squadron took over in the Spring. Surprisingly, the invasion of Iraq and the downfall of Saddam Hussein's regime was accomplished without the need for the involvement of 230 Squadron!

The tradition of artistic embellishment at Aldergrove was revived later in the year when the roof of the house occupied by the CO of 5 Regiment Army Air Corps was decorated with a large yellow tiger's head. It is believed that the 2I/C, Squadron Leader 'Stir' Howard, and the OC 'A' Flight, Squadron Leader Martin Cowie, may not have been entirely blameless, having been seen in possession of a ladder, a stencil and a spray can.

After the initial hostilities of 'Operation Telic' in Iraq had ended, the British forces were deployed into the Multinational Division (South East) (MND(SE)) centred on Iraq's second town of Basra. The task was a daunting one, attempting to keep the peace between the various factions vying over their disparate aims. As well as tribal in-fighting, there were frequent attacks directly against Coalition Forces (CF), cross-border smuggling and the removal of electricity cables from pylons. The gangs would then melt the cables and sell the valuable copper cores in Iran.

It became obvious that the CF would be able to focus its efforts more effectively and protect its troops more efficiently with some form of surveillance asset and it was thought that 230 Squadron's highly specialised P4 capability might provide the answer as regards night time cover. The Puma had a well-proven track record of desert operations but there were concerns about the P4. Would equipment designed for the damp but mild

Northern Ireland climate be able to cope with the vastly different conditions in southern Iraq?

Flight Lieutenant Simon O'Brien, 230's lead Reconnaissance Sensor Operator (RSO), went to Iraq early in October. He reported favourably and approval was given for deployment. An intense period of training concentrated on NBC drills, qualifying on the new A2 variant of the SA-80 rifle, first aid, desert survival and the operational situation in Iraq. The Squadron's admin office came in for much well-deserved praise by shouldering the burden of the seemingly endless flood of paperwork, reducing the individual's requirement to, "sign here, here and here and take this, this and this with you." The detachment was led by OC 'B' Flight, Squadron Leader Phil Gilling and was composed of eight additional aircrew, to form three crews and 20 engineers, commanded by the SEngO, Squadron Leader Paul Baldwin.

On 13 October 2003, a C-130 Hercules transported the engineering party with the P4 equipment to RAF Benson. It was then fitted into a 33 Squadron Puma – three of these were to be used as they had the Enhanced Self-Defence Suite (ESDS) which afforded greater protection against IR missiles. Only two days later the two Pumas, XW235 and ZA936, along with some 33 Squadron deployable engineering equipment, were transported into theatre from RAF Brize Norton. A number of 230 Squadron engineers accompanied the helicopters on a Boeing C-17A Globemaster III of No 99 Squadron (along with an armourer loaned from 33 Squadron for the ESDS flares), with the remainder being flown by VC-10 on the same day. On 16 October the Squadron aircrew flew on a civilian Boeing 757 into theatre, along with a 33 Squadron QHI loaned for the sand-landing qualification. The weather which greeted the 32 deployed personnel was hot and humid, often reaching over 40 degrees centigrade. The air-conditioned, rubberised tents did afford some respite, being a few degrees cooler inside. At first only two tents were available, one of which contained no less then 21 bunk beds.

Much work was needed to get the aircraft and crews operational by 25 October; not the least of the problems was the fact that the Squadron had virtually no deployable equipment to speak of. Therefore everything from accommodation, transport, hangarage (including power and air-conditioning to preserve the P4 avionics),

*A Puma is unloaded from a C-17A Globemaster III.*
Sqn Ldr Phil Gilling

*Living conditions on base were spartan.*
Sqn Ldr Phil Gilling

safety equipment and office space had to be begged or borrowed. Squadron Leader Baldwin's skills in this regard proved to be commensurate with the best traditions of the Service.

Meanwhile the flying training went on at a pace. All crews had to complete a local familiarisation of the Basra area and learn desert sand-landing techniques by day and night. Night sand landings are very demanding, even for highly experienced aircrew, due to the poor visual references and 'brown-out' at the final, critical stage. It takes smooth, accurate flying and robust crew co-operation to achieve successful sand landings in these conditions. The training target date was met and the P4 asset was operational from 25 October.

After the initial frenzy of activity, everyone settled into a less pressurised routine, with life concentrated around night flying and subsequent rest periods during the day. This allowed time to try and make the living conditions more comfortable. The number of tents was increased to five and

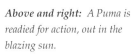

***Above and right:*** *A Puma is readied for action, out in the blazing sun.*
Sqn Ldr Phil Gilling

they were re-positioned further away from the sewage treatment plant. A tented rest facility was created with seating, a fridge, a water boiler, a DVD player and an outside decking area. Time was also found to produce a fortnightly newsletter – *The Big Cat Diary* – to send home.

Flying operations started off with routine overwatches of known trouble spots and CF patrols. The capability of P4 soon exceeded all expectations and performed even better than in Northern Ireland. This resulted in 20 Brigade using P4 for more demanding tasks including occasional daylight missions and the monitoring of smuggling activity along the Iraq/Iran border. Often tasking hours would be saved up for specific operations, thus allowing the greater utilisation of its capabilities. Due to the ever present threat, the crews soon became accomplished at tactical flying and operating the ESDS and its associated flares system.

Meanwhile, back in Northern Ireland, the new CO, Wing Commander Nick Laird, had the very rewarding task of flying four Puma loads of 230 Squadron Association members on the short hop from Aldergrove to Langford Lodge. This was part of the Association's Reunion Weekend in early November. The Ulster Aviation Society hosted the Association on a visit to its Aviation Heritage Centre. The veterans thoroughly enjoyed the visit and especially the lunch which was accompanied by several bottles of 'Black Bush', kindly donated by Old Bushmills. One former flying boat pilot was heard to remark, "We came to see the museum but stayed for a party!" The Society presented the Squadron with a model of the Sunderland JM673/P Black Peter and the Association made a most appropriate donation of £230 to the Society.

Within a few weeks Nick Laird was flying in a much more hostile environment – over Basra. The time and care devoted to training in the use of defensive systems and tactics paid off when the Puma in which he was flying with Flight Lieutenants 'Waffa' King and Lisa Peebles had a heat seeking missile launched against them. This was followed up by heavy machine gun fire from an area west of the city, known to be populated by a large number of former Republican extremists. Thankfully the tactics and equipment deployed on the day prevailed and the aircraft was recovered safely to base. Engagements at night from random small arms and tracer soon became the norm over the period from Christmas and on into 2004, with all

*230 Squadron Association visited the Ulster Aviation Society Heritage Centre on 8 November 2003 during their reunion at RAF Aldergrove. A presentation of a model of 230 Squadron Sunderland flying boat 'Black Peter' was made to the Squadron. Pictured left to right are Wing Commander (Retd) Bob Turner, Wing Commander Nick Laird RAF (OC 230 Squadron) & Mr Ernie Cromie (Chairman, Ulster Aviation Society).*

Eric Gray

crew reporting several incidents a week. From the turn of the year the detachment was renamed 1563 Flight, reviving the unit title used for the Pumas stationed in Belize. At the time of writing the Squadron is serving concurrently in two theatres, Northern Ireland and Iraq, and is being kept busy in both.

At the time of writing (August 2004), Aldergrove will remain the Squadron's base for the foreseeable future and the Puma will soldier on into the next decade of the 21st century. No major enhancements to the aircraft are planned beyond the Puma Integrated Modifications Programme, which will upgrade the instrumentation and radio fit to maintain capability. If the reduction of the military presence in Northern Ireland continues there will still be a role for the support helicopter but it will be diminished. It is anticipated that 230 will function as the 'Northern Support Helicopter Squadron', with more participation in training on the mainland and 'out of area' exercises.

The job in Northern Ireland creates great expertise and efficiency in performing the specific tasks required but inherent in this there is the danger of complacency and also of slightly losing sight of the bigger picture – the role of the SH helicopter force in the wider world. It is hoped that the next few years will bring the chance to

once again broaden the curriculum, to fly eastwards from Aldergrove across the water instead of just south and west. More opportunity could be given to aircrew and groundcrew to deploy into the field on exercise and to experience the 'joys' of camping out, thereby reducing the cultural gap with the other parts of the SH world.

There are no big names or glamour boys associated with the Squadron, no top brass. Therefore its history is all the more outstanding as it consists of the deeds of typical RAF types in the air and on the ground – the unsung heroes who have simply given their best and got on with the job, whatever the circumstances. The spirit that animates this remarkable squadron is evident

from the rapport enjoyed by retired, former and current members who meet at the annual Squadron Association Reunion. If the shades of Douglas Hallam, Cecil Clayton and Wilfred Dunn could be present, they too would feel at home and would, no doubt, join in with the rather tuneless but very enthusiastic renditions of the Squadron songs which always round off such a night.

Long may their work continue with the same professionalism, dedication and good humour as those who have served with the Squadron since its earliest days at Felixstowe and long may the Pumas continue to fly and to add more lustre to the name and reputation of No 230 Squadron, Royal Air Force – the Tiger Squadron.

*A sunny springtime evening at the junction of the Breagh and Knocknamuckley Roads near Portadown and 230 Squadron Puma XW213 arrives to extract a Royal Irish Regiment 'Eagle' patrol on 30 April 2000. Flt Lts Jason Bowes and Al Burgess and Flt Sgt Paul Granycome were, respectively, pilot, navigator and loadmaster.*

KA Boyd

# APPENDIX 1
### Squadron Art – The paintings of JK Fletcher

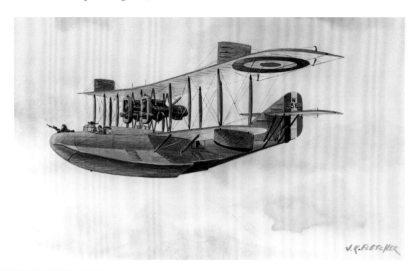

*During World War I 230 Squadron was equipped with the Felixstowe F2A flying boat. It was highly manoeuvrable and over 100 were constructed.*

*The Sopwith 2F1 Camel served with the Squadron during 1918. The type had been adapted to be launched from lighters towed by destroyers in order to increase its range.*

*In 1935 the graceful Short Singapore III arrived and served with the Squadron until 1938, and in many parts of the world.*

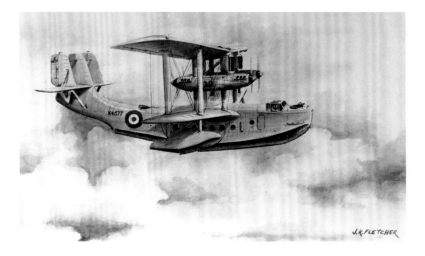

In 1941, following the occupation of their country some Yugoslav airman escaped, with their aircraft, and flew to Egypt where they were administered by 230 Squadron. The aircraft were eight Dornier Do22s (pictured right) and a single Rogozarski SIM XIV.

The hybrid Yugoslav and RAF markings are clearly shown in this delightful painting of the Rogozarski SIM XIV.

230 Squadron was the first to become operational on the Short Sunderland. This painting depicts a Mk V model. The Sunderland served with 230 from 1938 to 1957.

After several years with the Pioneer, in 1960 the first Twin Pioneers arrived. The 'Twin Pin' had the same short takeoff and landing (STOL) characteristics as the Pioneer and was equally rugged. It was equipped to carry out similar tasks but offered greater capacity and speed.

The move from fixed to rotary-wing flying came in 1962 when the Squadron was equipped with the Westland Whirlwind.

1971 saw another change of aircraft this time to the Westland/Aerospatiale Puma. In 2004 the Squadron is still flying the Puma from its base at RAF Aldergrove in Northern Ireland. This type has served the Squadron for longer than any other aircraft.

# APPENDIX 2
## No 230 Squadron Association

Those who have served on No 230 Squadron have immense pride in having done so and the spirit of comradeship which developed during operations, often on active service and in war conditions, is treasured. Life-long friendships have often developed amongst crews and other fellow Squadron members, so it was almost inevitable that an organisation to foster and encourage this fellowship would be formed.

However, it was not until 1984 when several old friends from WWII days met up at a VJ Day Memorial Service in London that a serious effort was made to start an Association. These founder members were extremely resourceful in their efforts to contact other potential members. They invoked the Squadron motto which translates to 'We seek afar' to the fullest possible extent. An appeal was printed on the front page of the Daily Telegraph and two of the team talked their way onto the Gloria Hunniford radio show with an appeal for former Squadron members to get in touch.

These early publicity efforts were very successful and soon telephones were ringing and new Association members were signed up. A committee was formed and Lord Gainford, a member of the Squadron from 1944 to 46, agreed to act as President. The first Reunion was organised at the RAF Museum at Hendon and initial contact was made with the current No 230 Squadron which at the time was stationed in Germany. Soon regular contact with the Squadron was taking place and Association members made several visits to RAF Gutersloh, before the Squadron was redeployed to Northern Ireland – its current base.

Since those early days the Association has gone from strength to strength in both numbers and the wide spectrum of membership from all periods of the unit's history during the last 60 to 70 years. Indeed, at the 18th Annual Reunion held in 2002 at RAF Aldergrove, there were members who served with the Squadron in 1935 and members of the current Squadron who had just joined. The Association has members living in many parts of the world as well as the UK and a regular newsletter helps members keep in touch. Naturally, a close liaison is maintained with the present Squadron and the current Commanding Officer is the Association's Vice-President.

The original objects of the Association's founding members – to foster good fellowship, to facilitate service by members to one another and to perpetuate the comradeship experienced by present and former serving members of No 230 Squadron is well and truly served.

*This group picture was taken at the 1997 Reunion and includes the then OC 230 Squadron, Wing Commander Gordon Evans, the Association President, Lord Joe Gainford, Bob Turner (Chairman), Don Holloway (Secretary), Ken Duckworth (Treasurer), committee members Joyce Wallace, Fred Coppard and Mike Taylor, along with air and ground crew members of the Squadron and many Association members.*

# APPENDIX 3
Examples of aircraft known to have served with the Squadron and its antecedents

| | |
|---|---|
| Borel Tractor Monoplane Seaplane | 88 (Felixstowe 1913) |
| Maurice Farman S11 Hydro Aeroplane | 29 (Felixstowe 1914) |
| Sopwith Bat Boat No 1 | 38 (Felixstowe 1914) |
| Maurice Farman S7 Longhorn | 67 (Felixstowe 1914) |
| Maurice Farman S7 Longhorn | 70 (Felixstowe 1914) |
| Maurice Farman S7 Longhorn Seaplane | 95 (Felixstowe 1914) |
| Maurice Farman Seaplane | 113,114, 115 (Felixstowe 1914) |
| Sopwith Pusher Biplane Seaplane | 123, 124 (Felixstowe 1915) |
| Deperdussin Monoplane | 885, 1377, 1378, 1379 (Felixstowe 1915) |
| BE2c | 977, 984, 985, 1131, 1132, 1153 (Felixstowe 1915) |
| Curtiss H1 | 950, 951 (Felixstowe 1915) |
| Curtiss H4 | 1228, 1230, 1238 (Felixstowe 1916) |
| Short Admiralty Type 827 | 3324, 3330 (Felixstowe 1916) |
| Short Admiralty Type 184 | 8063 (Felixstowe 1916) |
| Sopwith Baby Type 8200 | 8137, 8166, 8187, 8199,8200 (Felixstowe 1916) |
| Curtiss H8 (which when re-engined with 250 hp Rolls-Royce Eagle VIII became H12) | 8658, 8660, 8661*, 8662, 8663, 8667, 8676, 8677, 8682, 8683, 8689, 8693, 8694 (all Felixstowe War Flight 1917–18, 8661 also served with 230 Sqn) |
| Felixstowe F2c | N64, N65 (Felixstowe War Flight 1917) |
| Curtiss H.16 | N4060 |
| Felixstowe F2A | N4282, N4288, N4297, N4298, N4299, N4300, N4430, N4475, N4476, N4478, N4482, N4533, N4537, N4540, N4543, N4545, N4547, N4570, N4572 |
| Felixstowe F3 | N4033, N4191 |
| Felixstowe F5 | N4043, N4044, N4048, N4091, N4193, N4199, N4200, N4634, N4636, N4833, N4838 |
| Fairey IIID | N9485, N9640, N9733 (Calshot 1920s) |
| Supermarine Seagull II | N9607, N9646, N9647 (Calshot 1920s) |
| Supermarine Southampton Mk I | N9899, N9900, S1036, S1040, S1083, S1123 (480 Coastal Reconnaissance Flight) |
| Supermarine Southampton Mk II | S1232 (480 Coastal Reconnaissance Flight) |
| Short Singapore III | K4578, K4579, K4581, K4585 |
| Short S25 Sunderland Mk I | L2160 *Selangor*, L2161 *Negri-Sembilan*, L2164 *Pehang*, L2166 *Perak* |
| Dornier Do22Kj | 302, 306, 307, 308, 309, 311, 312, 313, (AX708 – 715) |
| Rogozarski SIM XIV–H | 157 |
| Short S25 Sunderland Mk II | W3987 / NM–X |
| Short S25 Sunderland MkIII | W4021 NM–W, W4022 NM–Z, W4023 NM–U |
| Short S25 Sunderland Mk V | DP180 / O, ML846 / W, NJ264 / 4X:R , PP117 / 4X:W |
| Supermarine Sea Otter | JM943 / Q |
| Scottish Aviation Pioneer CC Mk 1 | XK370, XL555, XL558 / W, XL666 / X, XL703 / Z |
| Scottish Aviation Twin Pioneer CC Mk 1 | XL996, XM285, XM940 |
| Scottish Aviation Twin Pioneer CC Mk 2 | XN318, XP295 |
| Westland Whirlwind HAR Mk 10 | XJ758, XP329 / V, XR453 / W |
| Westland / Aerospatiale Puma HC Mk 1 | XW202 / DM, XW217 / DA, XW220 / DD |

# APPENDIX 4
## Aircraft insignia

As far as is known no specific insignia was carried on the aircraft flown during World War One, though the dazzle colour schemes were applied to individual machines. Squadron code letters were introduced in 1938. 230 was originally allotted 'FV', at the outbreak of hostilities this was changed to 'NM' which was used until the Squadron went to East Africa in 1943 and when the use of markings was dropped. On return to UK waters in 1945 the code '4X' was allocated and this was painted on the side of the hull along with the Squadron badge. In 1951 the code changed again to 'B', which was replaced by the squadron number '230' in 1956. The Puma helicopters have carried a two–letter system, the first letter 'D' and later 'F' denoting the squadron, the Squadron badge being displayed on the side door. Since it began participating in NATO 'Tiger Meets' in 1977 a variety of special, temporary paint schemes have adorned the Pumas.

# APPENDIX 5
## Conditions of eligibility for Battle Honours won by the Squadron

| | |
|---|---|
| Home Waters 1918 | For operations over home waters, whether by land-based or carrier-borne aircraft. |
| Mediterranean 1940–1943 | For operations over Italy, Sicily and the Mediterranean and Aegean Seas by aircraft based in the Mediterranean Area between 10 June 1940 and 30 June 1943. |
| Egypt and Libya 1940–1943 | For operations in the defence of Egypt and the conquest of Libya, from the outbreak of war against Italy to the retreat of the Axis Forces into Tunisia 10 June 1940 to 6 February 1943. |
| Greece 1940–1941 | For operations over Albania and Greece during the Italian and German invasion, whether carried out by squadrons based in Greece or operating from external bases, 28 October 1940 to 30 April 1941. |
| Malta 1940–1942 | For squadrons participating in defensive, offensive and reconnaissance operations from Malta during the period of enemy action against the island 10 June 1940 to 31 December 1942. |
| Eastern Waters 1943–1945 | For operations over waters east of the Mediterranean and Red Sea including the Indian Ocean, Bay of Bengal, Java Sea and South China Sea throughout the war with Japan. |
| North Burma 1944 | For the air supply and support of General Wingate's second expedition 5 March to 26 June 1944. |
| Burma 1945 | For operations during the 14th Army's advance from Imphal to Rangoon. |
| Gulf 1991 | For operations against Iraqi invasion forces in Kuwait. |

# APPENDIX 6
## Comparative rank structure 1918–1919. RAF ranks were introduced in August 1919.

| RNAS | RFC | RAF |
|---|---|---|
| Wing Captain | Colonel | Group Captain |
| Wing Commander | Lieutenant Colonel | Wing Commander |
| Squadron Commander | Major | Squadron Leader |
| Flight Commander | Captain | Flight Lieutenant |
| Flight Lieutenant | Lieutenant | Flying Officer |
| Flight Sub-Lieutenant | 2nd Lieutenant | Pilot Officer |

# APPENDIX 7
## Commanding Officers

| | |
|---|---|
| Captain CE Risk RM | 5 August 1913 (Felixstowe) |
| Captain CEH Rathbone RM | August 1914 (Felixstowe) |
| Commander JC Porte RN | late 1914 (Felixstowe) |
| Flight Commander TD Hallam DSC | April 1917 (War Flight) |
| Captain CJ Clayton | 20 August 1918 |
| Wing Commander CE Risk OBE | 9 October 1919 |
| Squadron Leader FGD Hards DSC, DFC | 21 May 1920 |
| Wing Commander IT Courtney | December 1920 |
| {Squadron Leader WB Callaway AFC | April 1922 (230 Sqn / 480 CRF)} |
| {Squadron Leader A Durston AFC | January 1926 (480 Coastal Recce Flt)} |
| (Squadron Leader IT Lloyd | April 1927 (480 Coastal Recce Flt)} |
| {Squadron Leader DG Donald DFC, AFC | November 1928 (480 CRF / 201 Sqn)} |
| Wing Commander WH Dunn DSC and bar | 23 February 1935 |
| Wing Commander GM Bryer OBE, AFC | 3 November 1938 |
| Wing Commander G Francis AFC | 13 May 1940 |
| Wing Commander TWG Eady | 13 September 1941 |
| Wing Commander MC Collins | 9 October 1941 |

*Flight Commander TD Hallam DSC who commanded the War Flight from April 1917.*

Defence Forces of Canada Archive

*The current Commanding Officer is Wing Commander NWG Laird. Nick took command of the Squadron in September 2003.*

Crown copyright

| | |
|---|---|
| Wing Commander CR Taylor | 17 November 1942 |
| Wing Commander DK Bednall | 25 August 1943 |
| Wing Commander CEL Powell | 6 October 1944 |
| Wing Commander DE Hawkins DFC | 13 August 1945 |
| Wing Commander VHA McBratney AFC | 3 October 1946 |
| Squadron Leader GA Huxford | 17 June 1947 |
| Squadron Leader AJ Payn MBE | 5 April 1948 |
| Squadron Leader CJ Wells | 13 February 1950 |
| Squadron Leader AM Campbell | 20 November 1950 |
| Squadron Leader JG Higgins DFC, AFC | January 1952 |
| Squadron Leader EC Bennett DFM | 7 December 1953 |
| Squadron Leader CM Stavert AFC | 3 January 1955 |
| Squadron Leader PG Adams DSO | 28 December 1955 – February 1957 |
| Squadron Leader WJ Simpson DFC | 1 September 1958 |
| Squadron Leader HJ West DSO, DFC | 1 July 1960 |
| Squadron Leader DM Thomas | 15 October 1962 |
| Squadron Leader KR Cawdron | August 1965 |
| Squadron Leader DE Todd | October 1966 |
| Squadron Leader TSC Jones AFC | November 1968 |
| Squadron Leader PJ Maitland AFC | September 1971 |
| Wing Commander PDA Austin AFC | December 1971 |
| Wing Commander I Horrocks | November 1974 |
| Wing Commander DO Crwys-Williams | November 1975 |
| Wing Commander ANS Parker-Ashley | June 1977 |
| Wing Commander BA Wright AFC | January 1979 |
| Wing Commander DJ Hamilton-Rump | June 1981 |
| Squadron Leader PA Crawford | October 1983 |
| Wing Commander RE Turner | January 1984 |
| Wing Commander RE Wedge BSc | May 1986 |
| Wing Commander MR Trace MA | December 1988 |
| Wing Commander CR Williamson | June 1991 |
| Wing Commander IR McCluskie MSc | May 1992 |
| Wing Commander PH Rosentall | May 1994 |
| Wing Commander GR Evans | May 1996 |
| Wing Commander IK Bell | May 1998 |
| Wing Commander HW Nash MBE, MA | May 2000 |
| Wing Commander AWJ McAuley MA | April 2002 |
| Wing Commander NWG Laird MA | September 2003 |

# APPENDIX 8
## Awards and Honours
(Where a date is not shown it is assumed that the award was made on the same date as the previous entry.)

| Date | Name | Award |
|---|---|---|
| 1914 | Maj ER Moon | Legion of Honour |
| 22 Jun 1917 | Flt Cdr PL Holmes | DSC |
| | Flt Sub Lt CR Morrish | DSC |
| | Flt Sub Lt HC Boswell | DSC |
| | Flt Sub Lt BD Hobbs | DSC |
| | Flt Cdr D Hallam DSC | Bar |
| | AM2 WP Caston | DSM |
| | AM1 AE Shorter | DSM |
| | AM2 AG Flowers | DSM |
| | CPO JW Rose | DSM |
| | AM1 GB Clements | DSM |
| 20 Jul 1917 | Flt Lt BD Hobbs DSC | DSO |
| | Flt Sub Lt REL Dickey | DSC |
| | AM2 HM Davies | DSM |
| | AM1 AW Goody | DSM |
| 11 Aug 1917 | Flt Lt WR Mackenzie | DSC |
| | Flt Sub Lt REL Dickey DSC | Bar |
| | AM1 J Watts | DSM |
| | AM1 EE Hughes | DSM |
| | LM SF Anderson | DSM |
| | AM1 T Caird | DSM |
| 14 Sep 1917 | Flt Lt JO Galpin | DSC |
| | Flt Sub Lt CL Young | DSC |
| | Flt Lt WR Mackenzie DSC | Bar |
| | AM1 HL Curtis | DSM |
| | AM2 WH Grey | DSM |
| 1 Oct 1917 | Flt Cdr AQ Cooper | DSC |
| | Flt Lt TH Newton | DSC |
| | CPO JG Cockburn | DSM |
| | AM1 WN Blacklock | DSM |
| 17 Nov 1917 | Flt Lt BD Hobbs DSO DSC | Bar DSC |
| | Flt Lt REL Dickey DSC and Bar | 2nd Bar |
| | AM1 C Spikens | DSM |
| | AM1 LGS Boshier | DSM |
| 30 Nov 1917 | AM1 J Mortimer | DSM |
| 19 Dec 1917 | AM1 EH Clarke | DSM |
| 1918 | Maj ER Moon LoH | DSO |
| | Cdr OHK Macguire | DSO |
| | Maj K Blackburn | DSC and Bar |

| | | |
|---|---|---|
| 1918 | Sqn Ldr D Hallam DSC and Bar | 2nd Bar |
| | Flt Cdr R Scott | DSC |
| | Sqn Cdr ERC Nanson | DSC |
| | Flt Lt NA Magor | DSC |
| | Flt Lt C Hoare | DSC |
| | Capt A Carlisle | DSC |
| | Capt AT Barker | DFC |
| | Capt JO Galpin DSC | DFC |
| | Capt JL Gordon | DFC |
| | Capt EJ Webster | DFC |
| | Lt S Anderson | DFC BoTM |
| | Ensign KB Keys USN | DFC |
| | Sgt Maj Crispin | DSM |
| | Cpl Mech SF Anderson DSM | AM CGM |
| | AM1 Moyes | DFC |
| | AM1 AJ Kirby | DFC |
| | Cpl WN Blacklock DSM | DFC |
| | AM2 EM Nichol | DSM |
| | AM2 GH Robinson | DSM |
| | Sgt Mech T Caird DSM | DFC |
| | Cpl Mech TM Reid | DFC |
| 21 Nov 1918 | Lt B Armitt | DSM Bar 2 Roses |
| | 2 Lt R Fearn | DSM |
| | 2 Lt G Dyke | DSM |
| | Lt AG Galloway | MM |
| 14 Sep 1940 | Flt Lt WW Campbell | DFC |
| 3 Dec 1940 | Wg Cdr G Francis | DFC |
| 7 Jun 1941 | Flt Lt AMG Lywood | DFC |
| 17 Jun 1941 | Sgt GW Baxter | DFM |
| 9 Jul 1941 | Sqn Ldr PH Alington | DFC |
| 19 Jul 1941 | Wg Cdr G Francis DFC | DSO |
| 23 Jul 1941 | Sqn Ldr PR Woodward | DFC |
| 19 Aug 1941 | Sgt V Corderry | MM |
| | Sgt C Starkey | MM |
| 22 Aug 1941 | Flt Lt RF Martin DFC | Bar |
| | LAC JV Waterland | DFM |
| 3 Nov 1941 | Sgt WG Scarth | DFM |
| Nov 1941 | LAC WH Yates | DFM |
| 3 Mar 1942 | Sgt J Dupont | DFM |
| 1 Jun 1942 | Wg Cdr KV Garside | DFC |
| | Flt Lt DN Milligan | DFC |
| 7 Jul 1942 | FS BG Kemp | DFM |

| | | |
|---|---|---|
| 28 Jul 1942 | Sgt SE Gould | DFM |
| 18 Sep 1942 | FS D Barnett | DFM |
| | FS E Lewis | DFM |
| | Sgt WG McGhee | DFM |
| | Sgt KJ Cole | DFM |
| 26 Feb 1943 | Plt Off AGG Richmond | GM |
| 4 Aug 1943 | Fg Off SD Plummer | DFC |
| 25 Sep 1944 | Sqn Ldr LF Middleton | DFC |
| | Flt Lt J Rand | DFC |
| | Fg Off VN Verney | DFC |
| | FS RF Webber | DFM |
| 2 Jan 1945 | Sqn Ldr KV Ingham | DFC |
| 3 Apr 1945 | Fg Off EA Garside | DFC |
| | Flt Lt COP Watson | DFC |
| | Fg Off LEO List | DFC |
| 1945 | Sqn Ldr AW Deller | DFC |
| | Flt Lt AS Pedley | DFC |
| | Flt Lt CF Potter | DFC |
| 10 Dec 1948 | Flt Lt G Harkness | AFC |
| 1 Jan 1953 | Sqn Ldr JS Higgins DFC AFC | Bar-AFC |
| 31 May 1953 | Flt Lt CM Stavert | AFC |
| 1 Jan 1955 | Sqn Ldr EC Bennett DFM | OBE |
| | Flt Lt S Bowater DFC | AFC |
| 29 Mar 1955 | Sqn Ldr PR Woodward DFC | AFC |
| 1 Jan 1960 | WO CP Gilbert | MBE |
| 1 Jan 1970 | FS J Dungate | AFM |
| 24 Nov 1970 | Sqn Ldr TSC Jones | AFC |
| 1 Jul 1974 | Flt Lt RU Langworthy | AFC |
| 1 Jan 1976 | Flt Lt RC Atkinson | AFC |
| | Flt Lt R Hayward | MID |
| 12 Jun 1976 | Sqn Ldr BA Raphael | AFC |
| 6 Sep 1977 | Flt Lt AD Brown | AFC |
| 2 Jun 1978 | Sqn Ldr AFC Hunter | AFC |
| | Sgt D Jones | AFM |
| 26 Sep 1978 | Flt Lt CR Chaloner | AFC |
| 18 Jun 1979 | Flt Lt MJ Maclaine | AFC |
| 1 Jan 1981 | Sqn Ldr DA Waring | AFC |
| 1 Jul 1984 | Flt Lt GC Blackie | AFC |
| 1 Jan 1985 | Sqn Ldr KF Daykin | MBE |
| 1 Jan 1989 | Flt Lt RG Carpenter | AFC |
| 29 Jun 1991 | Wg Cdr MR Trace | OBE |
| | Ch Tech MW Callingham | BEM |

| | | |
|---|---|---|
| 1 Nov 1991 | Flt Lt G Duncan | QCVSA |
| Jun 1993 | Sqn Ldr PG Pyneger | AFC |
| | Sqn Ldr CW Dixon | MBE |
| | FS G Tucker | MBE |
| Apr 1994 | Flt Lt JJ Longmuir | MBE |
| Jan 1995 | Wg Cdr IR McLuskie | OBE |
| Apr 1995 | Sqn Ldr PW Gregory | MBE |
| | Sqn Ldr MF Strangroom | QCVS |
| | Flt Lt GJ Dobson | DFC |
| | MALM R Graham | QCVS |
| Jan 1996 | Ch Tech PJ Jamison | MBE |
| Nov 1996 | Flt Lt CJ Luck | MBE |
| Dec 1997 | Flt Lt SC Leach | QCVS |
| May 1998 | Sqn Ldr GK Wilson | QCVS |
| Nov 1998 | Flt Lt WH Creighton | QCVS |
| | Flt Lt RC Maddison | QCVS |
| May 1999 | Flt Lt PA Burlingham | QCVS |
| | Sgt D Boreham | QCVS |
| Apr 2002 | Sqn Ldr Charlton | QCVS |
| Oct 2002 | Flt Lt SJ Kovach | MID |
| Apr 2003 | Sgt RA Openshaw | QCB |
| Oct 2003 | Flt Lt A Palmer | QCVS |

# APPENDIX 9
A Chronology

| | |
|---|---|
| August 1913 | The establishment of a Royal Naval Air Station at Felixstowe |
| July 1914 | Aircraft from Felixstowe took part in the Royal Fleet Review at Spithead |
| 1914–1917 | Coastal patrols made by aircraft based at Felixstowe |
| April 1917 | The establishment of the Felixstowe 'War Flight' |
| April 1918 | The formation of the Royal Air Force |
| August 1918 | The formation of No 230 Squadron |
| March 1919 | Reduced to a cadre |
| Late 1919 | Re-establishment at peacetime strength |
| May 1922 | Relocation from Felixstowe to Calshot |
| April 1923 | Disbandment and re-numbering as No 480 Coastal Reconnaissance Flight |
| August 1925 | Flight re-equipped with Supermarine Southamptons |
| September 1925 and July 1926 | First visits to Belfast |
| January 1929 | Flight re-numbered as No 201 Squadron |
| December 1934 | No 230 Squadron re-formed at Pembroke Dock |
| October 1935 | Relocation to Aboukir in Egypt |
| August 1936 | Return to Pembroke Dock |
| October 1936 | Relocation to Singapore |
| March 1937 | The Squadron Badge received Royal approval |
| June 1938 | Arrival of the first Sunderland |
| October 1939 | Detachment sent to China Bay in Ceylon |
| February 1940 | Ceylon became Squadron's base |
| May 1940 | Relocation to Alexandria in Egypt |
| June 1940 | Detachment sent to Malta |
| June 1940 | Sinking of two Italian submarines |
| October 1940 | Detachment sent to Suda Bay in Crete |
| January 1941 | Detachment sent to Scaramanga in Greece |
| March 1941 | Involvement in Battle of Matapan |
| May 1941 | Administration of No 2 Yugoslav Squadron taken on |
| January 1942 | Sinking of U-577 |
| February 1942 | Final sortie made by No 2 Yugoslav Squadron |
| July 1942 | Relocation to Fanara on Great Bitter Lake for a month |
| Late 1942 | Re-equipment with Sunderland III |
| January 1943 | Relocation to Dar-es-Salaam in Tanganyika |
| February 1943 | Detachment sent to Tulear in Madagascar |
| June–July 1943 | Detachment sent to Bizerta in Tunisia |
| August 1943 | Detachment sent to Pamanzi in the Comoro Islands |
| September–November 1943 | Detachment sent to Dodecanese Islands in Greece |
| October 1943 | Pamanzi detachment moved to Mombasa in Kenya |
| November 1943 | Detachment operating Kisumu to Khartoum shuttle |
| February 1944 | Relocation to Koggala Lake in Ceylon |
| March 1944 | Advanced bases established at Addu Attol, Diego Garcia and Kelai |
| June 1944 | Detachment sent to for operations on Lake Indawgyi in Burma |
| January 1945 | Re-equipment with Sunderland V began |

| | |
|---|---|
| February 1945 | Detachment sent for operations on Chindwin River in Burma |
| April 1945 | Relocation to Akyab in Burma, detachment left at Koggala |
| May 1945 | Relocation to Rangoon in Burma |
| July 1945 | Relocation to Red Hills Lake near Madras in India |
| August 1945 | Detachment at Koggala withdrawn |
| September 1945 | Return of Squadron aircraft to Seletar in Singapore |
| November 1945 | Relocation to Seletar |
| January 1946 | Detachment sent to Labuan in Borneo |
| Early 1946 | Flights to Hong Kong, Vietnam, China, Japan and Australia |
| April 1946 | Return to the UK, Pembroke Dock and then Castle Archdale |
| September 1946 | Relocation to Calshot |
| July–December 1948 | Participation in the Berlin Airlift |
| February 1949 | Relocation to Pembroke Dock |
| July–August 1952 | The British North Greenland Expedition |
| May 1953 | Detachment sent to Malta, assisted with transport of troops to Egypt |
| July 1953 | Took part in Queen's Coronation Review at RAF Odiham |
| August 1953 | Relief flights from Malta to Ionian Islands |
| Summer 1954 | Return to Greenland to bring back expedition |
| May 1955 | Detachment sent to Seletar for SEATO exercise |
| August 1955 | Visit of Her Majesty the Queen to Pembroke Dock |
| September 1956 | Participation in the film Yangtse Incident |
| February 1957 | Disbandment along with No 201 Squadron |
| September 1958 | Re-formed at Dishforth with SA Pioneers |
| November 1958 | Relocated to Cyprus |
| April 1959 | Returned to Dishforth |
| May 1959 | Relocated to Upavon |
| February–March 1960 | At El Adem in Libya for 'Exercise Starlight One' |
| March 1960 | Arrival of Twin Pioneers |
| May 1960 | Relocation to Odiham |
| September 1960 | Detachment sent to the Southern Cameroons |
| February 1961 | Detachment sent to Northern Cameroons |
| November 1961 | Detachment to Northern Ireland |
| June 1962 | Formation of Helicopter Training Flight |
| Autumn 1962 | Gradual arrival of Westland Whirlwinds |
| October 1962 | Presentation of Squadron Standard |
| December 1962 | Final fixed-wing sorties |
| January 1963 | Relocation to Gutersloh in West Germany |
| February 1964 | Detachments to Cyprus and the UK |
| January 1965 | Return to Odiham |
| February–March 1965 | Relocation to Labuan in Borneo |
| March 1965 | Detachments sent to Tawau and Sepulot |
| July 1966 | Detachment sent to Bario and withdrawn from Tawau and Sepulot |
| October–November 1966 | Return to Odiham |
| January 1967 | Declared operational at Odiham |
| March 1968 | Detachment sent to Cyprus |
| February 1969 | Relocation to Wittering in Lincolnshire |

| | |
|---|---|
| February 1970 | Detachment sent to Cyprus |
| October 1971 | Creation of No 230 Squadron Puma Echelon at Odiham |
| December 1971 | Final sorties with Whirlwind and end of Cyprus detachment |
| January 1972 | Back at Odiham with new aircraft, Westland/Aerospatiale Puma |
| November 1972 | Deployment to Bahamas |
| April 1973 | Start of commitment to Northern Ireland |
| August 1973 | Deployment to Canada |
| July 1974 | Detachment sent to Cyprus |
| February 1975 | Detachment sent to Cyprus |
| June 1976 | Start of commitment to Belize |
| June 1977 | Participated in NATO Tiger Meet at RAF Greenham Common. |
| June 1978 | Awarded Tiger Spirit Trophy, voted into full membership |
| September 1978 | Belize detachment had to decamp to Mexico temporarily |
| December 1979 | Personnel deployed to Rhodesia |
| October 1980 | Relocation to RAF Gutersloh |
| August 1982 | 22nd International Tiger Meet held at Gutersloh |
| July 1983 | 70th Anniversary Open Day |
| January 1984 | Start of further detachments to Belize |
| Spring 1987 | Formation of 230 Squadron Association |
| October 1987 | Start of further detachments to Northern Ireland |
| July 1989 | First exchange to Montijo |
| March 1990 | End of Northern Ireland commitment |
| November 1990 | Deployment to Saudi Arabia for Operation Granby |
| April 1991 | Return to Gutersloh |
| May 1992 | Relocation to RAF Aldergrove |
| October 1992 | Presentation of new Standard |
| August 1993 | 75th Anniversary celebrations at RAF Aldergrove |
| August 1994 | Provisional IRA 'Cessation of hostilities' |
| October 1994 | Old Squadron Standard laid up in All Saints Church, Odiham |
| August–October 1995 | Detachment to Bosnia |
| February 1996 | End of IRA cease-fire |
| November 1998 | Mini–Tiger Meet to celebrate 80th Anniversary |
| October 2001 | Another mini–Tiger Meet at Aldergrove |
| March 2002 | With No 72 Squadron stood down, the Squadron becomes sole RAF SH unit in Northern Ireland |
| October 2003 | Start of detachment to Basra, Iraq |

# APPENDIX 10
Locations – the Squadron has travelled to many places around the world

## Europe
England, Scotland, Wales, Northern Ireland, Republic of Ireland, Isle of Man, Scilly Isles, Orkney Islands, Shetland Islands, Western Isles, Fair Isle, North Sea Gas Rig, Faroe Islands, Jersey, Guernsey, Norway, Denmark, Iceland, Greenland, France, Belgium, Holland, Italy, Portugal, Majorca, Germany, Switzerland, Austria, Gibraltar, Malta, Sicily, Sardinia, Cyprus, Greece, Ionian Islands, Dodecanese Islands, Crete, Federal Republic of Yugoslavia, Bosnia.

## Asia
Iraq, Saudi Arabia, Kuwait, Bahrein, Oman, Aden, Trucial States, India, Pakistan, , Singapore, Malaya, Indonesia, Philippines, Ceylon, Hong Kong, China, Vietnam, Japan, Burma, Sabah, Sarawak, Brunei

## Africa
Tunisia, Libya, Egypt, Tanganyika, Madagascar, North Cameroon, South Cameroon, Nigeria, Chad, Sudan, Rhodesia

## Indian Ocean Islands
Mauritius, Seychelles, Comoros Islands, Aldabra, Diego Suarez, Addu Atoll, Diego Garcia, Kelai, Nicobar Islands

## North America
Canada

## Central America and the Caribbean
Belize, Bahamas, Mexico

## Australasia
Australia, Papua-New Guinea

# APPENDIX 11
## Odiham to Aldergrove by Puma in 2002

There are many routes which can be taken to fly from England to Northern Ireland. One of the most unusual and enjoyable that I have experienced happened in a Westland Puma HC1 of No 230 Squadron RAF as I returned from the Squadron Association Reunion Weekend at RAF Odiham – the spiritual home of the Support Helicopter Force.

It was a bright, sunny, late September morning and members of the Squadron, past and present, had attended a service at Odiham Parish Church. Puma ZA940 was waiting on the grass just across from the Officers' Mess. Firstly two groups of cadets from No 230 Squadron Air Training Corps were flown around the circuit, kicking up a storm of autumn leaves on departure each time. The Association's Chairman, Wing Commander Bob Turner, looked wistfully at the chunky, purposeful looking helicopter – as he said, if the Queen had invited him to once more take the right-hand seat he would not have hesitated for a second. We said our goodbyes after a truly memorable weekend, most hospitably hosted by the Station, and boarded the aircraft.

Sitting on a webbing seat at the rear of the cabin – with a large mound of baggage – I was very glad of the proffered ear defenders. The Puma is a highly capable, fast and manoeuvrable machine, well-liked and even charismatic, but it could not be described as quiet. Two Turbomeca Turmo IIIC4 turboshaft engines of 1328 shp each produce a fair amount of noise. In the right-hand seat was Squadron Leader Jim Holland and beside him was Flight Lieutenant Dave Flynn, newly designated as the liaison officer between the Squadron and the Association. We rose from the grass at 12.25, the nose dipped down and we were away on the first leg of our journey. This was only a short hop of some 30 miles almost due north to RAF Benson in Oxfordshire, which took just over 10 minutes. Our stop there lasted about a minute, just enough time for the CO, Wing Commander Andy McAuley to disembark. He was on his way to a meeting and made a most debonair sight as he strode off in his best suit, luggage in each hand and a flying helmet on his head.

The Puma climbed to 1000 feet and with a good tailwind we were making about 160 knots over the ground as we headed north again, past Oxford, Bletchley, Northampton and Leicester. Our destination was Newark in Nottinghamshire, where a goodwill visit was to be made at the Air Museum. In a flight time of some 40 minutes, we covered about 100 miles and landed in a field, adjacent to the fine collection of aircraft, just after 13.15 and were met by one of the volunteer helpers at the museum. During World War Two it was the location of 1661 Heavy Conversion Unit, which flew Stirlings and was called RAF Winthorpe. We were given a swift guided tour and left again at 13.55, making a

low level departure before ascending with great rapidity to demonstrate the Puma's maximum rate of climb of 1200 feet per minute.

We were now heading southwest, on our way to East Midlands Airport (EMA) via the outskirts of Nottingham. Taking account of this brief diversion the 30 miles to EMA were covered in 20 minutes. We made a standard civil airliner type approach over the M1 and flew along Runway 28 before landing and taxiing to Stand 48. There both aircraft and crew were refuelled. A minor repair was made to the tail rotor, which necessitated the folding ladders being retrieved from the rear of the helicopter. The work was carried out by Sergeant Wayne Pettit, who had been the worthy winner the previous evening of the Association Award for the most valuable contribution by a Squadron member during the previous year. Wayne received a suitably inscribed tankard for his work in charge of the Safety Equipment Section. He was assisted at the tail rotor by the newest member of the Squadron, Avionics Technician Luke White, who was sampling his first detached duty.

Vortex 008 departed EMA at 15.10 and overflew Donington Park racing circuit, much to the pleasure of the spectators lying in the grass on a lovely, warm afternoon. Our next port of call was Blackpool Airport, which was 100 miles away to the northwest. As we neared our destination we observed a huge tailback on the M55 motorway – all heading away from the town – nothing to do with the Labour Party Conference I trust. We flew down the seafront past the famous Tower, the green trams and the enormous Big Dipper, arriving at 16.05, all very familiar to Dave Flynn, Blackpool being his home town. On landing at the airport it was necessary to refuel again and to don our immersion suits – mine was a lurid shade of orange. MALM Glyn Morgan gave me a safety briefing – brace, hold onto the strut by the door and when the door is jettisoned, simply follow your arm outwards and upwards.

We left Blackpool at 16.35 for the final stage of 130 miles across the Irish Sea. Our track was just to the north of the Isle of Man and past the Mull of Galloway to starboard and then on towards the Copeland Islands. Having met so many members of the Squadron Association who had flown and worked on Sunderlands, it seemed very appropriate to be concluding the weekend by flying over the steel grey sea, at a height of 2000 feet and a speed of around 130 mph. As we crossed Belfast Lough we passed over an outbound Stena Line High Speed Ferry (HSS) trailing its long wake and a Dash-8 on finals for Belfast City Airport. RAF Aldergrove was reached at 17.35 after a journey of 390 miles which took 185 minutes in the air.

# APPENDIX 12

A Brief History of 230 (Congleton) Squadron ATC by Flight Lieutenant Rod Goodier

**1971–1979**     230 Squadron started life as a Detached Flight (D/F) of 2151 (Biddulph) Squadron and was formed in 1971. Their first SHQ was in the crypt of St Mary's Church, Congleton. The D/F was resident there for six years until, in 1977, they relocated to the newly built Leisure & TA Centre sharing one room with the Army Cadet Force & TA.

**1980–1983**     Over the years the D/F had grown considerably with numbers reaching 40+ cadets, supervised by five staff. In 1979, with regular high cadet numbers the D/F became eligible to apply to Headquarters Air Cadets (HQAC) for Squadron status. The CO, Flying Officer Brian Mott and Pilot Officer Rod Goodier researched the squadron numbers offered by HQAC to discover that 230 Squadron was an active RAF Squadron based in Germany flying Puma helicopters. Thus 230 (Congleton) Squadron ATC was born in January 1980.

On 5 May 1981 a letter was written to Wing Commander Brian Wright OC 230 Squadron RAF Gütersloh to inform him of the formation of 230 Squadron ATC. Wing Commander Wright replied with a very positive letter offering to take two cadets for a week with the 'Tigers' in summer and so a 'Cadet of the Year' award was introduced to the newly formed squadron. In summer 1982 two Congleton cadets flew to Düsseldorf to be met by Warrant Officer B Golightly, 230 Squadron's Adjutant. Communication by mail continued and for three years the 'Tigers' hosted cadets of the year at RAF Gütersloh with the new OC 230, Wing Commander Hamilton-Rump giving his full support. The powers that be at HQAC did not like ATC squadrons making their own arrangements with overseas RAF squadrons; consequently both squadrons were banned from making direct arrangements to host cadets of the year. Attempts were made to use the official channel via HQAC but this proved fruitless.

The Squadron set out in search of land to build a new headquarters, headed by the Civilian Committee chairman, Squadron Leader Bernard Sandall DFC & Bar RAF Retd. After two years of searching, a suitable site was located and on 16 November 1982, planning permission was granted to build the existing HQ in Rope Walk, Congleton.

**1984**     The new Squadron HQ was officially opened on 29 April 1984 by the Lord Lieutenant of Cheshire – Viscount Leverhulme TD and the Mayor of Congleton. A representative from 230 Squadron RAF travelled from RAF Gütersloh to join the celebrations.

**1985–1990**     230 was designated an equal opportunities squadron and started to recruit female cadets. At the time there were serious misgivings by some about having female cadets. However this was soon dispelled and many girls joined Congleton ATC. On the building front, SHQ was complemented by a wooden garage complex, built by the staff and cadets to house the newly acquired minibus, radio room and NCO's mess. This was later extended to accommodate canoes and trailer.

**1991–1992**     Cadet Warrant Officer Richard Clowes was selected for an overseas camp at RAF Gütersloh in July 1991. On arrival Richard lost no time in befriending Flight Lieutenant Sean Leach. At Sean's suggestion Flight Lieutenant Goodier wrote to OC 230 Squadron RAF, Wing Commander C Williamson, requesting a visit by a Puma. On Friday 27 August 1991 a Puma helicopter piloted by Flight Lieutenant Leach landed on a school playing field in Congleton. Considerable local media coverage followed both in the press and on radio. As a result, the Squadron saw a massive influx of new cadets that more than doubled its strength, from 40 to 88. To cater for the new cadets, extra accommodation was sought; as a result, local companies donated four Portakabins. The cabins housed the modelling room, the probationer training room, the radio room, stores and an NCO's mess. Within the SHQ the computer room was reinstated to house two newly acquired computers and associated printers. Vigorous fund raising followed and the Squadron purchased seven new canoes with associated equipment – paddles, spray decks, helmets, etc.

**1993**     The CO, Flight Lieutenant Brian Mott, relocated to take up new employment in Poole having been with Congleton ATC since the mid '70s. Flight Lieutenant Rod Goodier was appointed CO having joined Congleton ATC in 1977.

**1994**        The first ever Dining In Night and Cadet Presentation Evening was held at a local hotel in January with over 100 cadets, parents and friends. In summer the CO took 12 cadets to RAF Odiham for the 230 Squadron Association re-union and the Laying-up of the old Squadron Standard.

During one week in November 1994, tragedy struck when the Squadron lost three cadets and a potential cadet in two separate road accidents. This tragedy brought out the 'family' in the Squadron, increasing its strength and resolve. As the Squadron had created a five-year plan to replace all the outbuildings with a permanent structure prior to the tragedy, the parents of the boys directed all donations in their memory into the Squadron. It was from this base that the Squadron set about raising funds culminating in a massive £85,000 that was used to build a Memorial Building in memory of the boys.

**1995**        Fund raising was the prime objective. Towing a Vulcan at Woodford Aerospace raised over £2,500, while coffee mornings, sales, letters to numerous individuals and charities and sponsored events such as parachuting, hill climbing and swimming all helped to raise the money needed for the new building.

On 20 January 1995, OC 230 Squadron RAF, Wing Commander Paul Rosentall, a Puma and crew attended the Squadron's second Dining In & Cadet Presentation Evening. Wing Commander Rosentall was so impressed with the evening that he issued an invitation to host the squadron's Cadet of the Year in the summer. The same year permission was granted by HQAC for 230 Squadron ATC to take 35 cadets on a weekend visit to RAF Aldergrove in December; this was the first recorded visit to the Province by a mainland ATC squadron for very many years.

**1996–1997**        Fundraising remained the squadron's prime objective during these two years and by the end of 1997 over £70,000 had been raised. At the end of May 1996 Squadron Leader Gavin Davey flew a Puma to Congleton to participate in the Congleton Carnival and Military Tattoo celebrations. A very successful three days ensued, during which the Puma and crew played a pivotal role.

In January 1997 the new OC 230 Squadron RAF, Wing Commander Gordon Evans flew a Puma to Congleton to attend the annual Dining In Night. In summer the Cadet of the Year spent a week at Aldergrove followed in December by 30 cadets for what was to become an annual visit.

**1998**        This was a proud year for all involved in the Squadron with the grand opening of the biggest squadron funded building project ever undertaken by an ATC Squadron. The Commandant Air Cadets, Air Commodore John

*230 Squadron ATC tow a Vulcan to raise funds.*

Rod Goodier

Kennedy and Ann Winterton MP officially opened the building. A Puma from 230 Squadron RAF Aldergrove flew over, by kind permission of the new OC, Wing Commander Ian Bell, landing on the school playing field opposite the Squadron. 200 people attended the opening, which warranted four full pages in the local newspaper. Ann Winterton MP (later to become Lady Winterton) accepted the position of Squadron President.

**1999** With the new purpose built memorial building facilities cadet numbers escalated to over 80, with parade strength two nights per week of 50. The CO held a special staff meeting to discuss the feasibility of entering 230 for the prestigious Lees Trophy Award – an annual award presented by HQAC to the squadron judged over a 12 month period to be the best in the Corps. With over 1100 ATC squadrons throughout the UK totalling 42,000 cadets and 10,000 staff it was to prove to be the biggest challenge in the history of 230 Squadron ATC. The decision to enter the Lees Trophy was made and plans were laid.

**2000–2001** From April 1999 to March 2000 every facet of life at 230 was recorded. Every ATC competition was entered from sports to shooting to drill. Staff taught and coached cadets for exams which were sat and passed with credits and distinctions. Community work, Duke of Edinburgh's Award Scheme, visits to RAF stations, camps and projects took place, culminating in three tough inspections, the first, by the Wing CO, placing 230 top of the 31 squadrons in the Wing. Next, the Regional Commandant inspected seven squadrons, one from each Wing under his command, choosing 230 and finally by COS HQAC, Group Captain Mike Cross who inspected the top squadron in each of the six ATC Regions. Some three weeks later the result was announced and 230 (Congleton) Squadron ATC was officially the number one squadron in the Corps. On 20 September 2000 the Commandant Air Cadets, Air Commodore John Kennedy, presented the Lees Trophy to OC 230 Squadron ATC, Flight Lieutenant Rod Goodier. Representatives from No 230 Squadron RAF were also there to witness the historic occasion, by kind permission of Wing Commander Howard Nash.

During the year 230 entered their SOV (Ford Transit minibus) dressed as a Puma helicopter in Congleton Carnival. It did not win a prize as the judges thought it was a real helicopter! The Millennium year saw the Squadron continue to maintain cadet numbers and further consolidated its position as a premier ATC squadron by improving the facilities in the SHQ with the addition of a dedicated radio room with a worldwide radio communications station, a purpose built room for two flight simulators and a multimedia room with a suite of four PCs and associated equipment.

The Memorial Building has transformed 230 Squadron ATC from a good squadron into the highly progressive, number one youth organisation in Congleton and area. The refurbished ATC building has allowed the squadron to re-class each room and produce excellent working facilities. The result of this, and the Memorial Building, have produced a massive change in 230 Squadron's outlook and significantly increased cadet numbers.

**2002–2003** In 2002 Wing Commander Gavin Davey, COS RAF Odiham, contacted the Squadron, requesting cadet participation at 230 Association's re-union. Two staff and 12 cadets travelled to RAF Odiham to assist, with cadets presenting a guard of honour in front of the Officers' Mess, followed by a spectacular silent drill display for all Association Members. Wing Commander Andy McAuley carried on tradition by hosting the cadet of the year, attending the Squadrons Dining In Night and granting permission for the annual December cadet camp at RAF Aldergrove.

Development of the squadron continues with a complete overhaul of the IT equipment with the latest flight simulators and a computer network and the refurbishment of several classrooms. A replacement caravan was purchased and a car-port to house it has been built adjoining the garage.

230 (Congleton) Squadron ATC is rated as one of the top ATC squadrons in the country. Its association with 230 Squadron RAF has flourished over the years and contact with past COs and many squadron members has been maintained. The current OC, Wing Commander Nick Laird, has assured his full support and it is hoped that this excellent relationship will continue for very many years to come.

# SOURCES

## Books

Burge, Squadron Leader CG, *Complete Book of Aviation*, Pitman, London, 1935

Brett, R Dallas, *The History of British Aviation 1908–1914*, John Hamilton Ltd, London, 1933

Raleigh, Walter and Jones, HA, *The War in the Air (Vols I to VI)*, Clarendon Press, Oxford, 1923–37

Cruddas, Colin, *In Hampshire's Skies*, Tempus Publishing, Stroud, 2001

Kinsey, Gordon, *Seaplanes Felixstowe*, Terence Dalton, Lavenham, 1978

Hallam, Squadron Leader TD, *The Spider Web*, Arms & Armour Press, London, 1979

Gamble, CF Snowden, *The Story of a North Sea Air Station*, Oxford University Press, 1928

Livock, Group Captain GE, *To the Ends of the Air*, HMSO, London, 1973

Wragg, David, *Boats of the Air*, Robert Hale Ltd, London, 1984

Sturtivant, Ray and Page G, *RN Aircraft Serials and Units 1911–19*, Air Britain, Tonbridge, 1992

King, Brad, *Royal Naval Air Service*, Hikoki Publications, Aldershot, 1997

Killen, John, *A History of Marine Aviation*, Frederick Muller, London, 1969

Johnson, Brian, *The History of Maritime Aviation*, David & Charles, Newton Abbot, 1981

Taylor, John WR, *Aircraft of World War 1*, Hippo Books, London, 1963

Jackson, Robert, *Aces Twilight*, Sphere Books, Harmondsworth, 1988

Vicary, Adrian, *Naval Wings*, Patrick Stephens Ltd, Cambridge, 1984

Campbell, Christopher, *Aces and Aircraft of World War One*, Blandford Press, Dorset, 1981

Jefford, Wing Commander CG, *RAF Squadrons*, Airlife Publishing Ltd, Shrewsbury, 1994

Whitehouse, Arch, *The Years of the Sky Kings*, Macdonald, London, 1960

Bruce, JM, *Felixstowe F2A*, Albatross Productions Ltd, Berkhamsted, 2000

Bruce, JM, *Short 184*, Albatross Productions Ltd, Berkhamsted, 2001

Jackson, AS, *Imperial Airways*, Terence Dalton, Lavenham, 1995

Bowyer, Chaz, *Coastal Command at War*, Ian Allan Ltd, London, 1979

Terraine, John, *The Right of the Line*, Hodder and Stoughton, London, 1985

Hendrie, Andrew, *Short Sunderland in World War II*, Airlife Publishing Ltd, Shrewsbury, 1994

*Sunderland at War*, Ian Allan Ltd, Shepperton, 1976

Bowyer, Chaz, *Coastal Command*, HMSO, London, 1942.

Bowman, Martin, *Wellington the Geodetic Giant*, Airlife Publishing Ltd, Shrewsbury, 1989

Andrews, CF and Morgan, EB, *Vickers Aircraft since 1908*, Putnam, London, 1989

Barnes, CH, *Handley Page Aircraft since 1907*, Putnam, London, 1987

James, Derek N, *Westland Aircraft since 1915*, Putnam, London, 1991

Barnes, CH, *Shorts Aircraft Since 1900*, Putnam, London, 1989

Banks, Arthur, *Wings of the Dawning*, Images Publishing, Malvern Wells, 1996

Probert, Air Commodore Henry, *The Forgotten Air Force*, Brassey's, London, 1995

Deller, Alan W, *The Kid Glove Pilot*, Colourpoint Books, Newtownards, 2004

Bednall, Dundas, *Sun on my Wings*, Paterchurch Publications, Pembroke Dock, 1989

Evans, John, *The Sunderland – Flying Boat Queen Vols 1 and 2*, Paterchurch Publications, Pembroke Dock, 1987 and 1993

*Airplane – the Complete Aviation Encyclopedia*, Orbis Publishing Ltd, London, 1990

Sharpe, Mike, *Aircraft of World War Two*, Grange Books, Rochester, 2000

*Royal Navy Warships 1939–1945*, Almark Publications, Edgware, 1971

Blundell, WDG, *The Battle for the Mediterranean*, Donald MacIntyre, Pan Books, London, 1970

Pack, SWC, *The Battle of Matapan*, Pan Books, London, 1968

Von der Porten, Edward P, *The German Navy in World War Two*, Pan Books, London, 1972

Arnold-Forster, Mark, *The World at War*, Thames-Methuen, London, 1983

Shores, Christopher and Cull, Brian with Malizia, Nicola, *Air War for Yugoslavia, Greece and Crete 1940–41*, Grub Street, London, 1987

Keegan, John, *Churchill's Generals*, Warner Books, London, 1993

Miller, Roger G, *To save a City – The Berlin Airlift*, United States Government, 1998

Dowling, Wing Commander JR, *RAF Helicopters The First Twenty Years (Parts 1 and 2)*, Air Historic Branch (RAF) , London, 1987

The *Sunday Times* Insight Team, *The Falklands War*, Sphere Books, London, 1982

Owen, David, *Air Accident Investigation*, Patrick Stephens Ltd, Sparkford, 1998

Geraghty, Tony, *The Irish War*, Harper Collins, London, 2000

Palmer, Alan, *The Penguin Dictionary of 20th Century History*, Penguin Books, Harmondsworth, 1979

Story, Richard, *A History of Modern Japan*, Penguin Books, London, 1990

## Articles

*The Wing*, RNAS Felixstowe Magazine, 1916

*The Wing*, Royal Air Force Felixstowe Magazine No 48, Christmas 1918 Victory, Anniversary and Souvenir Number

Smith, FDL, "Canadians in the Air, Major Douglas Hallam", *The Daily News*, September 1918

Meadows, Jack, "Diary of a North Sea Patroller", *Aeroplane Monthly*, August–September 1997

Rawlings, JDR, "History of No 230 Squadron", *Air Pictorial*, July 1969

Cole, Chris, "Boats for Airmen", Chris Cole, *RAF Yearbook,* 1980

Bruce, JM, "Sopwith 2F1 Camel", *Air Pictorial*, August 1964

"Visit of Southamptons to Belfast", *Belfast Evening Telegraph*, September 1925

"The Supermarine Southampton", *The Aeroplane*, July 1929

Jarrett, Philip, "Soaring Sea-Birds", *Rolls-Royce Magazine*

Manfield, SL, "Passage to Malaya", privately produced

Manfield, SL, "An 'Odd' Odyssey", privately produced

"The Sunderland Mk I", *Flight Magazine,* 1938

Newspaper accounts of No 230 Squadron activities, *The Straits Times,* 1938

de Normann, Roderick, "Seletar Sunderlands", *Fly-past*, June 1998

Crompton, TD, "Forced Landings in the tropical Nicobar Islands", Seletar Station Magazine, 1939

"The Saga of a Sunderland an Air, Sea and Desert Drama", *Illustrated London News*, February 1942

Isaic, Captain Vladimir, "Second Generation, Yugoslavia's Elegant SIM XIV Floatplanes", *Air Enthusiast*, November/December 2002

Brand, Squadron Leader RS and Busby, Gresham (201 Squadron), "Memories of the Berlin Airlift", *Talking Tangmere*, Summer 2001

Newspaper accounts of the British North Greenland Expedition 1952–54 in the *Daily Mail, Daily Telegraph, Daily Graphic, Western Mail*

"Farewell to the Flying Boat", *Flight Magazine*, February 1957.

Wynn, H, "Pioneering with the Army", *Flight Magazine*, December 1958

Newspaper accounts of the deployment to Cyprus 1958 in the *Times of Cyprus* and *Cyprus Mail*

Newspaper accounts of 'Exercise Winged Coachman' 1959 in the *Daily Telegraph* and *The Times*

Newspaper accounts of 'Exercise Starlight One' 1960 in the *Daily Telegraph*

"Desert Air Support", *The Aeroplane*, April 1960

Yoxall, John, "Exercise Starlight", *Flight Magazine*, April 1960

Rawlings, JDR, "Front-line Force – The RAF in Germany", *Air Pictorial*, October 1963

Fairbairn, AD, "The RAF in the Far East", *Air Pictorial*, April 1966

"Torrey Canyon", *Reading Evening News*, March 1967

UNFICYP, *Blue Beret*, March 1967

"Wing Commander Woodward", *Hants and Berks Gazette*, April 1967

"Dogmersfield Fete", *Hants and Berks Gazette*, September 1967

Hayes, Ian, Article on Belize, *The Herald,* 1978

Wheeler, Major JH AAC, "What was Belize?", *Army Air Corps Journal,* 1981

Holmes, Tony, "The Belize Experience", *RAF Yearbook* 1992

"No 230 Squadron in Germany 1980–1992", Wing Commander RE Turner

English, Malcolm, "RAF Germany", *Air Pictorial*, September 1981

Locke, Bill, Article about 230 Squadron's arrival at Gutersloh, *RAF News*, February 1981

"The flying 'docs'", *Soldier Magazine*, January 1991

Strickland, Brian , "The RAF's Year 1992" by , *RAF Yearbook,* 1993

Wise, Andrew, Article about No 230 Squadron, *RAF News*, February 1999

Flynn, Flight Lieutenant Dave, "230 Squadron Update", *230 Squadron Association Newsletter*, Spring 2003

*The Ulster Airmail* (the monthly journal of the Ulster Aviation Society), many issues

## Websites

The RNAS – www.fleetairarmarchive.net
Canadian Airmen – www.airforce.forces.ca, www.collection.nlc-bnc.ca
480 Coastal Reconnaissance Flight – www.rafweb.org/biographies
Supermarine Southampton – www.aeroplanemonthly.com
World War Two memories of Addu by John Rankin – www.rafgan.co.uk
World War Two memories of Alan Conrad – www.weiweb.com/raf
230 Tiger Squadron History – www.tiger-lair.org
230 Tiger Squadron History – www.esq301jaguares.home.sapo.pt
230 Tiger Squadron History – www.rafweb.org/Sqn226–230
230 Tiger Squadron History – www.raf.mod.uk/history
Coastal Command – www.rafcommands.currantbun.com
Rhodesia 'Operation Agila' – www.riv.co.nz
JASS – Ballykelly's Shackleton Era by David Hill – www.home.aone.net.au
*Herald of Free Enterprise* – www.business.unisa.edu.au
Article about the RAF in Bosnia – www.britains-smallwars.com/bosnia
Article about the RAF in Kosovo – www.raf.mod.uk/history/kosovo
Article about the RAF in Kosovo – www.britains-smallwars.com/kosovo

## Official sources

Files held at the Fleet Air Arm Museum, RNAS Yeovilton
Log books of Flight Lieutenants WJ Daddo-Langlois and JH Bentham (No 480 CRF)
Copy from 1930s RAF Form 540s made by Air Historical Branch (RAF)
Bound volumes of declassified Form 540s from the 1940s, 1950s & 1960s held by the Squadron
Unpublished memoir of N9029/V by Wing Commander AMG Lywood
Report written by Squadron Leader AW Deller on Chindwin Operation 2 Feb 1945 to 13 Mar 1945
Britain and the Berlin Airlift by Air Historical Branch (RAF) 1998
No 201 Squadron History Book – On the Step (Unclassified)
A history of 30 Years Service in support of the RUC and the British Army in Northern Ireland - No 72 Squadron (Unclassified)
Op Granby – The Support Helicopter Force Story by Wing Commander RE Best AFC – RAF 92 No 4 RAF (PR)
The Gulf Conflict Air Campaign – An Overview by Group Captain NR Irving AFC – RAF 92 No 4 RAF (PR)
230 Squadron in the Gulf by Squadron Leader Charles Gillow (Unclassified)
Operation Telic – Oct 2003 to date by Squadron Leader Phil Gilling (Unclassified)
*The Big-Cat Diary* – 230 'Tiger' Squadron Op Telic Newsletter (Unclassified)

## Correspondence by letter and e-mail

David J Barnes, Fred Mock, Ray Sturtivant, Stuart Leslie, Jack Meadows, Adrian Vicary, Gordon Kinsey, Wing Commander CG Jefford, Jack Beauchamp, DW McNichol, T Hulme, Alan Conrad, Alan Deller, Fred Maryon, Dennis Bracey, Tony Burt, Peter Price, WD Hallisey, Lewis Day, Graham Stevens, Eddy Bardgett, Bill Davis, Ian Mackie, Ronald O Hepburn, Duncan Donaldson, Bob Turner, Andrew Turner, Arnold Hutchison, Michael Stubbs, Flight Lieutenant Ron Goodier (230 Sqn ATC), Flight Lieutenant JC Gimenez (No 201 Sqn), Graham Day (AHB), Peter Devitt (RAF Museum), Jerry Shore (FAA Museum), Duncan Black (FAA Museum), Ian Leslie (Canada Aviation Museum), OC A Squadron (Canadian Forces Joint Imagery Centre), Gloria MacKenzie (National Archives of Canada)

## Conversations

Wing Commander Bob Turner, Wing Commander Andy McAuley, Wing Commander Nick Laird, Squadron Leader Brian Littley, Squadron Leader Jim Holland, Squadron Leader Dave Webber, Squadron Leader Phil Gilling, Squadron Leader Martin Cowie, Flight Lieutenant Dave Warren, Flight Lieutenant Dave Flynn, Flight Lieutenant Andrew Palmer, Flight Lieutenant Ron Goodier, Flight Lieutenant JC Gimenez, Chief Tech Pete Roberts, Chief Tech Miles McDowell, Mrs Carol Turner, Fred Coppard, John Sayers, Dennis Bracey, Alan Deller, Graham Stevens, Eddy Bardgett, Fred Maryon, Bill Hallisey, Duncan Donaldson, Peter Devitt, Steve Clarke (MoD), Nicola Hunt (MoD), Emma Crocker (Imperial War Museum), John Evans, United States Air Force Europe (Public Affairs Office, Ramstein).

Special thanks must go to Flight Lieutenant 'Harry' Palmer, who has acted as my liaison officer with the Squadron. His patience has been immense and his help equally so. Very many thanks also to Wing Commander Andy Turner, Wing Commander Nick Laird and Squadron Leader Phil Gilling for their splendid proof reading.